# The Grey Raiders
# Volume 1

# The Grey Raiders Volume 1

Accounts of Mosby & His Raiders During the American Civil War

Mosby's War Reminiscences

John S. Mosby

Reminiscences by the Surgeon of Mosby's Command

Aristedes Monteiro

*The Grey Raiders Volume 1*
*Accounts of Mosby & His Raiders During the American Civil War*
*Mosby's War Reminiscences*
by John S. Mosby
*Reminiscences by the Surgeon of Mosby's Command*
by Aristedes Monteiro

FIRST EDITION

First published under the titles
*Mosby's War Reminiscences*
and
*Reminiscences by the Surgeon of Mosby's Command*

Leonaur is an imprint
of Oakpast Ltd

Copyright in this form © 2014 Oakpast Ltd

ISBN: 978-1-78282-349-0 (hardcover)
ISBN: 978-1-78282-350-6 (softcover)

**http://www.leonaur.com**

Publisher's Notes
The views expressed in this book are not necessarily those of the publisher.

# Contents

Mosby's War Reminiscences                                  7

Reminiscences by the Surgeon of Mosby's Command     163

# Mosby's War Reminiscences

# Contents

| | |
|---|---|
| Opening of Hostilities | 11 |
| Experiences in the Confederate Cavalry | 16 |
| Christmastide Raids | 23 |
| Harassing the Army of the Potomac | 30 |
| How Major Gilmer Tried to Capture Mosby's Command | 36 |
| Sergeant Ames Deserts and Joins Mosby | 43 |
| Sudden Attacks upon Federal Cavalry Outposts | 52 |
| A Close Call | 64 |
| In Pursuit | 74 |
| In the Saddle | 82 |
| A Wrecked Train | 89 |
| On the Road to Gettysburg | 96 |
| General Stuart's Raid | 111 |
| Stuart's Cavalry | 129 |

## Chapter 1

# Opening of Hostilities

*Rebellion!*
*How many a spirit born to bless,*
*Hath sunk beneath that withering name,*
*Whom but a day's—an hour's—success*
*Had wafted to eternal fame.*—Tom Moore.

In April, 1861, I was attending court at Abingdon, Va., when I met a person who had just stepped out of the telegraph office, who informed me that tremendous tidings were passing over the wires. Going in, I inquired of the operator what it was, who told me that Lincoln had issued a proclamation calling out troops. Fort Sumter had fallen two days before. The public mind was already strained to a high pitch of excitement, and it required only a spark to produce an explosion. The indignation aroused by the President's proclamation spread like fire on a prairie, and the laws became silent in the midst of arms. People of every age, sex, and condition were borne away on the tide of excited feeling that swept over the land.

The home of Gov. John B. Floyd, who had resigned as secretary of war under Buchanan, was at Abingdon. I went to his house and told him the news. He immediately issued a call to arms, which resounded like the roll of Ziska's drum among the mountains of south-western Virginia. Many of the most influential families in that region were descendants of the men who had fought under Morgan and Campbell at Eutaw Springs and King's Mountain. Their military spirit was inflamed by stirring appeals to the memories of the deeds their sires had done. Women, too, came forward to inspire men with a spirit of heroic self-sacrifice, and a devotion that rivalled the maidens of Carthage and Saragossa.

All the pride and affection that Virginians had felt in the traditions of the government which their ancestors had made, and the great inheritance which they had bequeathed, were lost in the overpowering sentiment of sympathy with the people who were threatened with invasion. It is a mistake to suppose that the Virginia people went to war in obedience to any decree of their State, commanding them to go. On the contrary, the people were in a state of armed revolution before the State had acted in its corporate capacity. I went along with the flood like everybody else. A few individuals here and there attempted to breast the storm of passion, and appeared like Virgil's ship-wrecked mariners, "*Rari nantes in surgite vasto.*" Their fate did not encourage others to follow their example, and all that they did was to serve "like ocean wrecks to illuminate the storm." In anticipation of these events, a cavalry company had for some months been in process of organisation, which I had joined as a private. This company—known as the Washington Mounted Rifles—was immediately called together by its commanding officer, Capt. William E. Jones. Capt. Jones was a graduate of West Point, and had resigned some years before from the United States Army.

He was a stern disciplinarian, and devoted to duty. Under a rugged manner and impracticable temper he had a heart that beat with warm impulses. To his inferiors in rank he was just and kind, but too much inclined to cross the wishes and criticise the orders of his superiors. He had been a classmate of Stonewall Jackson at the military academy, and related to me many anecdotes of Jackson's piety, as well as his eccentricities. He was a hard swearer; and a few days after the battle of Bull Run he told me that he was at Jackson's headquarters, and Jackson got very much provoked at something a soldier had done, when Jones said, "Jackson, let me cuss him for you." He fell in battle with Gen. Hunter, in the valley of Virginia, in June, 1864. We went into barracks at Abingdon, and began drilling.

No service I ever had to perform during the war went as much against the grain as standing guard the first night I was in camp. I had no friends in the cavalry company, so I applied to Gov. Litchen for a transfer to an infantry company that had been raised in that part of the county where I resided. But on the very day I made the application, a telegraphic order came for us to start for Richmond immediately, and I never heard anything more of it. My company marched on horseback all the way to Richmond—about five hundred miles—while the infantry company went by rail. But how small is the control that mortals have over their own destinies. The company to which I unsuccessfully applied to be transferred became a part of the immortal division of Stonewall Jackson, in which I would have had only a slight chance of asserting my individuality, which would have been merged in the mass. I remember distinctly, now, how with a heart almost bursting with grief, in the midst of a rain, I bade my friends in the infantry company farewell just as they were about getting on the train. I had no dream then that I would ever be anything more than a private soldier. On the same day in rain and mud we started on the march to Richmond. A few days before a flag had been presented to our company by a young lady, with an address in which she reminded us that "*the coward dies a thousand deaths—the brave man dies but one.*" I am sure there was not a man among us who did not feel the ambition of the youth in Longfellow's poem, bearing

> *Onward amid the ice and snow of Alpine heights*
> *His banner with its strange device.*

The march to Richmond under a soldier who had bivouacked on the plains was a course of beneficial discipline. The grief of parting from home and friends soon wore away, and we all were as gay as if we were going to a wedding or a picnic. Gloom was succeeded by mirth and songs of gladness, and if Abraham Lincoln could have been sung out of the South as James II. was out of England, our company would have done it and saved the country all the fighting. The favorite songs were generally those of sentiment and sadness, intermingled with an occasional comic melody. I remember this refrain of one that often resounded from the head to the rear of the column as we passed some farmer's house:

> *He who has good buttermilk a plenty, and gives the soldiers none,*
> *He shan't have any of our buttermilk when his buttermilk is gone.*

The buttermilk, as well as everything else that the farmer had that was good, was generally given to the soldiers. The country was brimful of patriotism.

The gayety with which men marched into the face of death is not so remarkable as the fortitude and cheerfulness of the wives and mothers who stayed at home and waited for the news of the battles. In nearly every home of the South could be found an example of that Spartan mother who sent her son to the wars with her last injunction to return with his shield or return upon it. This courage, exhibited in the beginning, survived to the last, through all the long agony and bloody sweat of the struggle. On reaching Richmond, after a few days' rest, we were ordered to the Shenandoah valley. A day or so before we started, Capt. Jones made a requisition on the quartermaster's department for clothing for his company. We were furnished with suits of a very rough quality of goods manufactured in the Virginia penitentiary. It almost produced a mutiny in the camp. The men piled the clothes up in front of the captain's tent. Only two refused to wear them—Private Fountain Beattie and myself.

I do not think any clothes I ever wore did me more service than these. When I became a commander I made Beattie a lieutenant. I think we were both as contented on the picket line, dressed in our penitentiary suits, as we ever were in the gay uniforms we afterwards wore. Our march from Richmond to the Shenandoah valley was an ovation—our people had had no experiences of the misery and desolation that follow in the track of war; they were full of its romance, and expected us to win battles that would rival the glories of Wagram and Marengo. They never counted the cost of victory.

Our company was incorporated into the 1st regiment of Virginia cavalry, commanded by Col. J. E. B. Stuart. It was stationed at a village called Bunker Hill, on the turnpike leading from Winchester to Martinsburg, and was observing the Union army under Patterson, which was then stationed at the latter place, on the Baltimore & Ohio Railroad. Gen. Joseph E. Johnston then had his headquarters at Winchester. I first saw Stuart at Bunker Hill. He had then lately resigned from the United States army to link his fortunes with the Southern Confederacy. He was just twenty-eight years of age—one year older than myself—strongly built, with blue eyes, ruddy complexion, and a reddish beard. He wore a blouse and foraging cap with a linen cover, called a havelock, as a protection against the sun. His personal appearance indicated the distinguishing traits of his character—dash, great strength of will, and indomitable energy. Stuart soon showed that he possessed all the qualities of a great leader of cavalry—a sound judgment, a quick intelligence to penetrate the designs of an enemy, mingled with the brilliant courage of Rupert.

There was then such a wide chasm between me and him that I was only permitted to view him at a distance, and had no thought of ever rising to intimacy with him. He took us the next day on a scout down toward Martinsburg and gave us our first lesson in war and sight of the enemy. We saw the hills around the town covered with the white tents of the Union army, and caught two soldiers who had ventured too far outside the picket lines. Since then I have witnessed the capture of thousands, but have never felt the same joy as I did over these first two prisoners.

A few days after this, Patterson started out on a promenade toward Winchester, and then turned squarely off, and went back toward Charlestown. Patterson made a good deal of noise with the shells that he threw at us, but nobody was hurt. Stuart kept close on his flanks, both to watch his movements and to screen Johnston's, who had just begun to move to join Beauregard at Manassas. Fitz John Porter and George H. Thomas, who afterward became distinguished generals, were on his staff. Patterson has been greatly censured for not pressing Johnston, and detaining him in the Shenandoah valley, instead of making the retrograde movement to Charlestown that permitted his escape. He alleges that he acted under the advice of his staff officers. Patterson was a conspicuous figure as well as failure in the first scene of the first act of the drama of war; after that he disappeared forever. His campaign in the Shenandoah valley was a mere prologue to the great tragedy that was afterward acted there. Stuart left him in a position where he could neither be of advantage to the cause he upheld nor injury to that he opposed, and crossed the Blue Ridge to take part in the battle of Bull Run, on the 21st of July.

## Chapter 2

# Experiences in the Confederate Cavalry

*O! shadow of glory—dim image of war—
The chase hath no story—her hero no star."*
—Byron, *Deformed Transformed.*

After the first Battle of Bull Run, Stuart's cavalry was engaged in performing outpost duty on our front, which extended from the falls above Washington to Occoquan, on the lower Potomac. There were no opportunities for adventurous enterprise. McClellan's army was almost in a state of siege in Washington, and his cavalry but rarely showed themselves outside his infantry picket line. We had to go on picket duty three times a week and remain twenty-four hours. The work was pretty hard; but still, soldiers liked it better than the irksome life of the camp. I have often sat alone on my horse from midnight to daybreak, keeping watch over the sleeping army. During this period of inaction, the stereotyped message sent every night from Washington to the northern press was, "All quiet along the Potomac."

While I was a private in Stuart's cavalry, I never missed but one tour of outpost duty, and then I was confined in the hospital from an injury. With one other, I was stationed at the post on the road leading from Fall's Church to Lewinsville, in Fairfax. At night we relieved each other alternately, one sleeping while the other watched. About dusk, Capt. Jones had ridden to the post and instructed us that we had no troops outside our lines on that road, and that we must fire, without halting, on any body of men approaching from that direction, as they would be the enemy. The night was dark, and it had come my turn to sleep. I was lying on the ground, with the soft side of a stone for a pillow, when I was suddenly aroused by my companion, who called to me to mount, that the Yankees were coming. In an almost unconscious state I leaped into my saddle, and at the same instant threw forward my carbine, and both of us fired on a body of cavalry not fifty yards distant. Fortunately, we fired so low our bullets struck the ground just in front of them. The flash from my carbine in my horse's face frightened him terribly. He wheeled, and that is the last I remember about that night.

The next thing I recollect is that some time during the next day I became conscious, and found myself lying on a bed at the house of the keeper of the toll-gate. Capt. Jones and several of the men of my company were standing by me. It appears that the night before Stuart had sent a company of cavalry to Lewinsville for some purpose. This company had gone out by one road and returned on the one where I had been posted. My horse had run away and fallen over a cow that was lying down, and rolled over me. The company of cavalry coming along the same way, their horses in front started and snorted at something lying in the road. They halted, some of them dismounted to see what it was, and discovered me there in an insensible state. They picked me up and carried me into the village, apparently dying. I was bruised from head to foot, and felt like every bone in my body had been broken. I had to be carried to Fairbay Court House in an ambulance. There is a tradition that when Capt. Jones looked on me that night he swore harder than the army in Flanders. The feelings he expressed for the officer in fault were not so benevolent as my Uncle Toby's for the fly.

While the cavalry did not have an opportunity to do much fighting during the first year of the war, they learned to perform the duties and endure the privations of a soldier's life. My experience in this school was of great advantage to me in the after years when I became a commander. There was a thirst for adventure among the men in the cavalry, and a positive pleasure to get an occasional shot "from a rifleman hid in a thicket." There were often false alarms, and sometimes real ones, from scouting parties of infantry who would come up at night to surprise our pickets. A vivid imagination united with a nervous temperament can see in the dark the shapes of many things that have no real existence.

A rabbit making its nocturnal rounds, a cow grazing, a hog rooting for acorns, an owl hooting, or the screech of a night hawk could often arouse and sometimes stampede an outpost or draw the fire of a whole line of pickets. At the first shot, the reserve would mount; and soon the videttes would come running in at full speed. There was an old gray horse roaming about the fields at Fairfax Court House during the first winter of the war that must have been fired at a hundred times at night by our videttes, and yet was never touched. I have never heard whether Congress has voted him a pension. The last time that I was ever on picket was in February, 1862. The snow was deep and hard frozen.

My post was on the outskirts of Fairfax Court House, at the junction of the Washington road and turnpike. I wore a woollen hood to keep my ears from freezing, and a blanket thrown around me as a protection against the cold wind. The night was clear, and all that's best of dark and bright. I sat on my horse under the shadow of a tree, both as a protection from the piercing blast and as a screen from the sight of an enemy. I had gone on duty at midnight, to remain until daybreak. The deep silence was occasionally broken by the cry of "Halt!" from some distant sentinel, as he challenged the patrol or relief. The swaying branches of the trees in the moonlight cast all sorts of fantastic forms on the crystal snow. In this deep solitude, I was watching for danger and communing with the spirit of the past. At this very spot, a few nights before, the vidette had been fired on by a scouting party of infantry that had come up from McClellan's camps below. But the old gray horse had several times got up a panic there which raised a laugh on the soldiers.

Now I confess that I was about as much afraid of ridicule as of being shot, and so, unless I got killed or captured, I resolved to spend the night there. Horatius Cocles was not more determined to hold his position on the bridge of the Tiber, than I was to stay at my post, but perhaps his motives were less mixed than mine. I had been long pondering and remembering, and in my reverie had visited the fields that I had traversed "in life's morning march when my bosom was young." I was suddenly aroused by the crash of footsteps breaking the crust of the hard snow. The sound appeared to proceed from something approaching me with the measured tread of a file of soldiers. It was screened from my view by some houses near the roadside.

I was sure that it was an enemy creeping up to get a shot at me, for I thought that even the old horse would not have ventured out on such a night, unless under orders. My heart began to sicken within me pretty much like Hector's did when he had to face the wrath of Achilles. My horse, shivering with cold, with the instinct of danger, pricked up his ears and listened as eagerly as I did to the footsteps as they got near. I drew my pistol, cocked it, and took aim at the corner around which this object must come. I wanted to get the advantage of the first shot. Just then the hero of a hundred panics appeared—the old gray horse! I returned my pistol to my belt and relapsed into reverie. I was happy: my credit as a soldier had been saved.

A couple of days after this my company returned there, as usual, on picket. On this same morning Stuart came, making an inspection of the outposts. It happened that there were two young ladies living at Fairfax Court House, acquaintances of his, who did not like to stay in such an exposed situation, and so Stuart had arranged to send them to the house of a friend near Fryingpan, which was further within our lines. At that time the possibility of our army ever retiring to Richmond had not been conceived by the rank and file. Stuart had then become a brigadier-general, and Capt. Jones had been promoted to be colonel of the 1st Virginia cavalry.

Although I served under Stuart almost from the beginning of the war, I had no personal acquaintance with him before then. He asked Capt. Blackford to detail a man to go along as an escort for the two ladies. I had often been invited to the house of one of them by her father, so I was selected on that account to go with them. I left my horse with my friend Beattie to lead back to camp, and took a seat in the carriage with the ladies. This was on the 12th of February, 1862.

It began snowing just as we started, and it was late in the afternoon before we got to Fryingpan. I then went in the carriage to Stuart's headquarters a few miles off, at Centreville. It was dark when I got there. I reported to him the result of my mission to Fryingpan, and asked for a pass to go back to the camp of my regiment, which was about four miles off on Bull Run. Stuart told me that the weather was too bad for me to walk to camp that night, but to stay where I was until next morning. He and Generals Joseph E. Johnston and G. W. Smith occupied the Grigsby house and messed together. I sat down by a big wood fire in an open fireplace in the front room, where he and the other two generals were also sitting.

I never spoke a word, and would have been far happier trudging through the snow back to camp, or even as a vidette on a picket post. I felt just as much out of place and uneasy as a mortal would who had been lifted to a seat by the side of the gods on Olympus. Presently supper was announced. The generals all walked into the adjoining room, and Stuart told me to come in. After they had sat down at the table, Stuart observed that I was not there and sent for me. I was still sitting by the fire. I obeyed his summons like a good soldier, and took my place among the *dil majores*. I was pretty hungry, but did not enjoy my supper. I would have preferred fasting or eating with the couriers. I know I never spoke a word to anyone—I don't think I raised my eyes from off my plate while I was at the table.

Now, while I felt so much oppressed by the presence of men of such high rank, there was nothing in their deportment that produced it. It was the same way the next morning. Stuart had to send after me to come in to breakfast. I went pretty much in the same dutiful spirit that Gibbon says that he broke his marriage engagement: "I sighed as a lover and obeyed as a son." But now my courage rose; I actually got into conversation with Joe Johnston, whom I would have regarded it as a great privilege the day before to view through a long-range telescope. The generals talked of Judah P. Benjamin's (who was then Secretary of War) breach of courtesy to Stonewall Jackson that had caused Jackson to send in his resignation. They were all on Jackson's side. There was nothing going on about Centreville to indicate the evacuation that took place three weeks after that. Stuart let me have a horse to ride back to camp. As soon as I got there, Col. Jones sent for me to come to his tent. I went, and he offered me the place of adjutant of the regiment. I had had no more expectation of such a thing than of being translated on Elijah's chariot to the skies.

Of course, I accepted it. I was never half as much frightened in any fight I was in as I was on the first dress parade I conducted. But I was not permitted to hold the position long. About two months after that, when we had marched to meet McClellan at, Yorktown, my regiment reorganised under the new act of the Confederate Congress. Fitz Lee was elected colonel in place of Jones. This was the result of an attempt to mix democracy with military discipline. Fitz Lee did not reappoint me as adjutant, and so I lost my first commission on the spot where Cornwallis lost his sword. This was at the time an unrecognized favour. If I had been retained as adjutant, I would probably have never been anything else.

So at the close of the first year of the war I was, in point of rank, just where I had begun. Well, it did not break my heart. When the army was retiring from Centreville, Stuart's cavalry was the rear guard, and I had attracted his favourable notice by several expeditions I had led to the rear of the enemy. So Stuart told me to come to his headquarters and act as a scout for him. A scout is not a spy who goes in disguise, but a soldier in arms and uniform, who goes among as enemy's lines to get information about them. Among the survivors of the Army of the Potomac there are many legends afloat, and religiously believed to be true, of a mysterious person—a sort of Flying Dutchman or Wandering Jew—prowling among their camps in the daytime in the garb of a beggar or with a pilgrim's staff, and leading cavalry raids upon them at night. In popular imagination, I have been identified with that mythical character.

On the day after Mr. Lincoln's assassination, Secretary Stanton telegraphed to Gen. Hancock, then in command at Winchester, Va., that I had been seen at the theatre in Washington on that fatal night. Fortunately, I could prove an alibi by Hancock himself, as I was at that very time negotiating a truce with him. I recently heard an officer of the United States army tell a story of his being with the guard for a wagon train, and my passing him with my command on the pike, all of us dressed as Federal soldiers, and cutting the train out from behind him. I laughed at it, like everybody who heard it, and did not try to unsettle his faith. To have corrected it would have been as cruel as to dispel the illusion of childhood that the story of "Little Red Riding Hood" is literally true, or to doubt the real presence of Santa Claus. It was all pure fiction about our being dressed in blue uniforms, or riding with him.

I did capture the wagon train at the time and place mentioned, Oct. 26, 1863, at the Chestnut Fork, near Warrenton, Va., but we never even saw the guard. They had got sleepy, and gone on to camp, and left me to take care of their wagons—which I did. The quartermaster in charge of them, Capt. Stone, who was made prisoner, called to pay his respects to me a few days ago. I can now very well understand how the legendary heroes of Greece were created. I always wore the Confederate uniform, with the insignia of my rank. So did my men. So any success I may have had, either as an individual scout or partisan commander, cannot be accounted for on the theory that it was accomplished through disguise. The hundreds of prisoners I took are witnesses to the contrary.

Fauquier County, Va., Feb. 4, 1863.

General:—I arrived in this neighbourhood about one week ago. Since then I have been, despite the bad weather, quite actively engaged with the enemy. The result up to this time has been the capture of twenty-eight Yankee cavalry together with all their horses, arms, etc. The evidence of parole I forward with this. I have also paroled a number of deserters. Col. Sir Percy Wyndham, with over two hundred cavalry, came up to Middleburg last week to punish me, as he said, for my raids on his picket line. I had a slight skirmish with him, in which my loss was three men, captured by the falling of their horses; the enemy's loss, one man and three horses captured. He set a very nice trap a few days ago to catch me in. I went into it, but, contrary to the Colonel's expectations, brought the trap off with me, killing one, capturing twelve; the balance running. The extent of the annoyance I have been to the Yankees may be judged of by the fact that, baffled in their attempts to capture me, they threaten to retaliate on citizens for my acts.

I forward to you some correspondence I have had on the subject. The most of the infantry has left Fairfax and gone towards Fredericksburg. In Fairfax there are five or six regiments of cavalry; there are about three hundred at Dranesville. They are so isolated from the rest of the command, that nothing would be easier than their capture. I have harassed them so much that they do not keep their pickets over half a mile from camp. There is no artillery there. I start on another trip day after tomorrow.

I am, most respectfully, yours, etc.,

John S. Mosby.

Maj.-Gen. J. E. B. Stuart.

Headquarters Cavalry Division, Feb. 8, 1863.
Respectfully forwarded as additional proof of the prowess, daring, and efficiency of Mosby (without commission) and his band of a dozen chosen spirits.

J. E. B. Stuart,
Major-General Commanding.

Headquarters, Feb. 11, 1863.
Respectfully forwarded to the Adjutant and Inspector-General as evidence of merit of Capt. Mosby.

R. E. Lee,
General.

CHAPTER 3

# Christmastide Raids

After the Battle of Fredericksburg, in December, 1862, there was a lull in the storm of war. The men on the outposts along the Rappahannock had a sort of truce to hostilities, and began swapping tobacco and coffee, just as the soldiers of Wellington and Soult, on the eve of a great battle, filled their canteens from the same stream. At that time, Stuart determined to make a Christmas raid about Dumfries, which was on Hooker's line of communication with Washington. I went with him. He got many prisoners, and wagons loaded with *bonbons* and all the good things of the festive season. It made us happy, but almost broke the sutlers' hearts. A regiment of Pennsylvania cavalry left their camp on the Occoquan, and their Christmas turkeys, and came out to look for us. They had better have stayed at home; for all the good they did was to lead Stuart's cavalry into their camp as they ran through it. After leaving Dumfries, Stuart asked me to take Beattie and go on ahead. The road ran through a dense forest, and there was danger of an ambuscade, of which every soldier has a horror who has read of Braddock's defeat. Beattie and I went forward at a gallop, until we met a large body of cavalry.

As no support was in sight, several officers made a dash at us, and at the same time opened such a fire as to show that peace on earth and good will to men, which the angels and morning stars had sung on that day over 1800 years ago, was no part of their creed. The very fact that we did not run away ought to have warned them that somebody was behind us. When the whole body had got within a short distance of us, Stuart, who had heard the firing, came thundering up with the 1st Virginia cavalry. All the fun was over with the Pennsylvanians then. There was no more merry Christmas for them. Wade Hampton was riding by the side of Stuart. He went into the fight and fought like a common (or, rather, an uncommon) trooper. The combat was short and sharp, and soon became a rout; the Federal cavalry ran right through their camp, and gave a last look at their turkeys as they passed. But alas! they were "grease, but living grease no more" for them. There was probably some method in their madness in running through their camp. They calculated, with good reason, that the temptation would stop the pursuit.

A few days ago I read, in a book giving the history of the telegraph in the war, the despatch sent to Washington by the operator near there: "The 17th Pennsylvania Cavalry just passed here, furiously charging to the rear." When we got to Burke's Station, on the Orange and Alexandria Railroad, while his command was closing up, Stuart put his own operator in charge of the instrument, and listened to a telegraphic conversation between the general commanding at Fairfax Court-House and the authorities at Washington. In order to bewilder and puzzle them, he sent several messages, which put them on a false scent. Just before leaving, he sent a message to Quartermaster-General Meigs, complaining of the inferior quality of the mules recently furnished by him. The wire was then cut.

Having learned by the telegraph that Fairfax Court-House was held by a brigade of infantry, Stuart marched around north of it, and went into Loudoun—a land flowing with plenty. He made his headquarters at Col. Rogers's, near Dover, and rested until the next day. On the morning he left, I went to his room, and asked him to let me stay behind for a few days with a squad of men. I thought I could do something with them. He readily assented. I got nine men—including, of course, Beattie—who volunteered to go with me.

This was the beginning of my career as a partisan. The work I accomplished in two or three days with this squad induced him to let me have a larger force to try my fortune. I took my men down into Fairfax, and in two days captured twenty cavalrymen, with their horses, arms, and equipments. I had the good luck, by mere chance, to come across a forester named John Underwood, who knew every rabbit-path in the county. He was a brave soldier, as well as a good guide. His death a few months afterward, at the hands of a deserter from our own army, was one of the greatest losses I sustained in the war. I dismounted to capture one of the picket posts, who could be seen by the light of their fire in the woods. We walked up within a few yards of it. The men, never suspecting danger, were absorbed in a game of euchre. I halted, and looked on for a minute or two, for I hated to spoil their sport. At last I fired a shot, to let them know that their relief had come. Nobody was hurt; but one fellow was so much frightened that he nearly jumped over the tops of the trees.

They submitted gracefully to the fate of war. I made them lie down by a fence, and left a mounted man to stand guard over them while I went to capture another post about two miles off. These were Vermont cavalry, and being from the land of steady habits did not indulge in cards like their New York friends, whom I had just left in the fence corner. I found them all sound asleep in a house, except the sentinel. Their horses were tied to the trees around it. The night was clear and crisp and cold. As we came from the direction of their camp, we were mistaken for the patrol until we got upon them. The challenge of the sentinel was answered by an order to charge, and it was all over with the boys from the Green Mountains.

Their surprise was so great that they forgot that they had only pistols and carbines. If they had used them, being in a house, they might have driven us off. They made no resistance. The next day I started back to rejoin Stuart, who was near Fredericksburg. I found him in his tent, and when I reported what I had done, he expressed great delight. So he agreed to let me go back with fifteen men and try my luck again. I went and never returned. I was not permitted to keep the men long. Fitz Lee complained of his men being with me, and so I had to send them back to him. But while I had them I kept things lively and humming. I made many raids on the cavalry outposts, capturing men, arms, and horses. Old men and boys had joined my band. Some had run the gauntlet of Yankee pickets, and others swam the Potomac to get to me. Most men love the excitement of fighting, but abhor the drudgery of camps. I mounted, armed and equipped my command at the expense of the United States government.

There was a Confederate hospital in Middleburg, where a good many wounded Confederate soldiers had been left during our Maryland campaign a few months before. These were now convalescent. I utilized them. They would go down to Fairfax on a raid with me, and then return to the hospital. When the Federal cavalry came in pursuit, they never suspected that the cripples they saw lying on their couches or hobbling about on crutches were the men who created the panic at night in their camps. At last I got one of the cripples killed, and that somewhat abated their ardour.

There are many comic as well as tragic elements that fill up the drama of war. One night I went down to Fairfax to take a cavalry picket. When I got near the post I stopped at the house of one Ben Hatton. I had heard that he had visited the picket post that day to give some information to them about me. I gave him the choice of Castle Thunder or guiding me through the pines to the rear of the picket.

Ben did not hesitate to go with me. Like the Vicar of Bray, he was in favour of the party in power. There was a deep snow on the ground, and when we got in sight of the picket fire, I halted and dismounted my men. As Ben had done all I wanted of him, and was a non-combatant, I did not want to expose him to the risk of getting shot, and so I left him with a man named Gall (generally called "Coonskin," from the cap he wore), and Jimmie, an Irishman, to guard our horses, which we left in the pines. With the other men, I went to make the attack on foot. The snow being soft, we made no noise, and had them all prisoners almost before they got their eyes open. But just then a fusillade was opened in the rear, where our horses were. Leaving a part of my men to bring on the prisoners, we mounted the captured horses and dashed back to the place where I had dismounted, to meet what I supposed was an attempt of the enemy to make a reprisal on me. When I got there I found Ben Hatton lying in a snowbank, shot through the thigh, but Jimmy and Coonskin had vanished.

All that Ben knew was that he had been shot; he said that the Yankees had attacked their party, but whether they had carried off Jimmie and Coonskin, or Jimmie and Coonskin had carried them, he couldn't tell. What made the mystery greater was that all our horses were standing just as we left them, including the two belonging to the missing men. With our prisoners and spoil, we started home, Ben Hatton riding behind one of the men. Ben had lost a good deal of blood, but he managed to hold on. When we got into the road we met a body of Wyndham's cavalry coming up to cut us off. They stopped and opened fire on us. I knew this was a good sign, and that they were not coming to close quarters in the dark. We went on by them. By daybreak I was twenty miles away. As soon as it was daylight, Wyndham set out full speed up the pike to catch me. He might as well have been chasing the silver-footed antelope,

*That gracefully and gayly springs,*
*As o'er the marble courts of kings.*

I was at a safe distance before he started. He got to Middleburg during the day, with his horses all jaded and blown. He learned there that I had passed through about the dawn of day. He returned to camp with the most of his command leading their broken-down horses. In fact, his pursuit had done him more damage than my attack. He was an English officer, trained in the cavalry schools of Europe; but he did not understand such business. This affair was rather hard on Ben Hatton. He was the only man that got a hurt; and that was all he got. As it was only a flesh wound, it healed quickly; but, even if he had died from it, fame would have denied her requiem to his name.

His going with me had been as purely involuntary as if he had been carried out with a halter round his neck to be hanged. I left him at his house, coiled up in bed, within a few hundred yards of the Yankee pickets. He was too close to the enemy for me to give him any surgical assistance; and he had to keep his wound a profound secret in the neighbourhood, for fear the Yankees would hear of it and how he got it. If they had ever found it out, Ben's wife would have been made a widow. In a day or so, Coonskin and Jimmie came in, but by different directions. We had given them up for lost. They trudged on foot through the snow all the way up from Fairfax.

Neither one knew that Ben Hatton had been shot. Each one supposed that all the others were prisoners, and he the only one left to tell the tale of the disaster. Both firmly believed that they had been attacked by the enemy, and, after fighting as long as Sir John Falstaff did by Shrewsbury clock, had been forced to yield; but they could not account for all our horses being where we left them. The mistakes of the night had been more ludicrous than any of the incidents of Goldsmith's immortal comedy, *She Stoops to Conquer*. By a comparison of the statements of the three, I found out that the true facts were these: In order to keep themselves warm, they had walked around the horses a good deal and got separated. Coonskin saw Jimmie and Ben Hatton moving about in the shadow of a tree, and took them to be Yankees. He immediately opened on them, and drew blood at the first fire.

Hatton yelled and fell. Jimmie, taking it for granted that Coonskin was a Yankee, returned his fire; and so they were dodging and shooting at each other from behind trees, until they saw us come dashing up. As we had left them on foot a short while before, it never occurred to them that we were coming back on the captured horses. After fighting each other by mistake and wounding Ben Hatton, they had run away from us. It was an agreeable surprise to them to find that I had their horses.

Ben Hatton will die in the belief that the Yankees shot him; for I never told him any better. I regret that historical truth forbids my concluding this comedy according to the rules of the drama—with a marriage.

Fauquier County, Va., Feb. 28, 1863.

General:—I have the honour to report, that at four o'clock on the morning of the 26th instant I attacked and routed, on the Ox road, in Fairfax, about two miles from Germantown, a cavalry outpost, consisting of a lieutenant and fifty men. The enemy's loss was one lieutenant and three men killed, and five captured; number of wounded not known; also thirty-nine horses, with all their accoutrements, brought off. There were also three horses killed.

I did not succeed in gaining the rear of the post, as I expected, having been discovered by a vidette when several hundred yards off, who fired, and gave the alarm, which compelled me to charge them in front. In the terror and confusion occasioned by our terrific yells, the most of them saved themselves by taking refuge in a dense thicket, where the darkness effectually concealed them. There was also a reserve of one hundred men half a mile off who might come to the rescue. Already encumbered with prisoners and horses, we were in no condition for fighting. I sustained no loss. The enemy made a small show of fight, but quickly yielded. They were in log houses, with the chinking knocked out, and ought to have held them against a greatly superior force, as they all had carbines.

My men behaved very gallantly, although mostly raw recruits. I had only twenty-seven men with me. I am still receiving additions to my numbers.

If you would let me have some of the dismounted men of the First Cavalry, I would undertake to mount them. I desire some written instructions from you with reference to exportation of products within the enemy's lines. I wish the bearer of this to bring back some ammunition, also some large-size envelopes and blank paroles.

I have failed to mention the fact the enemy pursued me as far as Middleburg, without accomplishing anything, etc..

Jno. S. Mosby.

Maj.-Gen. J. E. B. Stuart.

Fairfax Court House, Jan. 27, 1863.

Sir:—Last night my pickets were driven in by some of Stuart's cavalry, wounding one and capturing nine. I then started with some two hundred men in pursuit.

Some twenty-seven miles beyond my pickets at Middleburg, I came up with them, and after a short skirmish, captured twenty-four of them. I have just returned.

P. Wyndham.

Capt. Carroll H. Porter,
Assistant Adjutant-General

CHAPTER 4

# Harassing the Army of the Potomac

It was the latter part of January, 1863, when I crossed the Rappahannock into Northern Virginia, which from that time until the close of the war was the theatre on which I conducted partisan operations. The country had been abandoned to the occupation of the Federal army the year before, when Johnston retired from Centreville, and had never been held by us afterward, except during the short time when the Confederate army was passing through in Gen. Lee's first campaign into Maryland. I told Stuart that I would, by incessant attacks, compel the enemy either greatly to contract his lines or to reinforce them; either of which would be of great advantage to the Southern cause. The means supplied me were hardly adequate to the end I proposed, but I thought that zeal and celerity of movement would go far to compensate for the deficiency of my numbers.

There was a great stake to be won, and I resolved to play a bold game to win it. I think that Stuart was the only man in the army of Northern Virginia, except two or three who accompanied me and knew me well, who expected that I would accomplish anything. Other detachments of cavalry had been sent there at different times that had done little or nothing.

Nearly every one thought that I was starting out on a quixotic enterprise, that would result in doing no harm to the enemy, but simply in getting all of my own men killed or captured. When at last I secured an independent command, for which I had so longed, I was as happy as Columbus when he set forth from the port of Palos with the three little barks Isabella had given him to search for an unknown continent. My faith was strong, and I never for a moment had a feeling of discouragement or doubted my ability to reap a rich harvest from what I knew was still an ungleaned field. I stopped an hour or so at Warrenton, which has always been a sort of political shrine from which the Delphian Apollo issues his oracles. After the war I made it my home, and it is generally supposed that I resided there before the war; the fact is that I never was in that section of Virginia until I went there as a soldier. The Union soldiers knew just as much about the country as I did.

I recall vividly to mind the looks of surprise and the ominous shaking of the heads of the augurs when I told them that I proposed going farther North to begin the war again along the Potomac. Their criticism on my command was pretty much the same as that pronounced on the English mission to Cabul some years ago—that it was too small for an army and too large for an embassy.

When I bade my friends at the Warren-Green Hotel "goodbye," I had their best wishes for my success, but nothing more. They all thought that I was going on the foolhardy enterprise of an Arctic voyager in search of the North Pole. My idea was to make the Piedmont region of the country lying between the Rappahannock and Potomac Rivers the base of my operations. This embraces the upper portion of the counties of Fauquier and Loudoun. It is a rich, pastoral country, which afforded subsistence for my command, while the Blue Ridge was a safe point to which to retreat if hard pressed by the superior numbers that could be sent against us. It was inhabited by a highly refined and cultivated population, who were thoroughly devoted to the Southern cause. Although that region was the Flanders of the war, and harried worse than any of which history furnishes an example since the desolation of the Palatinates by Louis XIV., (see note following), yet the stubborn faith of the people never wavered. When Sheridan started in March, 1865, from Winchester, to join Grant in front of Petersburg, he left my command behind him, more flourishing than it ever had been. The *"intense hatred"* he had hoped to excite in the people of the valley for me, by burning their homes, was only felt for him. They were not willing that I should be a scapegoat to bear another's sins.

★★★★★★

Note:— Telegram

Kernstown, Va., Nov. 26, 1864.

Sheridan to Halleck:—I will soon commence work on Mosby. Heretofore I have made no attempt to break him up, as I would have employed ten men to his one, and for the reason that I have made a scapegoat of him for the destruction of private rights. Now there is going to be an intense hatred of him in that portion of the valley which is nearly a desert. I will soon commence on Loudoun County, and let them know there is a God in Israel. Mosby has annoyed me considerably; but the people are beginning to see that he does not injure me a great deal, but causes a loss to them of all that they have spent their lives in accumulating. Those people who live in the vicinity of Harper's Ferry are the most villainous in this valley, and have not yet been hurt much. If the railroad is interfered with, I will make some of them poor. Those who live at home in peace and plenty want the *duello* part of this war to go on; but when they have to bear the burden by loss of property and comforts, they will cry for peace.

★★★★★★

Amid fire and sword they remained true to the last, and supported me through all the trials of the war. While the country afforded an abundance of subsistence, it was open and scant of forests, with no natural defensive advantages for repelling hostile incursions. There was no such shelter there as Marion had in the swamps of the Pedee, to which he retreated. It was always my policy to avoid fighting at home as much as possible, for the plain reason that it would have encouraged an overwhelming force to come again, and that the services of my own command would have been neutralized by the force sent against it. Even if I defeated them, they would return with treble numbers. On the contrary, it was safer for me, and greater results could be secured, by being the aggressor and striking the enemy at unguarded points. I could thus compel him to guard a hundred points, while I could select any one of them for attack. If I could do so, I generally slipped over when my territory was invaded and imitated Scipio by carrying the war into the enemy's camps.

I have seen it stated in the reports of some Federal officers that they would throw down the gage of battle to me in my own country and that I would not accept it. I was not in the habit of doing what they wanted me to do. Events showed that my judgment was correct. After I had once occupied I never abandoned it, although the wave of invasion several times rolled over it.

News of the surrender, or, rather, the evacuation, of Richmond came to me one morning in April, 1865, at North Fork, in Loudoun County, where my command had assembled to go on a raid.

Just two or three days before that I had defeated Colonel Reno, with the Twelfth Pennsylvania Cavalry, at Hamilton, a few miles from there, which was the last fight in which I commanded. Reno afterward enjoyed some notoriety in connection with the Custer massacre. My purpose was to weaken the armies invading Virginia, by harassing their rear. As a line is only as strong as its weakest point, it was necessary for it to be stronger than I was at every point, in order to resist my attacks. It is easy, therefore, to see the great results that may be accomplished by a small body of cavalry moving rapidly from point to point on the communications of an army.

To destroy supply trains, to break up the means of conveying intelligence, and thus isolating an army from its base, as well as its different corps from each other, to confuse their plans by capturing despatches, are the objects of partisan war. It is just as legitimate to fight an enemy in the rear as in front. The only difference is in the danger. Now, to prevent all these things from being done, heavy detachments must be made to guard against them. The military value of a partisan's work is not measured by the amount of property destroyed, or the number of men killed or captured, but by the number he keeps watching. Every soldier withdrawn from the front to guard the rear of an army is so much taken from its fighting strength.

I endeavoured, as far as I was able, to diminish this aggressive power of the army of the Potomac, by compelling it to keep a large force on the defensive. I assailed its rear, for there was its most vulnerable point. My men had no camps. If they had gone into camp, they would soon have all been captured. They would scatter for safety, and gather at my call, like the Children of the Mist. A blow would be struck at a weak or unguarded point, and then a quick retreat. The alarm would spread through the sleeping camp, the long roll would be beaten or the bugles would sound to horse, there would be mounting in hot haste and a rapid pursuit. But the partisans generally got off with their prey. Their pursuers were striking at an invisible foe.

I often sent small squads at night to attack and run in the pickets along a line of several miles. Of course, these alarms were very annoying, for no human being knows how sweet sleep is but a soldier. I wanted to use and consume the Northern cavalry in hard work. I have often thought that their fierce hostility to me was more on account of the sleep I made them lose than the number we killed and captured. It has always been a wonder with people how I managed to collect my men after dispersing them. The true secret was that it was a fascinating life, and its attractions far more than counterbalanced its hardships and dangers. They had no camp duty to do, which, however necessary, is disgusting to soldiers of high spirit. To put them to such routine work is pretty much like hitching a race-horse to a plough.

Many expeditions were undertaken and traps laid to capture us, but all failed, and my command continued to grow and flourish until the final scene at Appomattox. It had just reached its highest point of efficiency when the time came to surrender. We did not go into a number of traps set to catch us, but somehow we always brought the traps off with us. One stratagem was after the model of the Grecian horse, and would have done credit to Ulysses. They sent a train of wagons up the Little River turnpike from Fairfax, apparently without any guard, thinking that such a bait would surely catch me. But in each wagon were concealed six of the Bucktails, who would, no doubt, have stopped my career, if I had given them a chance. Fortunately, I never saw them, for on that very day I had gone by another route down to Fairfax.

When the Bucktails returned, they had the satisfaction of knowing that I had been there in their absence. At that time Hooker's army was in winter quarters on the Rappahannock, with a line of communication with Washington, both by land and water. The troops belonging to the defences at Washington were mostly cantoned in Fairfax, with their advance post at Centreville. West of the Blue Ridge, Milroy occupied Winchester. From my rendezvous east of the ridge I could move on the radius and strike any point on the circumference of the circle which was not too strongly guarded. But if I compelled them to be stronger everywhere than I was, then so much the better. I had done my work. Panics had often occurred in the camp when we were not near; the pickets became so nervous, expecting attacks, that they fired at every noise. It was thought that the honour as well as the safety of the army required that these depredations should no longer be endured, and that something must be done to stop them. Of course, the best way to do it was to exterminate the band, as William of Orange did the Macdonald of Glencoe.

A cavalry expedition, under a Major Gilmer, was sent up to Loudoun to do the work. He had conceived the idea that I had my headquarters in Middleburg, and might be caught by surrounding the place in the night-time. He arrived before daybreak, and threw a cordon of pickets around it. At the dawn of day he had the village as completely invested as Metz was by the Germans. He then gradually contracted his lines, and proceeded in person to the hotel where he supposed I was in bed. I was not there; I never had been. Soldiers were sent around to every house with orders to arrest every man they could find. When he drew in his net there was not a single soldier in it. He had, however, caught a number of old men. It was a frosty morning, and he amused himself by making a soldier take them through a squad drill to keep them warm; occasionally he would make them mark time in the street front of the hotel.

All this afforded a good deal of fun to the major, but was rather rough on the old men. He thought, or pretended to think, that they were the parties who had attacked his pickets. After a night march of twenty-five miles, he did not like to return to camp without some trophies, so he determined to carry the graybeards with him. He mounted each one behind a trooper, and started off. Now, it so happened that I had notified my men to meet that morning at Rector's Cross Roads, which is about four miles above Middleburg. When I got there I heard that the latter place was occupied by Federal cavalry. With seventeen men I started down the pike to look after them.

Of course, with my small force, all that I could expect to do was to cut off some straggling parties who might be marauding about the neighbourhood. When I got near Middleburg I learned that they had gone. We entered the town at a gallop. The ladies all immediately crowded around us. There were, of course, no men among them; Major Gilmer had taken them with him. There was, of course, great indignation at the rough usage they had received, and their wives never expected to see them again.

And then, to add to the *pathos* of the scene, were the tears and lamentations of the daughters. There were many as pure and as bright as any pearl that ever shone in Oman's green water. Their beauty had won the hearts of many of my men. To avenge the wrongs of distressed damsels is one of the vows of knighthood; so we spurred on to overtake the Federal cavalry, in hopes that by some accident of war we might be able to liberate the prisoners.

CHAPTER 5

# How Major Gilmer Tried to Capture Mosby's Command

*Still o'er these scenes my memory wakes,*
*And fondly broods with miser care!*
*Time but the impression stronger makes,*
*As streams their channels deeper wear.*—Burns.

About five miles below Middleburg is the village of Aldie, where I expected that the Federal cavalry would halt. But when I got within a mile of it I met a citizen, just from the place, who told me the cavalry had passed through. With five or six men I rode forward while the others followed on more slowly. Just as I rose to the top of the hill on the outskirts of the village, I suddenly came upon two Federal cavalrymen ascending from the opposite side. Neither party had been aware of the approach of the other, and our meeting was so unexpected that our horses' heads nearly butted together before we could stop. They surrendered, of course, and were sent to the rear. They said that they had been sent out as videttes. Looking down the hill, I saw before me several mounted men in the road, whom I took to be a part of the rear-guard of Major Gilmer's column. We dashed after them. I was riding a splendid horse—a noble bay—Job's war-horse was a mustang compared to him—who had now got his mettle up and carried me at headlong speed right among them.

I had no more control over him than Mazeppa had over the Ukraine steed to which he was bound. I had scarcely started in the charge, before I discovered that there was a body of cavalry dismounted at a mill near the roadside, which I had not before seen. They were preparing to feed their horses. As their pickets had given no alarm, they had no idea that an enemy was near, and were stunned and dazed by the apparition of a body of men who they imagined must have dropped from the clouds upon them. The fact was that we were as much surprised as they were. I was unable to stop my horse when I got to them, but he kept straight on like a streak of lightning.

Fortunately, the dismounted troopers were so much startled that it never occurred to them to take a shot at me *in transitu*. They took it for granted that an overwhelming force was on them, and every man was for saving himself. Some took to the Bull Run mountain, which was near by, and others ran into the mill and buried themselves like rats in the wheat bins. The mill was grinding, and some were so much frightened that they jumped into the hoppers and came near being ground up into flour. When we pulled them out there was nothing blue about them.

As I have stated, my horse ran with me past the mill. My men stopped there and went to work, but I kept on. And now another danger loomed up in front of me. Just ahead was the bridge over Little River, and on the opposite bank I saw another body of cavalry looking on in a state of bewildered excitement. They saw the stampede at the mill and a solitary horseman, pistol in hand, riding full speed right into their ranks. They never fired a shot. Just as I got to the bridge I jumped off my horse to save myself from capture; but just at the same moment they wheeled and took to their heels down the pike. They had seen the rest of my men coming up. If I had known that they were going to run I would have stayed on my horse. They went clattering down the pike, with my horse thundering after them. He chased them all the way into the camp.

They never drew rein until they got inside their picket lines. I returned on foot to the mill; not a half a dozen shots were fired. All that couldn't get away surrendered. But just then a Federal officer made his appearance at the bridge. He had ridden down the river, and, having just returned, had heard the firing, but did not comprehend the situation. Tom Turner of Maryland, one of the bravest of my men, dashed at him. As Turner was alone, I followed him. I now witnessed a single-handed fight between him and the officer. For want of numbers, it was not so picturesque as the combat, described by Livy, between the Horatii and the Curatii, nor did such momentous issues depend upon it. But the gallantry displayed was equally as great.

Before I got up I saw the horse of the Federal officer fall dead upon him, and at the same time Turner seemed about to fall from his horse. The Federal officer, who was Capt. Worthington of the Vermont cavalry, had fired while lying under his horse at Turner and inflicted quite a severe wound. The first thing Turner said to me was that his adversary had first surrendered, which threw him off his guard, and then fired on him. Worthington denied it, and said his shot was fired in fair fight. I called some of the men to get him out from under his horse. He was too much injured by the fall to be taken away, so I paroled and left him with a family there to be cared for.

While all this was going on, the men were busy at the mill. They had a good deal of fun pulling the Vermont boys out of the wheat bins. The first one they brought out was so caked with flour that I thought they had the miller. We got the commanding officer, Capt. Huttoon, and nineteen men and twenty-three horses, with their arms and equipments. I lingered behind with one man, and sent the captures back to Middleburg. Now, all the ladies there had been watching and listening as anxiously to hear from us as Andromache and her maids did for the news of the combat between Hector and Achilles. Presently they saw a line of blue coats coming up the pike, with some gray ones mixed among them.

Then the last ray of hope departed—they thought we were all prisoners, and that the foe was returning to insult them. One of the most famous of my men—Dick Moran—rode forward as a herald of victory. He had the voice of a fog horn, and proclaimed the glad tidings to the town. While I was still sitting on my horse at the mill, three more of the Vermont men, thinking that all of us had gone, came out from their hiding place. I sent them on after the others. Up to this time I had been under the impression that it was Maj. Gilmer's rear-guard that I had overtaken. I now learned that this was a body of Vermont cavalry that had started that morning several hours after Gilmer had left. They had halted to feed their horses at the mill. As they came up they had seen a body of cavalry turn off toward Centreville. That was all they knew. I then rode down the road to look after my horse that I had lost. I had not gone far before I met the old men that Maj. Gilmer had taken off.

They were all happy at the ludicrous streak of fortune that had brought them deliverance. It seems that Maj. Gilmer knew nothing of the intention of Capt. Huttoon to pay Middleburg a visit that day. When he got below Aldie he saw a considerable body of cavalry coming from the direction of Fairfax. It never occurred to him that they were his own people. He took them for my men, and thought I was trying to surround him. Even if he did think the force he saw was my command, it is hard to understand why he should run away from the very thing that he was in search of. But so he did. Just at the point where he was when he saw the Vermont men the pike crosses the old Braddock road. It is the same on which the British general marched with young George Washington to death and defeat on the Monongahela. Maj. Gilmer turned and started down the Braddock road at about the speed that John Gilpin rode to Edmonton on his wedding day. The ground was soft, and his horses sank knee deep in the mud at every jump. Of course, those broke down first that were carrying two. As he thought he was hard pressed, he kept on fast and furious, taking no heed of those he left on the roadside. It was necessary to sacrifice a part to save the rest.

Long before he got to Centreville, about one-half of his horses were sticking in the mud, and all his prisoners had been abandoned. They had to walk home. Maj. Gilmer never came after me again. I heard that he resigned his commission in disgust, and, with Othello, "bade farewell to the big wars that make ambition virtue." There was rejoicing in Middleburg that evening; all ascribed to a special providence the advent of the Vermont cavalry just in time to stampede the New Yorkers, and make them drop their prisoners; and that my horse had run away, and carried me safely through the Vermont squadron. The miller, too, was happy, because I had appeared just in time to save his corn. At night, with song and dance, we celebrated the events, and forgot the dangers of the day.

Headquarters Cavalry Brigade,<br>Fairfax Court-House, Va., March 3, 1863.

Sir:—By order of Col. R. B. Price, I directed, on the night of the 1st instant, a reconnoissance to go in direction of Aldie.

The officer who commanded this reconnoissance was Major Joseph Gilmer, of the Eighteenth Pennsylvania Cavalry. He had two hundred men. The orders to him were to proceed carefully, and send back couriers through the night with information whether they saw any enemy or not. This last order was disobeyed. They were not to cross Cub Run until daylight, and then try and gain all information possible by flankers and small detached scouting parties.

Major Gilmer went to Middleburg, and, while returning, the videttes of the First Vermont Cavalry noticed a part of his advance and prepared to skirmish. The advance fell back toward Aldie. Major Gilmer, instead of throwing out a party to reconnoitre, turned off with nearly the whole of his command in the direction of Groveton, to gain Centreville. The horses returned exhausted from being run at full speed for miles. A few of Major Gilmer's men left his command and went along the Little River turnpike toward the Vermont detachment. They reported that the men seen were a part of a scouting party under Major Gilmer, and that no enemy were in Aldie.

Capt. Huttoon then entered the town, and halted to have the horses fed near a mill. Immediately beyond was a rising ground which hid the guerillas. While the horses were unbridled and feeding, the surprise occurred. As both the officers have been captured, and as the detachment was not under my command, and is not attached to this brigade, I have no means of receiving any official or exact report from them, nor is there any one belonging to that detachment here. All men belonging to this detachment seem to have fought well; the enemy did not pursue them; they fell back in good order.

Major Gilmer, when he returned, was unable to make a report to Lieut.-Col. (John S.) Krepps, who during the time I was confined from sickness, had charge of the camp. I ordered Major Gilmer under arrest early this morning, and have sent to Col. R. B. Price charges, of which the annexed is a copy. Major Gilmer lost but one man, belonging to the Fifth New York Cavalry, who was mortally wounded by the enemy and afterwards robbed. He was away from the command and on this side of Aldie, his horse having given out. The enemy seemed to have been concealed along the line of march and murdered this man, when returning, without provocation.

I have the honour to be, very respectfully, your obedient servant,

            Robt. Johnstone,
     Lieut.-Col. Commanding Cavalry Brigade.

Capt. C. H. Potter,
Assistant Adjutant-General.

| | |
|---|---|
| General Orders | War Department. |
| No. 229. | Adjutant-General's Office. |
| | Washington, July 23, 1863. |

I. Before a General Court Martial, which convened in the city of Washington, D.C, March 27, 1863, pursuant to General Orders, No. 20, dated Headquarters Cavalry, Defences of Washington, near Fort Scott, Virginia, February 2, 1863, and Special Orders, No. 146, dated February 10, 1863; No. 150, dated February 16, 1863; No. 161, dated March 6, 1863; and No. 164, dated March 21, 1863, Headquarters Cavalry, Department of Washington, and of which Colonel E. B. SAWYER, 1st Vermont Cavalry, is President, was arraigned and tried—

Major Joseph Gilmer, 18th Pennsylvania Cavalry.

Charge 1.—"Drunkenness."

Specification—"In this; that Joseph Gilmer, a Major of the 18th Pennsylvania Cavalry, he then being in the service of the United States, and while in command of a reconnoitring party, on the second day of March, 1863, was so intoxicated from the effects of spirituous liquors as to be incapacitated to perform his duties in an officer-like manner. This at or near the village of Aldie, in the State of Virginia."

Charge 2—"Cowardice."

Specification—"In this; that Joseph Gilmer, a Major in the 18th Pennsylvania Cavalry, he then being in the service of the United States, upon the second day of March, 1863, did permit and encourage a detachment of cavalry, in the service of the United States, and under his command, to fly from a small body of the 1st Vermont Cavalry, who were mistaken for the enemy, without sending out any person or persons to ascertain who they were, or what were their numbers; and that the said cavalry under his command, as above stated, were much demoralised, and fled many miles through the country in great confusion and disorder. This near Aldie, in the State of Virginia."

To which charges and specifications the accused, Major Joseph Gilmer; 18th Pennsylvania Cavalry, pleaded "Not Guilty."

Finding.

The Court, having maturely considered the evidence adduced, finds the accused, Major Joseph Gilmer, 18th Pennsylvania Cavalry, as follows:—

                        Charge 1.

    Of the Specification,    Guilty.
    Of the Charge,         Guilty.

                    Charge 2.
    Of the Specification,     Guilty.
    Of the Charge,            Not Guilty.
                    Sentence.
And the Court does therefore sentence him, Major Joseph Gilmer, 18th Pennsylvania Cavalry, "To be cashiered."

2. The proceedings of the Court in the above case were disapproved by the Major-General commanding the Department of Washington, on account of fatal defects and irregularities in the record. But the testimony shows that the accused was *drunk* on duty, and brought disgrace upon himself and the service. The President directs that, as recommended by the Department Commander, he be dismissed the service; and Major Joseph Gilmer, 18th Pennsylvania Cavalry, accordingly ceases to be an officer in the United States Service since the 20th day of July, 1863.

    By Order of the Secretary Of War:

                                    E. D. Townsend,
                        Assistant Adjutant-General.

                Fairfax Court House, March 2, 1863.
Sir:—Fifty men of the First Vermont Cavalry, from Companies H and M, under Captains Huttoon and Woodward, were surprised in Aldie while feeding their horses by about 70 of the enemy. Both captains captured and about 15 men. They saw no enemy but the attacking party. Major Gilmer has returned with the scouting party that left last night. They were to Middleburg and saw but one rebel. I have anticipated the report of Lieutenant-Colonel Krepps, now in command, which will be forwarded in probably one hour.

                                    Robt. Johnstone,
            Lieutenant-Colonel, commanding Cavalry Brigade.
Capt. C. H. Potter,
Assistant Adjutant-General.

CHAPTER 6

# Sergeant Ames Deserts and Joins Mosby

Within a few weeks after I began operations in Northern Virginia, I received accessions to my command from various sources. I have before spoken of the convalescents in the hospital at Middleburg, out of whom I got some valuable service. The Confederate government did not furnish horses to the cavalry, but paid each man forty cents a day compensation for the use of his horse. When the trooper lost his horse, or it became disabled, he was given a furlough to go to get another. A great many of this class of men came to me, to whom I would furnish captured horses in consideration of their going with me on a few raids. I made a proposition to mount all the dismounted men of Fitz Lee's brigade in consideration of their serving with me a short time.

It was declined, and they were sent over to Fauquier under command of an ambitious officer, who thought, like Sam Patch when he leaped over Genesee falls, that some things could be done as well as others. Reports of my forays, which had been almost uniformly successful, had spread through the army, and it seemed, after the thing had been done, to be a very easy thing to surprise and capture cavalry outposts. The result of this attempt at imitation was that all the dismounted men were returned as prisoners of war via Fort Monroe, the mounted officer who commanded them alone escaping capture.

About this time I received a valuable recruit in the person of Sergt. Ames of the 5th New York cavalry, who deserted his regiment to join me. I never really understood what his motives were in doing so. I never cared to inquire. The men of my command insisted that I should treat him simply as a prisoner, and send him back to join many of his comrades whom I had sent to Richmond. After a long conversation with him I felt an instinctive confidence in his sincerity. He came to me on foot, but proposed to return to camp and mount himself if I would receive him. It happened that a young man named Walter Frankland was present, who also came on foot to join my standard. With my consent they agreed to walk down to Fairfax that night, enter the cavalry camp on foot and ride out on two of the best horses they could find.

At the same time, I started off on an expedition in another direction. I had not gone far before I struck the trail of a raiding party of cavalry that had been off into Loudoun committing depredations on the citizens. I met old Dr. Drake walking home through snow and mud knee deep. He told me that the Federal cavalry had met him in the road, while he was going around to attend to the sick, and had not only taken his horse but also his saddle-bags, with all his medicines. As the Confederacy was then in a state of blockade, medicine was more valuable than gold, and great suffering would be inflicted on a community by the loss even of Dr. Drake's small stock. He told us that the marauders were not far ahead, and we spurred on to overtake them. Fortunately, as they were not far from their camps, they deemed themselves safe, and scattered over the country a good deal.

Before going very far we overtook a party that had stopped to plunder a house. As they were more intent on saving their plunder than fighting, they scampered off, but we were close on their heels. We had intercepted them and were between them and their camp, so they had to run in an opposite direction. But very soon they came to a narrow stream, the Horsepen Run, which was booming with the melted snow. The man on the fleetest horse, who was some distance in advance of the others, plunged in and narrowly escaped being drowned. He was glad to get back even as a prisoner. The others did not care to follow his example, but quietly submitted to manifest destiny. We got them all. They were loaded down mostly with silver spoons, of which they had despoiled the houses they had visited. But the richest prize of all we got was old Dr. Drake's saddle-bags. I was strongly tempted to administer to each one of the prisoners a purge by way of making them expiate their offence.

Now, when Dr. Drake parted with his saddle-bags, he never expected to see them again, and supposed that as long as the war lasted his occupation would be gone, as a doctor without medicine and implements of surgery is like a soldier without arms. His surprise and delight may be imagined when a few hours afterward his saddle-bags and the captured silver were brought to him to be restored to the owners.

We then proceeded on toward Fryingpan, where I had heard that a cavalry picket was stationed and waiting for me to come after them. I did not want them to be disappointed in their desire to visit Richmond. When I got within a mile of it and had stopped for a few minutes to make my disposition for attack, I observed two ladies walking rapidly toward me. One was Miss Laura Ratcliffe, a young lady to whom Stuart had introduced me a few weeks before, when returning from his raid on Dumfries—with her sister. Their home was near Fryingpan, and they had got information of a plan to capture me, and were just going to the house of a citizen to get him to put me on my guard, when fortune brought them across my path. But for meeting them, my life as a partisan would have closed that day. There was a cavalry post in sight at Fryingpan, but near there, in the pines, a large body of cavalry had been concealed. It was expected that I would attack the picket, but that my momentary triumph would be like the fabled Dead Sea's fruit—ashes to the taste—as the party in the pines would pounce from their hiding-place upon me.

A garrulous lieutenant had disclosed the plot to the young lady, never dreaming that she would walk through the snow to get the news to me. This was not the only time during the war when I owed my escape from danger to the tact of a Southern woman. I concluded then to go in the direction of Dranesville in search of game. When we reached Herndon Station, I learned that the contents of a sutler's wagon, that had broken down when passing there that day, were concealed in a barn near by. The sutler had gone into camp to get another team to haul his goods in. In the exercise of our belligerent rights, we proceeded to relieve him of any further trouble in taking care of them. He had a splendid stock of cavalry boots, with which he seemed to have been provided in anticipation of the wants of my men. Now, loaded down with what was to us a richer prize than the Golden Fleece, we started back, but could not forbear taking along a cavalry picket near by which was not looking for us, as it had been understood that we were to attack Fryingpan that night, where preparations had been made to receive us. Once more I had tempted fortune, and from "*the nettle danger had plucked the flower safety.*"

On my return to Middleburg I found Ames and Frankland there in advance of me. They had entered the camp of the Fifth New York cavalry at night on foot, and had ridden out on two of the finest horses they could find in the stables. They had passed in and out without ever having been molested or challenged by the guard. Ames had not had time to exchange his suit of blue for a gray one, but Frankland was in full Confederate uniform. It was a perfectly legitimate enterprise, certainly, as open and bold as the capture in the night-time of the Palladium of Troy by Ulysses and Diomede. But still the men were not satisfied of Ames's good faith. They said that he had not betrayed Frankland because he wanted to entrap us all at one time.

A few days after that, I once more put him to a test which convinced the men of his truth and fidelity. He seemed to burn with an implacable feeling of revenge toward his old companions in arms. I never had a truer or more devoted follower. He was killed in a skirmish in October, 1864, and carried the secret of his desertion to the grave. I had made him a lieutenant, and he had won by his courage and general deportment the respect and affection of my men. They all sincerely mourned his death.

Since the war I have often passed his lonely grave in a clump of trees on the very spot where he fell. The soldier who killed him was in the act of taking his arms off when one of my men rode up and shot him. Ames is a prominent figure in the history of my command. It was my habit either to go myself, with one or two men, or to send scouts, to find out some weak and exposed place in the enemy's lines. I rarely rested for more than one day at a time. As soon as I knew of a point offering a chance for a successful attack, I gathered my men together and struck a blow. From the rapidity with which these attacks were delivered and repeated, and the distant points at which they were made, a most exaggerated estimate of the number of my force was made. I have before spoken of John Underwood, to whose courage and skill as a guide I was so much indebted for my earlier successes. He was equally at home threading a thick labyrinth of pines in Fairfax or leading a charge. He was among the first everywhere, and I always rewarded his zeal.

About this time I had sent him down on a scout, from which he returned informing me that a picket of thirty or forty cavalry had been placed at Herndon Station on the Loudoun & Hampshire Railroad. This was the very place where I had got the sutler's wagon the week before. I could hardly believe it—I thought it must be another trap—for I could not imagine why such a number of men should be put there, except for the purpose of getting caught. I had supposed that the enemy had been taught something by experience. I collected my men and started down, though I did not expect to find any one at Herndon when I got there.

Fearing an ambuscade, and also hearing that the reserve at the post stayed in a house, I thought I would try my luck in the daytime. Besides, as most of my attacks had been made at night, I knew they would not expect me in the day. Underwood conducted me by all sorts of crooked paths through the dense forests until we got in their rear. We then advanced at a walk along the road leading to their camp at Dranesville, until we came upon a vidette, who saw us, but did not have time either to fire or to run away. He was ours before he recovered his senses, he was so much surprised. About 200 yards in front of us, I could see the boys in blue lounging around an old sawmill, with their horses tied by their halters to the fence.

It was past twelve o'clock, and the sun was shining brightly, but there was a deep snow on the ground. They were as unconscious of the presence of danger as if they had been at their own peaceful homes among the Green Mountains. It happened to be just the hour for the relief to come from their camp at Dranesville. They saw us approaching, but mistook us for friends. When we got within 100 yards, I ordered a charge. They had no time to mount their horses, and fled, panic-stricken, into the sawmill and took refuge on the upper floor. I knew that if I gave them time to recover from the shock of their surprise they could hold the mill with their carbines against my force until re-enforcements reached them.

The promptness with which the opportunity was seized is the reason that they were lost and we were saved. They were superior in numbers, with the advantage of being under cover. The last ones had hardly got inside the mill before we were upon them. I dismounted and rushed into the mill after them, followed by John De Butts. The enemy were all above me. As I started up the steps I ordered the men to set fire to the mill. I knew that this order would be heard overhead and increase the panic. The mill was full of dry timber and shavings that would have burned them to cinders in ten minutes. As I reached the head of the stairway I ordered a surrender. They all did so. They had the alternative of doing this or being roasted alive. In a minute more the mill would have been in flames.

Against such an enemy they had no weapon of defence, and, in preference to cremation, chose to be prisoners. On going out and remounting, I observed four finely caparisoned horses standing in front of the house of Nat Hanna, a Union man. I knew that the horses must have riders, and that from their equipments they must be officers. I ordered some of the men to go into the house and bring them out. They found a table spread with milk, honey, and all sorts of nice delicacies for a lunch.

But no soldiers could be seen, and Mrs. Hanna was too good a Union woman to betray them. Some of the men went upstairs, but by the dim light could see nothing on the floor. Ames opened the door to the garret; he peeped in and called, but it was pitch dark, and no one answered. He thought it would do no harm to fire a shot into the darkness. It had a magical effect. There was a stir and a crash, and instantly a human being was seen descending through the ceiling. He fell on the floor right among the men. The flash of the pistol in his face had caused him to change his position, and in doing so he had stepped on the lathing and fallen through. His descent had been easy and without injury to his person. He was thickly covered with lime dust and mortar.

After he was brushed off, we discovered that we had a major. His three companions in the dark hole were a captain and two lieutenants, who came out through the trap-door, and rather enjoyed the laugh we had on the major. As we left the house the lunch disappeared with us. It was put there to be eaten. The major was rather dilatory in mounting. He knew that the relief was due there, and was in hope not only of a rescue, but of turning the tables and taking us with him to his camp. But fate had decreed otherwise. He was admonished of the importance of time to us, and that he must go right on to Richmond, where he had started to go the year before.

As soon as possible, John Underwood, with a guard, went on in advance with the prisoners. Just as we left the railroad station the relief appeared in sight. I remained behind with a dozen men as a rear-guard, to keep them back until Underwood had got far ahead. The relief party hung on in sight of me for some distance, but never attacked. After I crossed the Horsepen, which almost swam our horses, I started off at a gallop, thinking the pursuit was over. This emboldened the pursuers, and a few came on and crossed after me. I saw that they were divided, and I halted, wheeled, and started back at them. They did not wait for me, but got over the stream as fast as they could. One fellow got a good ducking. I was now master of the situation. I drew up on a hill and invited them to come across, but they declined. I was not molested any more that day. A rather ludicrous thing occurred when we made the attack at the station.

There was a so-called Union man there, named Mayo Janney. As he lived just on the outskirts of the picket line, he was permitted to conduct a small store, and trade with Washington. He had been down to the city, and, with other things, had brought out a hogshead of molasses, which he intended to retail to his neighbours at speculative prices. The element of danger in such a trade was, of course, largely considered in estimating the market value of the merchandise. Janney had his store in the vacant railroad depot. He had just knocked out the bung of the barrel of molasses, and was in the act of drawing some to fill the jug of a customer, when he heard the clatter and yell of my men, as they rushed down on the terrified pickets.

As Herndon Station and the region round about was supposed to be in the exclusive occupation of the army of the United States, he could not have been more surprised at an earthquake, or if a comet had struck the earth. Forgetting all about the molasses, which he had left pouring out of the barrel, he rushed wildly to the door to see what was the matter. He saw the Vermont cavalry flying in every direction in confusion, and whizzing bullets passing unpleasantly close to his ears.

Now, to be a martyr in any cause was just the last thing which a man in Fairfax, who had taken an oath to support the constitution of the United States, had any idea of being. Janney's idea of supporting the Union was to make some money out of it, and a living for his family. But he did not consider that his oath required him to stay there to be shot, or to help to bury or bind up the wounds of those who might be. His idea of honour was as selfish and material as Sir John Falstaff's. He preferred remaining a live man without it, to being a dead one who died with it yesterday.

So Janney ran away as fast as his legs could carry him, and, if possible, his molasses ran faster than he did. He did not return for several hours to view the field. When he at last mustered up courage to go back, he found the molasses about shoe-deep all over the floor, but not a drop in the barrel.

Now, Janney's loyalty to the Union was not altogether above suspicion. It was suspected that he had taken the oath for profit, and probably to enable him to act as a spy for me. The loss of his molasses proved his innocence; but for that fact he would have been arrested and sent to board at the Old Capitol on the charge of having given me the information on which I had acted.

When I overtook my command at Middleburg, I found Dick Moran, after the style of the ancient bards, in the street, rehearsing the incidents of the day to an admiring crowd. I paroled the privates and let them go home, as I could not then spare a guard to take them back to the Confederate lines, which were at Culpepper. I put the four officers on their parole to report at Culpepper to Fitz Lee, and sent with them, simply as an escort, a Hungarian whom we called Jake. On the way out they spent one night at a farmer's house.

Now, Jake had been a soldier under Kossuth, and having had some experience in Austrian perfidy, had no sort of confidence in the military value of a parole. When time came for the officers to go to bed, Jake volunteered to take their boots down to the kitchen to be blacked. He had no fears of their leaving, barefooted, in the snow, as long as he held on to their boots. Jake told me, with a chuckle, of his stratagem, on his return. He never doubted that it kept his prisoners from going away that night.

Dranesville, Va., March 24, 1863.

Colonel:—I have the honor to report, on the 17th instant, at 1 p.m., the reserve picket post at Herndon Station, consisting of twenty-five men, under command of Second Lieut. Alexander G. Watson, Company L, First Vermont Cavalry, was surprised by Capt. Mosby, with a force of forty-two men, and twenty-one of our men, together with Maj. William Wells, Capt. Robert Schofield, Company F, and Second Lieut. Alexander G. Watson, Company L, and Perley C. J. Cheney, Company C (second lieutenant) captured, all of First Vermont Cavalry; the three first were visiting the post. The surprise was so complete the men made but little or no resistance. The enemy were led on by citizens and entered on foot by a bridle-path in rear of the post, capturing the vidette stationed on the road before he was able to give the alarm.

Every effort was made, on receipt of the intelligence by me, to capture the party, but without avail. Had Second Lieut. Edwin H. Higley, Company K, First Vermont Cavalry, who had started with the relief for the post, consisting of forty men, together with ten of the old guard, who joined him, performed his duty, the whole party could, and would, have been taken. I cannot too strongly urge that orders may be given that all citizens near outpost must remove beyond the lines.

Such occurrences are exceedingly discreditable, but sometimes unavoidable, not only calculated to embolden the enemy, but dispirit our men. I am, &c.,

Charles F. Taggart,<br>Major, Commanding Post.

Col. R. Butler Price,
Commanding, &c.

Near Piedmont, Va., March 18, 1863.

General:—Yesterday I attacked a body of the enemy's cavalry at Herndon Station, in Fairfax County, completely routing them. I brought off twenty-five prisoners—a major (Wells), one captain, two lieutenants, and twenty-one men, all their arms, twenty-six horses and equipments. One, severely wounded, was left on the ground. The enemy pursued me in force, but were checked by my rear-guard and gave up the pursuit. My loss was nothing.

The enemy have moved their cavalry from Germantown back of Fairfax Court House on the Alexandria pike.

In this affair my officers and men behaved splendidly, &c.

Jno. S. Mosby,<br>Captain, &c.

Indorsement.
Maj.-Gen. J. E. B. Stuart.

Headquarters Army of Northern Virginia,<br>March 21, 1863.

Respectfully forwarded for the information of the department and as evidence of the merit and continued success of Captain Mosby.

R. E. Lee,<br>General.

CHAPTER 7

# Sudden Attacks upon Federal Cavalry Outposts

*'Tis sweet to win, no matter how, one's laurels.*
*By blood or ink.—Don Juan.*

During the time I had been operating against the outposts of the Union Army in Northern Virginia I kept up a regular correspondence with Stuart by means of couriers, and reported to him the result of every action. The base from where I operated was on its flank, and so I compelled it to present a double front. The prisoners taken were sometimes released on their paroles, but generally sent out under charge of a guard to the provost marshal at Culpepper Court House. The necessity of making the details for guard duty seriously diminished my effective strength. It would take nearly a week for them to go over and return, and I was often compelled to wait on that account before undertaking an expedition.

The men, too, who would join me to go on a raid just to get a horse would generally quit as soon as it was over to return to their own regiments. When an enterprise had been accomplished, I was often left as forlorn as Montrose after fighting and winning a battle with the undisciplined Highland clans—they had all scattered and gone home with their plunder. I would have to give notice of my place and time of meeting several days in advance, in order to make sure of a sufficient number answering the call to effect any good work.

The longer I remained in the country, successful raids became more difficult, as the enemy was all the time on the lookout, and kept every point closely guarded. I had promised Stuart, as an inducement to let me have some men, either to compel the enemy to contract their lines in Fairfax County or to reinforce them heavily. Having no fixed lines to guard or defined territory to hold, it was always my policy to elude the enemy when they came in search of me, and carry the war into their own camps.

This was the best way to keep them at home. To have fought my own command daily, on equal terms and in open combats against the thousands that could have been brought against it by the North, would soon have resulted in its entire annihilation. I endeavoured to compensate for my limited resources by stratagems, surprises, and night attacks, in which the advantage was generally on my side, notwithstanding the superior numbers we assailed. For this reason, the complaint has often been made against me that I would not fight fair. So an old Austrian general complained that Bonaparte violated all military maxims and traditions by flying about from post to post in Italy, breaking up his cantonments and fighting battles in the winter time. The accusations that have been made against my mode of warfare are about as reasonable. In one sense the charge that I did not fight fair is true. I fought for success and not for display. There was no man in the Confederate Army who had less of the spirit of knight-errantry in him, or took a more practical view of war than I did.

The combat between Richard and Saladin by the Diamond of the Desert is a beautiful picture for the imagination to dwell on, but it isn't war, and was no model for me. The poets have invested the deeds of the Templars with the colours of romance; but if they were half as generous as they were said to have been, it was because their swords, and not their hearts, were dedicated to a cause.

I never admired and did not imitate the example of the commander who declined the advantage of the first fire. But, while I conducted war on the theory that the end of it is to secure peace by the destruction of the resources of the enemy, with as small a loss as possible to my own side, there is no authenticated act of mine which is not perfectly in accordance with approved military usage. Grant, Sheridan, and Stonewall Jackson had about the same ideas that I had on the subject of war. I will further add that I was directly under the orders of Stuart up to the time of his death, in May, 1864, and after that time, of Gen. Robert E. Lee, until the end of the war. With both of these two great Christian soldiers I had the most confidential relations. My military conduct received from them not only approbation, but many encomiums. In a letter received from Stuart about this, he said, "I heartily wish you great and increasing success in the glorious career on which you have entered."

In September, 1864, I visited Gen. Lee at his headquarters, near Petersburg. I had been badly wounded a week or so before by a bullet, which I still carry in me. When he saw me hobbling up to him on my crutches, he came to meet me, and said, as he extended his hand, "Colonel, I have never had but one fault to find with you—you are always getting wounded." I mention this circumstance to show that all I did had the sanction of the commander of the army of Northern Virginia, of which my own command—the Forty-third Battalion of Virginia Cavalry—was a part. I was independent simply in the sense that both Gen. Lee and Gen. Stuart had such confidence in me that they never undertook to trammel me with orders, but gave me full discretion to act as I chose. After the death of Stuart, Gen. Lee frequently wrote to me, although we were separated by a distance of over a hundred miles. All of his letters are in his own handwriting. What were called my depredations had caused another brigade of cavalry to be sent into Fairfax to protect Washington. The frequent incursions we had made down there created great alarm and an apprehension that they might be extended across the Potomac. The deliberations of the Senate were frequently disturbed by the cry that the Gauls were at the gate.

One day I rode down on a scout in sight of the dome of the Capitol, when a wagon came along, going to Washington, which was driven by the wife of a Union man who had left his home in Virginia and taken refuge there. I stopped it, and, after some conversation with the driver, told her who I was. With a pair of scissors she had I cut off a lock of my hair and sent it to Mr. Lincoln, with a message that I was coming to get one of his soon. A few days after this, I saw in the *Star* that it had been delivered to him, and that the President enjoyed the joke.

After returning from my last expedition to Herndon Station, I had sent John Underwood down to search along the lines for a weak point where I might make a successful attack. This had now become very difficult to do. There had been so many real and false alarms that the pickets were always on the watch, and slept with their eyes open. The videttes were stationed so close together that it was impossible to pass them without being discovered; and a snowbird could not fly by without being fired at. They had so strengthened their lines that, where formerly there had been not over a dozen men, there were now a hundred. If there was a hole anywhere, I knew that John Underwood would find it.

I had about that time received another recruit, who became famous in the annals of my command. His home was in Loudoun, and his name was William Hibbs. He was always called the "Major," although he never held a commission. He was a blacksmith by trade, over fifty years old, and had already fully discharged the duty he owed to the Southern Confederacy by sending his two sons into the army. But for my appearance in the vicinity, he would probably have lived and died unheard.

The fame of the exploits of my men, and the rich prizes they won, aroused his martial ambition; and he determined to quit the forge and become a warrior bold. The country soon echoed the notes of his fame, as the anvil had once rung with the strokes of his hammer. Around the *triumvirate*—Dick Moran, John Underwood, and Major Hibbs—recruits now gathered as iron filings cluster around a magnet. They were the germs from which my command grew and spread like a banyan tree. Beattie, who was always my faithful Achates, had been captured, but was soon afterward exchanged. Underwood, on his return from his scout, reported a body of about 100 cavalry at Chantilly, which was in supporting distance of several other bodies of about equal numbers. An attack on the post there would be extremely hazardous, on account of the proximity of the others.

The chance of success was a poor one; but, as about fifty men had assembled to go with me, I did not like to disappoint them. Each man wanted a horse, as well as a leader to show him how to get one. They were all willing to risk a good deal, and so was I. We started off for Chantilly, down the Little River Turnpike, as the mud prevented our travelling any other route. The advantage of attacking at Chantilly was not only that we had a good road to travel on, but I knew it was the very last place they expected I would attack. They did not look for my approach in broad daylight along the pike, but thought I would come by some crooked path after dark through the pines.

I had never asked a commission of the Confederate government, but the warfare I had been conducting had attracted the attention of Gen. Robert E. Lee, who not only complimented me in general orders published to the army, but at his request the President of the Confederate States sent me a commission as captain, with authority to organise a company of cavalry. This was succeeded, in the course of two or three weeks, with a commission of major. Before the close of the war I became a full colonel, which was the highest rank I got. My first commission was accompanied by the following letter:—

Headquarters Army of Northern Virginia,<br>March 23, 1863.

Capt. J. S. Mosby, through Major-General Stuart.

Captain:—You will perceive from the copy of the order herewith enclosed that the President has appointed you captain of partisan rangers. The general commanding directs me to say that it is desired that you proceed at once to organise your company, with the understanding that it is to be placed on a footing with all the troops of the line, and to be mustered unconditionally in the Confederate service for and during the war. Though you are to be its captain, the men will have the privilege of electing the lieutenants so soon as its members reach the legal standard. You will report your progress from time to time, and when the requisite number of men are enrolled, an officer will be designated to muster the company into the service.

I am, very respectfully, your obedient servant,

W. W. Taylor, A.A.G.

The partisan ranger law was an act of the Confederate Congress authorising the President to issue commissions to officers to organise partisan corps. They stood on the same footing with other cavalry organisations in respect to rank and pay, but, in addition, were given the benefit of the law of maritime prize. There was really no novelty in applying this principle to land forces. England has always done so in her Majesty's East Indian service, and the spoils of Waterloo were divided among the captors, of which Wellington took his share. The booty of Delhi was the subject of litigation in the English Court of Chancery, and Havelock, Campbell and Outram returned home from the East loaded with barbaric spoils.

As there is a good deal of human nature in people, and as Major Dalgetty is still the type of a class, it will be seen how the peculiar privileges given to my men served to whet their zeal. I have often heard them disputing over the division of the horses before they were captured, and it was no uncommon thing for a man to remind me just as he was about going into a fight that he did not get a horse from the last one.

On the Chantilly raid I was accompanied by Captain Hoskins, an English officer, who had just reported to me with a letter from Stuart. He had been a captain in the English army and had won the Crimean medal. After the conclusion of peace he had returned home, but disliking the monotonous life of the barracks, had sold his commission and joined Garibaldi in his Sicilian expedition. He was a thorough soldier of fortune, devoted to the profession of arms, and loved the excitement of danger and the joy of battle. He had been attracted to our shores by the great American war, which offered a field for the display of his courage and the gratification of his military tastes. He was a noble gentleman and a splendid soldier, but his career with me was short. A few weeks after that he fell fighting by my side.

I mounted Hoskins and his companion, Captain Kennon, on captured horses, and they went to try their luck with me. The post at Chantilly was only two miles from the camp of a division of cavalry, and flanked by strong supporting parties on each side. When I got within two or three miles of it, I turned obliquely off to the right, in order to penetrate, if possible, between them and Centreville, and gain their rear. But they were looking out for me, and I found there was no chance for a surprise. I despaired almost of doing anything; but as I did not want to go back without trying to do something, I ordered a few men to chase in the pickets, in hopes that this would draw their main body out for some distance. They did so, and several were killed and captured.

From a high position I saw the reserve mount, form, and move up the pike. I regained the pike also, so as not to be cut off. I got ready to charge as soon as they were near, although I did not have half their number, when I discovered another large body of cavalry, that had heard the firing, coming rapidly from the direction of Fryingpan to reinforce them. These were more than I had bargained to fight in the open, so I ordered a retreat at a trot up the turnpike.

I was certain that they would pursue rapidly, thinking I was running away, and, getting strung out along the pike, would lose their advantage in numbers, and give me a chance to turn and strike back. My calculation was right. I kept my men well closed up, with two some distance behind, to give me notice when they got near. I had just passed over a hill, and was descending on the other side, when one of my men dashed up and said the enemy was right upon me. I looked back, but they were not in sight. I could distinctly hear their loud cheers and the hoof-strokes of their horses on the hard pike. I had either to suffer a stampede or make a fight. The cavalry officer is like the woman who deliberates—he's lost. If I had gone a step further my retreat would have degenerated into a rout.

My horses were jaded by a long day's march, while the enemies' were fresh. I promptly ordered the men to halt, right about wheel, and draw sabres. It was all done in the twinkling of an eye. Fortunately, just at the place where I halted was an abattis, formed of fallen trees, which had been made by the army the year before. The men formed behind these, as I knew that when they darted out it would create the impression on my pursuers that I had drawn them into an ambuscade. As they stood there, calmly waiting for me to give the word for the onset,

*A horrid front they form,*
*Still as the breeze, but dreadful as the storm.*

I had no faith in the sabre as a weapon. I only made the men draw their sabres to prevent them from wasting their fire before they got to closer quarters. I knew that when they got among them the pistol would be used. My success had been so uninterrupted that the men thought that victory was chained to my standard. Men who go into a fight under the influence of such feelings are next to invincible, and are generally victors before it begins. We had hardly got into position before the head of the pursuing column appeared over the hill, less than 100 yards off. They had expected to see our backs, and not our faces. It was a rule from which, during the war, I never departed, not to stand still and receive a charge, but always to act on the offensive. This was the maxim of Frederick the Great, and the key to the wonderful successes he won with his cavalry.

At the order to charge, my men dashed forward with a yell that startled and stunned those who were foremost in pursuit. I saw them halt, and I knew then that they had lost heart and were beaten. Before they could wheel, my men were among them. Those who were coming up behind them, seeing those in front turn their backs, did the same thing. They had no idea they were running away from the same number of men they had been chasing. My men had returned their sabres to their scabbards, and the death-dealing revolver was now doing its work.

The Union cavalry had assumed, as I thought they would, that my retreat had only been feigned to draw them into a trap. They could not understand why I ran away just to run back again. They had no time to ascertain our numbers or to recover from the shock of their surprise in finding us drawn up to receive them. I never witnessed a more complete rout, or one with less cause for it. The chase continued two or three miles. It was almost dark when we stopped. I remember that in the first set of fours that led the charge were three young men, James W. Poster, Thomas W. Richards, and William L. Hunter, to whom I gave commissions for their gallant conduct. They all have since won honourable positions in civil life.

We left the killed and wounded on the field, brought off thirty-six prisoners and about fifty horses. By strategy and hard fighting, four times our numbers had been defeated. The only casualty in my command happened to Major Hibbs, who had his boot-heel shot off. He had been one of the foremost leaders in the charge, and like Byron's *corsair*, everywhere in the thickest of the fight *"shone his mailed breast and flashed his sabre's ray."* When the "Major" rode up to me, after the fight was over, he was almost a maniac, he was so wild with delight. And when, in the presence of all the men, I praised his valour, he could no longer contain himself; he laughed and wept by turns. All that he could say in reply was: "Well, Captain, I knew the work had to be done, and that was the way to do it."

One thing is certain, the major got a good horse as a reward. The regiment we had fought happened to be the very one to which Ames had belonged, and from which he had deserted a few weeks before to join me. He had gone through their ranks like an avenging angel, shooting right and left. He took a malicious pleasure in introducing some of his old comrades to me. I could not help feeling a pang of regret that such courage as his should be stained with dishonour. It was Hoskins's first fight with me. He said it was better than a fox chase. I recall his image now as it rises above the flood of years, as he hewed his path through the broken ranks. It was a point of honour or of military etiquette with him to use his sword and not his pistol. In this way he lost his life. I reported to Stuart the result of the engagement and received from him the following letter in reply:

> Headquarters Cavalry Division,
> Army of Northern Virginia,
> March 27, 1863.

Captain:—Your telegram announcing your brilliant achievement near Chantilly was duly received and forwarded to General Lee. He exclaimed upon reading it:
"Hurrah for Mosby! I wish I had a hundred like him."
Heartily wishing you continued success, I remain your Obedient servant,

J. E. B. Stuart,<br>
Major-General Commanding.

Captain J. S. Mosby, Commanding, etc.

Fairfax Court-House, March 23, 1863.

Sir:—At 5 p.m., our picket in front of Chantilly was attacked. The videttes were on the alert, and gave the alarm. The reserve of about 70 men were immediately under arms, and charged the enemy, who fled for 2 miles along the Little River turnpike. Between Saunder's toll-gate and Cub Run there is a strip of woods about a half a mile wide through which the road runs. Within the woods, and about a quarter of a mile apart, are two barricades of fallen trees; our troops pursued the enemy between these barricades. Behind the latter, some of the enemy were concealed. The head of the column was here stopped by a fire of carbines and pistols, and also by a fire upon the flank from the woods.

The column broke, and was pursued by the enemy 1½ miles. It was then rallied by the exertions of Majors Bacon and White. Captains McGuinn and Hasbrouck, when they heard of the alarm, proceeded on a gallop from Fryingpan, and, joining Major White's command, pursued the enemy for 8 miles. Night coming on, and the enemy being more numerous than we were, and our horses exhausted, the column halted and returned to Chantilly. The line of pickets is now established. Our loss is, killed, Corporal Gilles, Company H. Fifth New York Cavalry; James Doyle, Company C; John Harris, Company L. Mortally wounded, Sergeant Leahey, Company C. Lieutenant Merritt taken prisoner.

Robt. Johnstone,<br>
Lieutenant Colonel Commanding.

Col. R. Butler Price,
Commanding Cav. Brig.

Endorsement.

Headquarters Army Northern Virginia,<br>
March 26, 1863.

General:—On the 25th (23) instant Capt. Mosby attacked and routed a body of the enemy's cavalry on the Little River turnpike, near Chantilly. He reports 10 killed and wounded—and a lieutenant and 30 (35) men, with their horses, arms, and equipments captured. He sustained no loss . ... etc.

R. E. Lee, General.

Fauquier County, Va., April 7, 1863.

General:—I have the honour to submit the following report of the operations of the cavalry under my command since rendering my last report. On Monday, March 16, I proceeded down the Little River pike to capture two outposts of the enemy, each numbering 60 or 70 men. I did not succeed in gaining their rear as I expected, and only captured 4 or 5 videttes. It being late in the evening, and our horses very much jaded, I concluded to return. I had gone not over a mile back when we saw a large body of the enemy's cavalry, which, according to their own reports, numbered 200 men, rapidly pursuing. I feigned a retreat, desiring to draw them off from their camps.

At a point where the enemy had blockaded the road with fallen trees, I formed to receive them, for with my knowledge of the Yankee character I knew they would imagine themselves fallen into an ambuscade. When they had come within 100 yards of me I ordered a charge, to which my men responded with a vim that swept everything before them. The Yankees broke when we got in 75 yards of them; and it was more of a chase than a fight for 4 or 5 miles. We killed 5, wounded a considerable number, and brought off 1 lieutenant and 35 men prisoners. I did not have over 50 men with me, some having gone back with the prisoners and others having gone on ahead, when we started back, not anticipating any pursuit.

On Monday, March 31, I went down in the direction of Dranesville to capture several strong outposts in the vicinity of that place. On reaching there I discovered that they had fallen back about 10 miles down the Alexandria pike. I then returned 6 or 8 miles back and stopped about 10 o'clock at night at a point about 2 miles from the pike. Early the next morning one of my men, whom I had left over on the Leesburg pike, came dashing in, and announced the rapid approach of the enemy. But he had scarcely given us the information when the enemy appeared a few hundred yards off, coming up at a gallop. At this time our horses were eating; all had their bridles off, and some even their saddles—they were all tied in a barnyard.

Throwing open the gate I ordered a counter-charge, to which

my men promptly responded. The Yankees never dreaming of our assuming the offensive, terrified at the yells of the men as they dashed on, they broke and fled in every direction. We drove them in confusion seven or eight miles down the pike. We left on the field nine of them killed—among them a captain and lieutenant—and about fifteen too badly wounded for removal; in this lot two lieutenants. We brought off 82 prisoners, many of these also wounded. I have since visited the scene of the fight. The enemy sent up a flag of truce for their dead and wounded, but many of them being severely wounded, they established a hospital on the ground. The surgeon who attended them informs me that a great number of those who escaped were wounded.

The force of the enemy was six companies of the First Vermont Cavalry, one of their oldest and best regiments, and the prisoners inform me that they had every available man with them. There were certainly not less than 200; the prisoners say it was more than that. I had about 65 men in this affair. In addition to the prisoners, we took all their arms and about 100 horses and equipments. Privates Hart, Hurst, Keyes and Davis were wounded. The latter has since died. Both on this and several other occasions they have borne themselves with conspicuous gallantry. In addition to those mentioned above I desire to place on record the names of several others, whose promptitude and boldness in closing in with the enemy contributed much to the success of the fight. They are Lieutenant Chapman (late of Dixie Artillery), Sergt. Hunter and Privates Wellington and Harry Hatcher, Turner, Wild, Sowers, Ames and Sibert.

There are many others, I have no doubt, deserving of honourable mention, but the above are only those who came under my personal observation. I confess that on this occasion I had not taken sufficient precautions to guard against surprise. It was 10 o'clock at night when I reached the place where the fight came off on the succeeding day. We had ridden through snow and mud upwards of 40 miles, and both men and horses were nearly broken down; besides, the enemy had fallen back a distance of about 18 miles. . . .

John S. Mosby,<br>Captain Commanding.

Maj.-Gen. J. E. B. Stuart.

Endorsements.

Headquarters Cavalry Division,
April 11, 1863.

Respectfully forwarded, as in perfect keeping with his other brilliant achievements. Recommended for promotion.

J. E. B. Stuart,
Major-General.

Headquarters Army Northern Virginia,
April 13, 1863.

Respectfully forwarded for the information of the Department. Telegraphic reports already sent in.

R. E. Lee, General.

April 22, 1863.

Adjutant-General:—Nominate as major if it has not been previously done.

J. A. S. (Seddon), Secretary.

## Chapter 8

# A Close Call

*Olympicum pulverem collegisse juvat.*—Horace.

After the fight at Chantilly and division of the booty the men who were with me, as usual, disappeared. Of the original fifteen who had come with me from the army for temporary service, five or six had been captured one night at a dancing frolic. Beattie was not in this party when he was made a prisoner, but was captured in a fight. I gave notice of a meeting at Rector's X roads, in Loudoun County, for the 31st of March. I had no idea until I got on the ground how many men I would have to go with me on my next raid, although I was confident that the success of my last one would attract a good many soldiers who were then at their homes on furlough. I was promptly there at the appointed time, and very soon sixty-nine men mustered to go with me.

This was the largest force I had ever commanded up to that time. The shaking up of a kaleidoscope does not produce more variegated colours than the number of strange faces that appeared among them. I had never seen more than a dozen of them before, and very few of them had ever seen each other. I remember that there were several of the Black Horse Company with them. The force, therefore, lacked the cohesion and esprit de corps which springs from discipline and the mutual confidence of men who have long been associated together. I had no subordinate officer to aid me in command. They were better dressed, but almost as motley a crowd as Falstaff's regiment. There were representatives of nearly all the cavalry regiments in the army, with a sprinkling of men from the infantry, who had determined to try their luck on horseback.

A good many of this latter class had been disabled for performing infantry duty by wounds; there were others who had been absent from their regiments without leave ever since the first battle of Bull Run. There were a number of the wounded men who carried their crutches along tied to their saddle bows. As soon as their commanders heard that I had reclaimed and converted them once more into good soldiers they not only made requisition to have them returned to their regiments, but actually complained to General Lee of their being with me.

Now I took a practical and not a technical view of the question, and when a man volunteered to go into a fight with me I did not consider it to be any more a duty of mine to investigate his military record than his pedigree. Although a revolutionary government, none was ever so much under the domination of red tape as the one at Richmond. The martinets who controlled it were a good deal like the hero of Moliere's comedy, who complained that his antagonist had wounded him by thrusting in *carte*, when, according to the rule, it should have been in *tierce*. I cared nothing for the form of a thrust if it brought blood. I did not play with foils. The person selected to feed the army was a metaphysical dyspeptic, who it is said, lived on rice-water, and had a theory that soldiers could do the same.

A man, to fill such a position well, should be in sympathy with hungry men, on the principle that he who drives fat oxen must himself be fat. When I received these complaints, which were sent through, but did not emanate from headquarters, I notified the men that they were forbidden any longer to assist me in destroying the enemy. They would sorrowfully return to their homes. It was no part of my contract to spend my time in the ignoble duty of catching deserters. I left that to those whose taste was gratified in doing the work. Several of these men, who had been very efficient with me, were, on my application, transferred to me by the Secretary of War. I always had a Confederate fire in my rear as well as that of the public enemy in my front. I will add that I never appealed in vain for justice either to General R. E. Lee, General Stuart, or the Secretary of War, Mr. Seddon.

And now, again, on the 31st of March, I set out once more to tempt fortune in the Fairfax forests. The men who followed me with so much zeal were not, perhaps, altogether of the saintly character or excited by the pious aspirations of the Canterbury pilgrims who knelt at the shrine of Thomas à Becket. Patriotism, as well as love of adventure, impelled them. If they got rewards in the shape of horses and arms, these were devoted, like their lives, to the cause in which they were fighting. They were made no richer by what they got, except in the ability to serve their country. I did not hope for much on this expedition. The enemy had grown wary and were prepared for attack at every point. But I knew that if I dispersed the men without trying to do something I would never see them again.

The spring campaign was about to open, and most of them would soon be recalled to the army, and I would be left a major without a command. I concluded to attack the detached cavalry camp at Dranesville. In a letter to Stuart a few weeks before, I had suggested that the cavalry brigade then stationed at Culpepper Court House should do this. I said:

"There are about three hundred cavalry at Dranesville who are isolated from the rest of the command, so that nothing would be easier than to capture the whole force. I have harassed them so much that they do not keep their pickets over half a mile from camp."

For some reason, Stuart did not undertake it. The reason was, I suppose, that he was saving his cavalry for the hard work they would have to do as soon as Hooker crossed the Rappahannock.

The enterprise looked hazardous, but I calculated on being able to surprise the camp, and trusted a good deal to my usual good luck. Ames, Dick Moran, Major Hibbs, and John Underwood, who never failed to be on time, went with me. I thought I would vary my tactics a little this time, and attack about dusk. They would hardly look for me at vespers; heretofore I had always appeared either in the daytime or late at night. I got to Herndon Station, where I had had the encounter two weeks before with the Vermont cavalry, about sundown, and learned there that the camp at Dranesville, which was about three miles off, had been broken up on the day before, and the cavalry had been withdrawn beyond Difficult Run, several miles below. This stream has its proper name, as there are few places where it can be crossed, and I knew that these would be strongly guarded.

So it was hopeless to attempt anything in that direction. As I was so near, I concluded to go on to Dranesville that night, in hopes that by chance I might pick up some game. After spending an hour or so there, we started up the Leesburg pike to find a good place with forage for camping that night. I expected that our presence would be reported to the cavalry camps below, which would probably draw out a force which I could venture to meet. As all the forage had been consumed for several miles around, we had to march five or six miles to find any. About midnight we stopped at Miskel's farm, which is about a mile from the turnpike and just in the forks of Goose Creek and the Potomac.

Although it was the last day of March, snow was still lying on the ground, and winter lingered on the banks of the Potomac. My authority over the men was of such a transitory nature that I disliked to order them to do anything but fight. Hence I did not put out any pickets on the pike. The men had been marching all day, and were cold and tired. The enemy's camps were about fifteen miles below, and I did not think they could possibly hear of us before the next morning, when we would be ready for them, if they came after us. We fed and picketed our horses inside the barnyard, which was surrounded by a strong fence. Sentinels were stationed as a guard over the horses, and to arouse us in the event of alarm. Many of the men went to bed in the hayloft, while others, including myself, lay down on the floor in the front room of the dwelling-house, before a big log fire.

With my head on my saddle as a pillow, I was soon in a deep sleep. We were within a few hundred yards of the river, and there were Union camps on the other side; but I had no fear of them that night. About sunrise the next morning, I had just risen and put on my boots when one of the men came in and said that the enemy on the hill over the river was making signals. I immediately went out into the back yard to look at them. I had hardly done so, when I saw Dick Moran coming at full speed across the field, waving his hat, and calling out, "The Yankees are coming!"

He had stopped about two miles below, near the pike, and spent the night with a friend; and just as he woke up, about daylight, he had seen the column of Union cavalry going up the pike on our trail. By taking a short cut across the fields, he managed to get to us ahead of them. The barnyard was not a hundred yards from the house; and we all rushed to it. But not more than one-third of our horses were then bridled and saddled. I had buckled on my arms as I came out of the house. By the time we got to the enclosure where our horses were, I saw the enemy coming through a gate just on the edge of a clump of woods about two hundred yards off. The first thing I said to the men was that they must fight. The enemy was upon us so quick that I had no time to bridle or saddle my horse, as I was busy giving orders. I directed the men not to fire, but to saddle and mount quickly. The Union cavalry were so sure of their prey that they shut the gates after passing through, in order to prevent any of us from escaping.

As Capt. Flint dashed forward at the head of his squadron, their sabres flashing in the rays of the morning sun, I felt like my final hour had come. Another squadron, after getting into the open field, was at the same time moving around to our rear. In every sense, things looked rather blue for us. We were in the angle of two impassable streams and surrounded by at least four times our number, with more than half of my men unprepared for a fight. But I did not despair. I had great faith in the efficacy of a charge; and in the affair at Chantilly had learned the superiority of the revolver over the sabre. I was confident that we could at least cut our way through them.

The Potomac resounded with the cheers of the troops on the northern bank, who were anxious spectators, but could not participate in the conflict. When I saw Capt. Flint divide his command, I knew that my chances had improved at least fifty per cent. When he got to within fifty yards of the gate of the barnyard, I opened the gate and advanced, pistol in hand, on foot to meet him, and at the same time called to the men that had already got mounted to follow me. They responded with one of those demoniac yells which those who once heard never forgot, and dashed forward to the conflict "*as reapers descend to the harvest of death.*"

Just as I passed through the gate, at the head of the men, one of them, Harry Hatcher, the bravest of the brave, seeing me on foot, dismounted, and gave me his horse. Our assailants were confounded by the tactics adopted, and were now in turn as much surprised as we had been. They had thought that we would remain on the defensive, and were not prepared to receive an attack. I mounted Harry Hatcher's horse, and led the charge. In a few seconds Harry was mounted on a captured one whose rider had been killed. When the enemy saw us coming to meet them they halted, and were lost.

The powerful moral effect of our assuming the offensive, when nothing but surrender had been expected, seemed to bewilder them. Before they could recover from the shock of their surprise Captain Flint, the leader, had fallen dead in their sight. Before the impetuous onset of my men they now broke and fled. No time was given them to re-form and rally. The remorseless revolver was doing its work of death in their ranks, while their swords were as harmless as the wooden sword of harlequin. Unlike my adversaries, I was trammelled with no tradition that required me to use an obsolete weapon. The combat was short, sharp and decisive. In the first moment of collision, they wheeled and made for the gate which they had already closed against themselves.

The other squadron that had gone around us, when they saw their companions turn and fly, were panic-stricken and forgot what they had been sent to do. Their thoughts were now how to save themselves. Our capture was now out of the question. They now started pell-mell for the gate in order to reach it ahead of us. But by this time our men had all mounted, and like so many furies were riding and shooting among their scattered ranks. The gate was at last broken through by the pressure, but they became so packed and jammed in the narrow passage that they could only offer a feeble resistance, and at this point many fell under the deadly fire that was poured in from behind.

Everywhere above the storm of battle could be heard the voices and seen the forms of the Dioscuri—"Major" Hibbs and Dick Moran—cheering on the men as they rode headlong in the fight. Dick Moran got into a hand-to-hand conflict in the woods with a party, and the issue was doubtful, when Harry Hatcher came up and decided it. There was with me that day a young artillery officer—Samuel F. Chapman—who at the first call of his State to arms had quit the study of divinity and become, like Stonewall Jackson, a sort of military Calvin, singing the psalms of David as he marched into battle.

I must confess that his character as a soldier was more on the model of the Hebrew prophets than the Evangelist or the Baptist in whom he was so devout a believer. Before he got to the gate Sam had already exhausted every barrel of his two pistols and drawn his sabre. As the fiery Covenanter rode on his predestined course the enemy's ranks withered wherever he went. He was just in front of me—he was generally in front of everybody in a fight—at the gate. It was no fault of the Union cavalry that they did not get through faster than they did, but Sam seemed to think that it was. Even at that supreme moment in my life, when I had just stood on the brink of ruin and had barely escaped, I could not restrain a propensity to laugh.

Sam, to give more vigour to his blows, was standing straight up in his stirrups, dealing them right and left with all the theological fervour of Burly of Balfour. I doubt whether he prayed that day for the souls of those he sent over the Stygian river. I made him a captain for it. The chase was kept up for several miles down the pike. When the people at Dranesville saw Capt. Flint pass through that morning in search of me, they expected to see him return soon with all of us prisoners. Among the first fugitives who had passed through, and showed the day's disasters in his face, was a citizen who had hurried down the night before to the camp of the Vermont cavalry to tell them where I was. Thinking that Captain Flint had an easy thing of it, he had ridden with him as a pilot, to witness my humiliation and surrender. He escaped capture, but never returned to his home during the war. I doubt whether his loyalty ever received any reward. He was also the first man to get back to the camp he had left that morning on Difficult Run, where he was about as welcome as the messenger who bore to Rome the tidings of Cannæ.

The reverend Sam was not satisfied with the amount of execution he had done at the gate, but continued his slaughter until, getting separated in the woods from the other men, he dashed into a squad of the Vermont men, who were doing their best to get away, and received a cut with a sabre. But one of my men, Hunter, came to his rescue, and the matter in dispute was quickly settled. Down the pike the Vermont cavalry sped, with my men close at their heels. Lieutenant Woodbury had got three miles away, when a shot from Ames laid him low. They never drew rein or looked back to see how many were behind them. I got pretty close to one, who, seeing that he was bound to be shot or caught, jumped off his horse and sat down on the roadside.

As I passed him he called out to me, "You have played us a nice April fool, boys!" This reminded me that it was the first day of April. Some of the men kept up the pursuit beyond Dranesville, but I stopped there. The dead and wounded were strewn from where the fight began, at Miskel's, for several miles along the road. I had one man killed and three slightly wounded. I knew that as soon as the news reached the camps in Fairfax a heavy force would be sent against me, so I started off immediately, carrying eighty-three prisoners and ninety-five horses, with all their equipments.

At Dranesville were two sutlers' stores that had not been removed by their owners when the camps were broken up. These were, of course, appropriated, and helped to swell the joy of the partisans.

A more hilarious party never went to war or a wedding than my men were returning home. Danger always gives a keener relish for the joys of life. They struck up a favourite song of Tom Moore's, "The wine cup is sparkling before us," and the woods resounded with the melody. The dead and wounded were left on the field to be cared for by citizens until their friends could come after them. The number of prisoners I took exceeded the number of my men. One of my command—Frank Williams—had ridden early that morning to the house of a farmer to get his breakfast.

The Vermont cavalry came up and got between him and us, and so

Frank had to retreat. He, however, took two of them prisoners who had straggled off on the same errand, and carried them along with him. As he had seen such an overwhelming force go down upon us, and as he knew that we were hemmed in by deep water on two sides, Frank took it for granted that my star had set forever. He started off to carry the news, and reached Middleburg that day, when he informed the citizen of what he supposed was our fate. There was, of course, loud lamentation over it, for many had a son or a brother or a lover there. Frank had been there an hour or so anxiously waiting to hear something from us, but dreading the worst, when suddenly a blue column was seen coming up the pike. As blue was the predominant colour, the first impression was that the men in gray were prisoners. But soon Dick Moran, who was riding in front, solved all doubts and fears as, with a voice louder than a Triton's shell, he proclaimed, "All right."

Headquarters, Camp Fred's, April 4, 1863.

Mr. President:—Maj. John S. Mosby reports that he was attacked early on the morning of the 2nd (1st) instant, near Dranesville, by about 200 Vermont cavalry. He promptly repulsed them, leaving on the field 25 killed and wounded, including 3 officers, and brought off 82 prisoners, with their horses, arms, and equipments. His force consisted of 65 men, and his loss was 4 wounded.

The enemy has evacuated Dranesville.

I had the pleasure to send by return courier to Major Mosby his commission of major of Partisan Rangers, for which I am obliged to your Excellency.

I am, with great respect, your obedient servant,

R. E. Lee,
General.

His Excellency Jefferson Davis,
President Confederate States of America, Richmond, Va.

Headquarters, Stahel's Cavalry Division,
Fairfax Court House, Va.,
April 2, 1863.

General:—I have the honour to submit the following report, which is, however, made up from verbal information received from Col. Price, Lieutenant-Colonel Johnstone, and Major Taggart. I will forward the written report as soon as it is received, and shall take all possible means to ascertain the true state of the case. It appears that on the evening of the 31st *ultimo*, Major Taggart, at Union Church, 2 miles above Peach Grove, received information that Mosby, with about 65 men, was near Dranesville. He immediately despatched Captain Flint, with 150 men of the First Vermont, to rout or capture Mosby and his force. Captain Flint followed the Leesburg and Alexandria road to the road which branches off to the right, just this side of Broad Run. Turning to the right, they followed up the Broad Run toward the Potomac, to a place marked "J. Mesed" (Miskel). Here, at a house, they came on to Mosby, who was completely surprised and wholly unprepared for an attack from our forces.

Had a proper disposition been made of our troops, Mosby could not, by any possible means, have escaped. It seems that around this house was a high board fence and a stone wall, between which and the road was also another fence and ordinary farm gate. Captain Flint took his men through the gate, and, at a distance from the house, fired a volley at Mosby and his men, who were assembled about the house, doing but slight damage to them. He then ordered a sabre charge, which was also ineffectual, on account of the fence which intervened.

Mosby waited until the men were checked by the fence, and then opened his fire upon them, killing and wounding several. The men here became panic-stricken, and fled precipitately toward this gate, through which to make their escape. The opening was small, and they got wedged together, and a fearful state of confusion followed; while Mosby's men followed them up, and poured into the crowd a severe fire. Here, while endeavouring to rally his men, Captain Flint was killed, and Lieutenant Grout, of the same company, mortally wounded (will probably die today).

Mosby's men followed in pursuit, and sabred several of our men on the road. Mosby, during his pursuit, is supposed to have received a sabre wound across the face which unhorsed him. The rebels took some prisoners, and a number of horses, and fell back in great haste. In comparison to the number engaged, our loss was very heavy. As soon as Major Taggart received the report, he sent Major Hall in pursuit of Mosby, and to bring in our killed and wounded.

Upon receiving the first intelligence, I immediately sent out

Colonel Price with a detachment of the Sixth and Seventh Michigan and First Virginia (Union) Cavalry, who searched in every direction; but no trace could be found of Mosby or his men, as information reached me too late.

I regret to be obliged to inform the commanding general that the forces sent out by Major Taggart missed so good an opportunity of capturing this rebel guerilla. It is only to be ascribed to the bad management on the part of the officers and the cowardice of the men. I have ordered Colonel Price to make a thorough investigation of this matter, and shall recommend those officers who are guilty to be stricken from the rolls.

The list of killed and wounded will be forwarded as soon as received.

I have the honour to remain, your obedient servant,

Jul. Stahel,
Major-General.

Maj. Gen. S. P. Heintzelman,
Commanding, &c.

CHAPTER 9

# In Pursuit

*And thou, Dalhousie, thou great god of war,*
*Lieutenant-Colonel to the Earl of Mar.*—Waller.

What in the newspaper slang of the day were termed "the depredations of guerillas," in the vicinity of Washington, induced the authorities there to make a change in outpost commanders. Wyndham, having played an unsuccessful game for over two months, during which time his headquarters had been raided, and his coat and hat carried off by us in his absence, had given it up in despair, and been sent to join his regiment at the front. The new person selected for the position was a major-general in the army, and a whiskered *pandour*, whose experience in foreign wars, it was hoped, would devise a remedy to suppress these annoyances.

As soon as he took command, the cavalry camps in Fairfax resounded with the busy notes of preparation for a grand expedition, which he had resolved to undertake against us. It could no longer be endured that the war should be waged in full view of the dome of the Capitol, and the outposts could not stand the wear and tear of a perpetual skirmish, and the worry of lying awake all night waiting for an invisible foe to come and kill or capture them.

The spring campaign was about to open, and if the hostile band that created this trouble could be exterminated, the cavalry division, then doing duty in Fairfax, might be thrown forward to the Rappahannock to aid Hooker's operations. The major-general was firmly persuaded, as no one had ever seen our camp, that the so-called guerillas were nobody but the country farmers, who collected together at night to make their incursions, and dispersed by day to take care of their fields and flocks. The fights at Chantilly and Dranesville ought to have convinced him that the men who had routed his best regiments had some training in war, and were no such irregular band as he imagined. It is true that, after I began operations in that region, many took up arms and joined me, who up to that time had followed peaceful pursuits. But whenever a citizen joined me and became a soldier, he discarded the habiliments of peace, put on his arms and uniform, and laid aside every other occupation.

When the struggle was over, they relapsed into the habits of their former life, and like the Puritan soldiers of Cromwell, became as marked for devotion to their civil duties as they had ever been in war. As for myself, it was for a long time maintained that I was a pure myth, and my personal identity was as stoutly denied as that of Homer or the Devil. All historic doubts about my own existence have, I believe, been settled; but the fables published by the Bohemians who followed the army made an impression that still lives in popular recollection.

There is a lingering belief that my command was not a part of the regularly organised military force of the Southern Confederacy. The theory of the major-general, though contradicted by facts staring him in the face every day, got a lodgement in the minds of some people which has never been effaced. It was to confirm it that he now undertook to make a reconnoissance through the region infested by us. It happened that just at that time Hooker was preparing once more to cross the Rappahannock, and as a preliminary movement had sent Stoneman with the cavalry corps up the river to seize the Orange and Alexandria railroad and hold it as the line of communication with Washington.

The line that connects an army with its base of supplies is the heel of Achilles—its most vital and vulnerable point. It is a great achievement in war to compel an enemy to make heavy detachments to guard it; it is equally as great a one to destroy the force that threatens it. It was to effect this latter object that in April, 1863, the Major-General set out on his expedition against me with two brigades of cavalry and a battery of artillery, which was to be the prelude of the opening of the campaign on the Rappahannock. Now it so happened that just about that time I received a letter from Stuart suggesting the capture of a train on the railroad. The effect of such a stroke of course would be to create uneasiness and alarm about the safety of Hooker's supplies.

The following is an extract from Stuart's letter:

There is now a splendid opportunity to strike the enemy in the rear of Warrenton Junction; the trains are running regularly to that point. Capture a train and interrupt the operation of the railroad, though it may be, by the time you get this, the opportunity may be gone. Stoneman's main body of cavalry is located near Warrenton Junction, Bealeton and Warrenton Springs. Keep far enough away from a brigade camp to give you time to get off your plunder and prisoners. Information of the movements of large bodies is of the greatest importance to us just now. The marching or transportation of divisions will often indicate the plan of a campaign. Be sure to give dates and numbers and names, as far as possible.

I could offer no better proof than this letter of the useful services that may be rendered by an active partisan corps in co-operation with the movements of an army. It not only cripples an adversary, but communicates intelligence of his movements. Accordingly I gave notice for a meeting at Upperville to undertake an enterprise against the railroad. I was willing to let the Union troops down in Fairfax rest while I turned my attention to Joe Hooker. On the evening of the day before the meeting I had been with Beattie up to the mountain to get a fresh horse to ride on the raid, and we returned about dark. I met a citizen, who informed me that a large Federal force was camped at Middleburg, and that there had been artillery firing there during the afternoon. I thought it was merely a false report that had gotten up a stampede, for I had not heard the firing, and I could not conceive what they could have been firing at, as we had no troops about there. I supposed that if they had come after me they would have tried to keep it a secret and make as little noise as possible.

About nine o'clock that night Beattie and I rode down in the direction of Middleburg to find out if there was any truth in the rumor. When we got on a high hill, about a mile off, that overlooks the town, we stopped to reconnoitre. The night was very cold, with a drizzling rain. Not a single camp-fire could be seen anywhere; and there was nothing to indicate the bivouacs of a military force. I said to Beattie: "This is just as I said—nothing but a stampede about nothing. If there were any troops about there, they would have camp-fires on such a cold night as this." We then rode forward, but had only gone a few hundred yards farther when we were halted and fired on by a picket. This, of course, proved that the rumour was true.

We fell back. But it was a mystery I could not solve, why there should be an encampment of troops in such weather without fires. Then, too, there had been artillery firing; what could possibly have been the reason for that? The next morning I went, according to appointment, to meet my men at Upperville, having sent out some scouts toward Middleburg, which is eight miles distant. My desire was to let the Union cavalry alone at Middleburg and strike the meditated blow at Hooker, on the railroad. The force that had come up from Fairfax after me had now been practically eliminated from the campaign. I wanted, therefore, if possible, to slip away from them undiscovered. Early that morning the major-general put his column in motion on the pike for Upperville; but he had only gone a couple of miles before his advance-guard was driven in by Tom Richards and a few men. This caused him to halt and get ready for action. On the day before, on his march up the turnpike, he had seen horsemen on the hills watching him, who, like the Arab when he folds his tent, had silently stolen away.

On reaching Middleburg, the clouds seemed to thicken around him; for he had seen at least a dozen perched on the heights at different places gazing at him. They were evidently ready to light down on any stragglers, and bear them off in their talons. The major-general unlimbered his guns, and opened fire on every moving object in his sight. He did no damage to anybody; but his firing gave notice for miles around to people to get out of his way. There was a large grove near Middleburg, in which he proposed to bivouac that night. But before entering it, he shelled it so effectively as not only to expel any guerillas that might be lurking there, but all animated nature. He carried along a newspaper correspondent to chronicle his exploits. His letter, published in the New York *Tribune* shortly after that, made clear a number of things which I had not been able to understand before reading it.

It praised his consummate skill and prudence in allowing no camp-fires during the night, as they would have lighted the way for the guerillas to attack him; while the destructive artillery fire with which he had raked the forest showed that he possessed the foresight of a great general. It was also stated that he would only permit one half of his command to sleep at a time or unbridle and unsaddle their horses. With unconscious irony the letter concluded by stating that the result of the expedition had demonstrated that Mosby hadn't over twenty-five men, who had been totally exterminated. After remaining in line of battle for some time, waiting for me to attack him, the Major-General determined not to advance any farther toward Upperville, which lies just at the base of the Blue Ridge.

It was surmised that the guerillas, like the Cyclops, had taken refuge in caves on the mountainside, and there might be danger in approaching too closely, so he turned squarely off to his left. On his line of march he had swept the country of all the old men he could find, for he was firmly persuaded that in doing so he was breaking up my band. No plea in defence would be heard. A man named Hutchison, who was 70 years old, and had always used crutches, was among the prisoners. In vain he pleaded his age and infirmities as proof of the impossibility of his being a guerilla. A Vermont soldier stepped forward, and swore that he saw him leading the charge in the fight at Miskel's farm. He was sent to Washington as a trophy. The captives under guard marched in the rear of the column.

About eighty men had met me at Upperville. In order to elude the major-general, and execute my plan of capturing a train on the railroad, I made a detour by Salem, going on toward Thoroughfare Gap in the Bull Run Mountains. The major-general and myself, being ignorant of each other's plans, had also gone the same way, in order to avoid meeting the force that had driven in his advance from Upperville. Somehow he had got the idea in his head that a large body of Stuart's cavalry was in the neighbourhood, and he was not looking for them. An hour or so after I had passed through Salem, the major-general arrived there. He had started to return to Fairfax by making a circuit around through Thoroughfare Gap.

Without any design on his part, he had struck right on my track. As I was marching very leisurely,—for I did not want to get to the railroad until about dark,—he might easily have overtaken me; but he did not seem to have the least desire to do so. He followed me at the rate of half a mile an hour. Having got all the old farmers prisoners, the measure of his ambition was full. He had at last destroyed the nest of vipers. He did not believe the body of cavalry that had gone on ahead were the very men he pretended to be looking for.

Just as I reached Thoroughfare Gap, two of my men—Alfred Glasscock and Norman Smith—came galloping up, and said that the enemy was pursuing me. They had, for some reason, remained behind at Salem, and saw the Major-General's command march through along the same road I was on. As he was only one hour behind me there, I felt certain that he was almost upon me. Some four miles back of where I was, the roads forked at a village called the Plains, one leading to Thoroughfare, and the other to Hopewell Gap in the Bull Run Mountains. I immediately wheeled around, and crossed over on the Hopewell road and started back toward the Plains.

I supposed the major-general was in pursuit of me, and as I could not undertake with less than 100 men to attack in front 4000 cavalry and a battery of artillery, my intention was to try to cut off his rear-guard before it passed the forks or the gap. But when I got on a high hill overlooking the Plains, instead of meeting his rear-guard, when I rode forward to reconnoitre, I saw his advance, that had just got to the forks. I halted, so did they, while their whole column rapidly deployed in line of battle, and the guns were placed in battery, ready for the expected onset.

Every disposition was made by him to receive an attack. We stayed there facing each other over one hour, until it grew dark, when I disbanded my men. I had abandoned my enterprise against the railroad because I supposed that it had been discovered where I was going, and that if I went on, with the major-general behind me and Stoneman's cavalry in front, we would all be captured. He had learned at Salem that a body of cavalry had passed through just ahead of him, and at the Plains he saw that they had gone on the Thoroughfare road.

After giving us, as he supposed, ample time to get away, he started on the same route, when, with surprise, he saw a body of cavalry threatening him on the Hopewell road. He had no idea they were the same cavalry whose track he was on. If he continued his line of march he must go through one of the mountain passes, and remembering the fate of the Persians at Thermopylæ, he determined now to halt. I took it for granted that he had stopped to go into camp at the Plains. But he, not knowing that I had disbanded my command and fearing a night attack, as soon as it became dark began a retreat back toward Middleburg.

Being a cautious general, he did not go along the main public road, but cut across fields and took private ways. The bridges across every stream he crossed were broken down after he passed, although some were so narrow that a man could jump over them, and trees were felled across the road to prevent us from charging his rear. After marching all night he reached the vicinity of Middleburg about daybreak and went into camp. He had no idea that I had disbanded my men and gone off, but thought he had eluded us.

Now, it had never entered my head that he was going to run away from me. Beattie and I had ridden on the same night over near Middleburg, and I stopped at the house of George McArty. About daybreak he came running to where we were sleeping and called out to us: "Boys! get up quick—the Yankees are all around you." We jumped up, and two or three hundred yards away we could see the field was blue with the major-general's command. We bridled and saddled our horses quickly and rode off unmolested in full view of them.

The major-general and I had been running away from each other a whole day and night, and then came very near sleeping together. After taking a short rest from the fatigue of his night march, he started back to Fairfax with the battalion of graybeards he had taken prisoners, riding bareback with blind bridles on broken-down plough-horses. They were marched down to Washington and paraded through the streets to gratify the curiosity of the people. They created a greater sensation than a circus. Such was the grand anti-climax to the major-general's Anabasis. It is so unique and complete in itself that I will not mar its epic unity by adding anything more to the narrative.

Provost-Marshal's Office, Fairfax Court House, Va.,
March 9, 1863, 3.30 a.m.

Capt. Mosby, with his command, entered this town this morning at 2 a.m. They captured my patrols, horses, &c. They took Brigadier-General Stoughton and horses, and all his men detached from his brigade. They took every horse that could be found, public and private; and the commanding officer of the post, Colonel Johnstone, of the Fifth New York Cavalry, made his escape from them in a nude state by accident. They searched for me in every direction, but being on the Vienna road visiting outposts, I made my escape.

L. L. Connor, Provost-Marshal.

P.S. All our available cavalry forces are in pursuit of them.

Maj. Hunt, Asst. Adjt. Gen.

General Heintzelman's Headquarters.

Genl. Stahel's report to War Dept. says:

On the 13th day of March, 1863, the day after General Stoughton was captured at Fairfax C.H., I was on my way from Stafford Court House to New York, on eight days' leave of absence. Upon my arrival in Washington, I was summoned to report at once to President Lincoln. He told me of the capture of Genl. Stoughton and the insecure condition of our lines in front of

Washington. The President also said that he desired to have me in command in front of Washington to put a stop to these raids. He wrote a letter to Gen. Heintzelman, comdg. the Dept. of Washington, and directed me to go and see him. . . . On the same day, the 17th of March, I was appointed Major-General of Volunteers, to take date from the 14th of March, 1863.

Gen. Stahel was relieved of his cavalry command on June 28th, 1863.

Heqrs. Stahel's Cav. Div., Dept. of Washington,
Fairfax Court House, April 11, 1863.

General:—I have the honour to report with regard to the reconnoissance under command of Brig.-Gen. J. F. Copeland, which left this place on the 3rd day of April, and returned here early on the morning of the 6th instant, that it proceeded as far as Middleburg, and searched diligently through that whole section of country without meeting any enemy in force or ascertaining definitely the whereabouts of Mosby. Small detachments of rebels, however, were occasionally seen, but scattered on the approach of our troops.

On the 4th instant, early in the morning, in front of Middleburg, a collision occurred between one of his pickets and some of the enemy's, resulting in the death of one and the wounding of another on each side. During the expedition there were captured and arrested sixty-one prisoners, citizens and soldiers, fifty-three horses, two mules, a quantity of wheat, three wagons, saddles, bridles, guns, sabres, &c., all of which were turned over to the provost-marshal of this place, and by him to Colonel Baker Washington, a copy of whose receipt is enclosed within . . . &c.

Jul. Stahel,
Major-General.

Maj.-Gen. S. P. Heintzelman,
Commanding, &c.

There is no report on file of Major-General Stahel's expedition about two weeks after this in search of Mosby.

CHAPTER 10

# In the Saddle

*Our acts our angels are—or good or ill,*
*Our fatal shadows that walk by us still.*

If I had known at the time of the major-general's expedition to Fauquier all that I know now, I would not, of course, have abandoned the enterprise against the railroad. I had thought that after he struck my track at Salem, he was really in pursuit of me, although he only followed at a terrapin's pace. I could not have anticipated that a major-general, starting out to win his spurs, would retreat as soon as he got in sight of the object he was in search of. I had disbanded my men, with instructions to meet me again in a few days at a certain place. I wanted to give the major-general time to get home, while I could recruit my forces, pick my flint, and try again.

As the troops that belonged to the defences of Washington were now on the defensive, it was my policy to let them alone, and turn my attention to Hooker's army, which was then preparing to cross the Rappahannock. I could most efficiently aid Gen. Lee by assailing Hooker in the rear. A partisan commander who acts in co-operation with an army should always, if possible, operate against troops engaged in offensive movements. The major-general was now resting on his laurels. For two months preceding his raid into Fauquier, there had been incessant attacks on the outposts, and daily alarm through the camps. All this had now suddenly ceased, and the quiet that reigned was supposed to confirm the truth of the report of the annihilation of my band.

On May 2, 70 or 80 men assembled at my call. I had information that Stoneman's cavalry had left Warrenton and gone south, which indicated that the campaign had opened. My plan now was to strike

Hooker. The moral effect of a blow from behind might have an important influence on the result. I started for Warrenton, and reached there about dusk, and learned that Stoneman was over the river. It was not known whether or not the Orange & Alexandria railroad was still held by the Union troops. I went into camp near the town that night, and started by daylight the next morning on the road leading to Fredericksburg, which crosses the railroad. I was sure that Hooker would not repeat the blunder of Burnside, but would cross at some of the upper fords of the Rappahannock. It was toward one of these that my course was directed. The roar of the guns at Chancellorsville could be distinctly heard, and we knew that the two armies were once more in the deadly embrace of battle.

It was not more than fifteen or twenty miles off; and we could easily reach there early in the day. I wanted to contribute my mite of support to the Southern cause. When we were within a couple of miles of the railroad a bugle was heard; and I turned aside and marched to the sound. I thought it must come from a cavalry camp, which we might sweep through as we went along. Before we had gone very far, an infantry soldier was caught, who informed me that I was marching right into the camp of an infantry brigade. I found out that there was some cavalry on the railroad at another point, and so I made for that. These troops had just been sent up to replace Stoneman's.

I committed a great error in allowing myself to be diverted by their presence from the purpose of my expedition. They were perfectly harmless where they were, and could not help Hooker in the great battle then raging. I should, at least, have endeavoured to avoid a fight by marching around them. If I had succeeded in destroying them all, it would hardly have been the equivalent of the damage I might have done to Hooker by appearing at United States ford during the agony of the fight. There all of his wagons were packed. It would be difficult to calculate the demoralizing effect of the news on his army that the enemy was in their rear, and their trains and rations were burning up.

Just as we debouched from the woods in sight of Warrenton Junction, I saw, about 300 yards in front of us, a body of cavalry in the open field. It was a bright, warm morning; and the men were lounging on the grass, while their horses, with nothing but their halters on, had been turned loose to graze on the young clover. They were enjoying the music of the great battle, and had no dream that danger was near. Not a single patrol or picket had been put out. At first they mistook us for their own men, and had no suspicion as to who we were until

I ordered a charge and the men raised a yell. The shouting and firing stampeded the horses, and they scattered over a field of several hundred acres, while their riders took shelter in some houses near by. We very soon got all out of two houses; but the main body took refuge in a large frame building just by the railroad. I did not take time to dismount my men, but ordered a charge on the house; I did not want to give them time to recover from their panic.

I came up just in front of two windows by the chimney, from which a hot fire was poured that brought down several men by my side. But I paid them back with interest when I got to the window, into which I emptied two Colt's revolvers. The house was as densely packed as a sardine box; and it was almost impossible to fire into it without hitting somebody. The doors had been shut from the inside; but the Rev. Sam Chapman dismounted, and burst through, followed by John Debutts, Mountjoy, and Harry Sweeting. The soldiers in the lower rooms immediately surrendered; but those above held out. There was a haystack near by; and I ordered some of the hay to be brought into the house and fire to be set to it. Not being willing to be burned alive as martyrs to the Union, the men above now held out a white flag from a window. The house was densely filled with smoke and the floor covered with the blood of the wounded. The commanding officer, Maj. Steel, had received a mortal wound; and there were many others in the same condition. All who were able now came out of the house.

After a severe fight, I had taken three times my own number prisoners, together with all their horses, arms and equipments. Most of my men then dispersed over the field in pursuit of the frightened horses which had run away. I was sitting on my horse near the house, giving directions for getting ready to leave with the prisoners and spoil, when one of my men, named Wild, who had chased a horse some distance down the railroad, came at full speed, and reported a heavy column of cavalry coming up. I turned to one of my men, Alfred Glasscock, and said to him, "*Now we will whip them.*" I had hardly spoken the words when I saw a large body of Union cavalry, not over 200 or 300 yards off, rapidly advancing.

As I have stated, most of my command had scattered over the field, and the enemy was so close there was no time to rally and re-form before they got upon us. In attempting to do so, I remained on the ground until they were within 50 yards of me, and was nearly captured. So there was nothing to do but for every man to take care of himself. I have already described the kind of command I had at this time. They were a mere aggregation of men casually gathered, belonging to many different regiments, who happened to be in the country.[1] Of course, such a body has none of the cohesion and discipline that springs from organisation, no matter how brave the men may be individually. Men never fought better than they did at the house, while the defenders were inspired to greater resistance, knowing that relief was near. We had defeated and captured three times our own number, and now had to give up the fruits of victory, and in turn to fly to prevent capture. My men fled in every direction, taking off about 50 horses and a number of prisoners.

Only one of my men—Templeman—was killed, but I lost about 20 captured, nearly all of whom were wounded. Dick Moran was among them. I never made a better fight than this, although finally compelled to retreat before 10 times my own number.

As to its ulterior effects, it was about the same, as I shall hereafter show, as if I had not lost what I had won. The cavalry I had met was Deforest's brigade, that had come up the night before. As I have said, it was a mistake my making this fight, even if I had been completely successful. In all probability, it saved Hooker's transportation, just as the fight of the Prussians at the bridge of the Dyle saved Wellington, although they were beaten. It detained Grouchy long enough to keep him from Waterloo. I learned wisdom from experience, and after that always looked before I took a leap.

When I ordered the charge at Warrenton Junction, I had no idea whether I was attacking a hundred or a thousand men.

Just one year after that, I started with the purpose of attacking the rear of the army of the Potomac, at the same place where I had intended to strike Hooker. I found the railroad guarded, but I crossed it unnoticed in the dark, and went on. Lee and Grant had met in the Wilderness. Grant had all of his transportation south of the river, with cavalry pickets at the United States ford. There was no chance to get at it. Hooker had left his on the north bank where I was. I got one of Grant's trains near Aquia Creek, on the Lower Potomac; but when I returned, a few days after that, to get another, found that he had detached a cavalry force to protect that route.

This was what I wanted to make him do. It was that number of men subtracted from his strength. After striking one blow at the line of supply of an army, a demonstration will generally answer all the purposes of an attack. Hooker did not stay in the Wilderness long

---

1. I had no subordinate officer to help me in command.

enough for me to renew my attempt to get at his trains. When, after my rout, I appeared at Warrenton, attended by a single companion, where I had passed the night before with my command, I was apparently as forlorn as Charles,

> After dread Pultowa's day,
> When fortune left the royal Swede.

But I felt no discouragement. My faith in my ability to create a command and continue my warfare on the border was still as unwavering as Francis Xavier's when he left the Tagus, to plant the cross on the shores of Coromandel.

The enemy held the railroads as far south as the Rappahannock, and in a few days I got together 30 or 40 men, and started down again to strike them somewhere. I found the bridges over Broad Run and Kettle Run unguarded; we set fire to them and left them in a blaze. It had not been expected that we would come back so soon, hence their want of precaution to provide for their safety. While the bridges were burning, the soldiers who had been put there to protect them were dozing in their tents not a mile off. In a few days I again went as far as Dumfries, but could find no assailable point.

The trains all carried strong infantry guards, in addition to those stationed along the railroad. I started back without having effected anything, and stopped at the house of a man named Lynn, to rest and feed our horses. As we were far inside the enemy's lines, there was some risk in this; but we were tired and hungry. Our horses had been unbitted, and were eating their corn, and I was lying on the grass asleep, when I was aroused by the cry that the enemy was coming. We barely had time to bridle up and mount before they were upon us. They came full speed on our trail, and were strung out for a long distance on the road.

This was my opportunity. A lieutenant was gallantly leading them. I saved myself this time by the same counter-stroke that a few weeks before had rescued me from the brink of ruin in the fight at Miskel's farm. We did not wait for the danger, but went to meet it. There was a gate across the road, between us and the enemy, which I ordered to be opened. We dashed through, and in the moment of collision the lieutenant fell, severely wounded. Several others in the front met the same fate; they had drawn sabres, that hurt nobody, and we used pistols. Their companions halted, hesitated, and were overpowered before support could come up. Some turned and fled, and in doing so communicated their panic to those in their rear. They fled pell-mell back toward their camp, leaving their dead and wounded on the field and a number of prisoners and horses in our hands. I then had, in turn, to get away quickly. I knew they would soon return with reinforcements; they did come, but we were gone.

In returning, we crossed the railroad within a mile of Manassas, and in full view of the troops there, but were not molested. I found out from this raid the difficulty of making any impression with my small command on the force guarding the road. I could keep them on the watch, and in a state of anxiety and alarm; but, while this might satisfy Stuart and Gen. Lee, the men on whom I had to depend to do the work would not be content with such results. In order to retain them, it was necessary for me to stimulate their enthusiasm with something more tangible. War to them was not an abstraction; it meant prisoners, arms, horses and sutler's stores; remote consequences were not much considered. So I sent Beattie with a letter to explain the situation to Stuart, in which I said:

> If you will let me have a mountain howitzer, I think I could use it with great effect, especially on the railroad trains. I have several experienced artillerists with me. The effect of such annoyance is to force the enemy to make heavy details to guard their communications. I have not attacked any of their railroad trains, because I have no ammunition for my carbines, and they are pretty strongly guarded with infantry.

In this letter I suggested the theory on which my warfare was conducted. It would not only draw troops from the front, but prevent those doing duty on the railroad and around Washington from being sent to Hooker to make up his losses in the Wilderness. These operations were erratic simply in not being in accordance with the fixed rules taught by the academies; but in all that I did there was a unity of purpose, and a plan which my commanding general understood and approved. The Confederate drill sergeants could see no use in what they could not comprehend.

In reference to the fight at Warrenton Junction, Gen. Abercrombie reports:

> Between the hours of 9 and 10 a.m., on the morning of the 3rd *ult.*, an outpost of the 1st Va. (Union) Cavalry at Warrenton Junction, about 100 men, under Lieut.-Col. Krepp's command, were surprised and attacked by Maj. Mosby, with his

force of about 125 (75) men. The men of the 1st Va. were scattered about the station, their horses unsaddled, in order to be groomed and fed. Mosby's force came in upon them from the direction of Warrenton, which place they left at daylight. Their front rank was dressed in the uniform of the United States (we were all dressed in gray. J.S.M.), and they were supposed to be a force of Union cavalry until within a short distance, when they charged, and surrounded the house in and about which the 1st Va. lay. After a short fight, in which several of the rebels were killed and wounded, the men of the 1st Va. for the most part surrendered, and about 40 were being taken towards Warrenton by their captors, when a detachment of 70 men of the 5th N.Y. Cavalry, which was camped near by, under command of Maj. Hammond, came up, charged upon the rebels, and a running fight ensued, which was continued for five miles, in the course of which all the prisoners taken by Mosby were recaptured, with the exception of two.

Major-General Stahel reports:

> Our men being surprised and completely surrounded, rallied in a house close at hand, and where a sharp fight ensued. Our men defended themselves as long as their ammunition lasted, notwithstanding the Rebels built a large fire about the house, of hay and straw and brushwood; the flames reached the house, and their ammunition being entirely expended, they were obliged to surrender.

Maj. Steele, of the 1st. Va., was mortally wounded in the house.

CHAPTER 11

# A Wrecked Train

*Quis jam fluctus, quae regio in terris non nostri plena laboris.*
*—Æneid.*

At this time Gen. Lee was making the preliminary movement of the Gettysburg campaign up the left bank of the Rappahannock, while Hooker moved on a parallel line on the other. Pleasanton's cavalry corps was massed on the river, near Rappahannock station, about fifty miles from Washington, which was now covered by Hooker's army. In compliance with my request, Stuart sent me a small mountain howitzer by Beattie. A brigade of cavalry and one of infantry were lying between Manassas and Catlett's station; and here was the only possible chance of reaching the railroad without being discovered. On May 29, 1863, I set out with about forty men, and my little gun, to strike it somewhere between these points. I had no caisson; but carried fifteen rounds of ammunition in the limber-chest.

The enterprise on which I was going, when judged by the common standards of prudence, appeared not only hazardous but foolhardy. The camps of the enemy were distributed along the road at intervals of one or two miles, with patrols continually passing. Every train had on board a strong infantry guard. If I should succeed in penetrating their lines and making a capture, it could not be done without alarming the camps, which would make my retreat difficult, if not impossible. But I thought the end justified the risk. An attack, even by my small band, at such a critical time, might create an important diversion in favour of Gen. Lee. If this could be done, then the loss of the gun, and even of my whole command, would be as dust in the balance against the advantage of it.

We bivouacked that night in the pines near Catlett's, and were awakened in the morning by the reveille in the Union camps, which were a mile or so distant on either side of us. There was a narrow pathway through the pines, along which we marched until within a hundred yards of the railroad. The telegraph wire was cut, and a rail sufficiently removed to allow a train to run off the track. The howitzer was in charge of the Rev. Sam Chapman, who had been so conspicuous in the fight at Miskel's; it was now made ready for action. All of us were under cover, with one man near the road to give notice of an approaching train. We had not waited long before he gave the signal. I rode forward, and saw it puffing along.

Chapman rammed down a charge in his gun; and all awaited the event with breathless interest. I was in fear every moment of a patrol coming on the road who might give the alarm and stop the train. Fortunately, none came. The engineer, not suspecting danger, was driving at full speed, when suddenly the locomotive glided from the track. The infantry guard fired a volley, which did no injury to us except killing a horse. In an instant, a shell from Chapman's gun went crashing through the cars. They all jumped off and took to their heels through the pines.

In the stampede, they did not take time to count our number. If they had stood their ground, they could have easily driven us away. Another shell was sent through the boiler of the engine. The infernal noise of the escaping steam increased the panic among the fugitives. There were several bales of hay on the train that were set on fire. The whole was soon in flames. One car was loaded with sutlers' goods, which the men did not permit to be entirely consumed by the fire. There was also a number of fresh shad; and each man secured one of these. The blockade of the Potomac had for a long time deprived us of that luxury. The United States mail bags were tied to the carriage of the howitzer; and we started to retrace our steps.

I have been criticised a good deal at the North for capturing trains on railroads used for military purposes. To justify myself, it is not necessary for me to use the *tu quoque* argument, and retort that my adversaries did the same whenever they could; for the plain reason that I was simply exercising a belligerent right. There was nobody but soldiers on this train; but, if there had been women and children, too, it would have been all the same to me. Those who travel on a road running through a military district must accept the risk of the accidents of war. It does not hurt people any more to be killed in a railroad wreck than having their heads knocked off by a cannon shot. One of the most effective ways of impeding the march of an army is by cutting off its supplies; and this is just as legitimate as to attack it in line of battle. Jomini says that the irregular warfare of the Cossacks did more to destroy the French army on the expedition to Moscow than the élite regiments of the Russian guard. After the peace, all Europe hailed their hetman, Platoff, as the hero of the war, and the corporation of London gave him a sword.

But to return to my story. I had penetrated the enemy's lines, and the difficulty was now to get out. The sound of the cannon had given the alarm. The long roll was beaten through all the infantry camps, and the bugles sounded—"to horse." As I had never used a piece of artillery before, it was not known that I had it. It was thought at first that Stuart had come in behind them, and hence they advanced on me cautiously. When I had got about a mile from the railroad I met a regiment of New York Cavalry (the 5th), in the road directly in front of me. It had come up from the camp below at Kettle Run to cut us off. We halted while Chapman unlimbered, and sent a shell at them, which, fortunately, burst at the head of the column, and killed the horse of the commanding officer.

This created a stampede, and they scattered before another shell could get to them. The way was now open, and we went on by the horse lying with his accoutrements in the road. I made Foster and a few others gallop forward, to produce the impression that we were pursuing, but soon recalled them to the gun, as I was expecting the enemy every moment in my rear. We were now girt with foes on every side. It would, of course, have been easy to save ourselves by scattering through the woods, but I was fighting on a point of honour. I wanted to save the howitzer, or, if I had to lose it, I was determined to exact all that it was worth in blood. After we got about a mile further on, the regiment we had broken rallied, and with reinforcements came on again in pursuit. Another shell was thrown at them, and they fell back. We were just on the edge of a wood, and I ordered Chapman to go forward with his gun at a gallop, while I remained behind with six men as a rear-guard to cover the retreat.

Clouds of cavalry which had been attracted by the firing were now seen in different directions, and the enemy once more moved toward us. With less than 50 men I was confronting Deforest's brigade of cavalry. At one time we had been entirely enveloped by them, but had broken through their line. As the enemy came near we slowly withdrew. Their advance guard of 12 or 15 men suddenly dashed upon us as we were retiring through the woods. We wheeled and had a fierce hand-to-hand fight, in which they were routed and driven back. Several of their dead and wounded were left on the ground. I have before spoken of Capt. Hoskins, an English officer, who had recently joined me. He was riding by my side when the fight began. The tradition of chivalry inherited from the ancient knights of using the sword in single combat still asserted its dominion over him, but my other men had no more use for that antiquated weapon than a coat of mail. They had discarded it as a useless incumbrance.

Hoskins was in the act of giving a thrust when he was shot. In an instant after, his adversary fell before a deadly revolver. Hoskins's wound was mortal. When the fight was over, he was taken to the house of an Englishman near by, and lived a day or two. Thus died as gallant a gentleman as ever pricked his steed over Palestine's plains. He had passed without a scar through the fire of the Redan and the Malakoff to fall in a petty skirmish in the American forests. I could not stay by him, and I had no means of carrying him off. The overwhelming numbers pressing upon us forced a retreat, and we had to leave him by the roadside with his life-blood ebbing fast away. The horse that I had presented to him disdained capture and followed us. I gave it to Beattie. He was buried in his martial cloak at Greenwich church, and now, like Lara,

*Sleeps not where his fathers sleep.*

Seeing that no hope was left us but to save our honour and stand by the gun, I sent Foster with an order to Chapman to halt and unlimber in a narrow lane on a hill. The high fences on both sides were some protection against a flank attack of cavalry. I knew we could hold the position as long as the ammunition lasted for the gun. Some of the men who had joined me, thinking that they were going on a picnic, had already left to fry their shad and eat the confectioneries they had got on the train. When I rode up to Chapman, he had his gun already shotted. Mountjoy and Beattie were standing by it. Their faces beamed with what the Romans called the *gaudia certaminis*, and they had never looked so happy in their lives. As for myself, realizing the desperate straits we were in, I wished I was somewhere else.

Sam Chapman and his brother William, who afterward became the lieutenant-colonel of my battalion, had commanded the battery which, under Longstreet's orders, had shattered Fitz John Porter's corps in its assault on Jackson's line at Groveton heights. When the Federal cavalry came in sight a couple of hundred yards off, he sent them a shell that exploded in their ranks, and they fell back in confusion to the woods. They re-formed and came again. If they had deployed as foragers, we would have been driven away without inflicting much loss on them. But they committed the error of charging up the road in a solid column of fours, where every discharge from the gun raked them with grape and canister. They made several successive onsets of this kind, which Chapman repulsed. In turn, we would charge and drive them a considerable distance, and then return to the gun. This was repeated several times over ground strewn with their killed and wounded men and horses. The damage done here to my side was that Bill Elzey had several teeth knocked out by a bullet. They used their sabres, and we the revolver.

At last the supreme moment came. Chapman had rammed home his last round of ammunition, and a heavy column was again advancing. I sat on my horse just behind the gun: when they got within 50 yards, it again belched with fire and knocked down a number of men and horses in their front. They halted, and, at the same time, I ordered a charge, and drove them down to the foot of the hill. I was riding a spirited sorrel horse, who carried me with so much force that I could not hold him up until I had gone some distance through their ranks. Charlie McDonough followed me. As I passed by a big cavalryman he struck me a blow with his sabre on the shoulder that nearly knocked me from my seat.

At the same instant my pistol flashed, and he reeled from his saddle. McDonough and I were now hemmed in by high fences on both sides; the Federal soldiers we had passed in the road, seeing that nearly all my men had left the gun, which had ceased firing, made a dash at it. Beattie managed to mount and get away. George Tuberville, who acted as driver, went off at full speed, and saved his two horses and limber-chest. Mountjoy, who was one of the bravest of the brave, was captured at the gun, after he had fired his last cartridge.

The Rev. Sam Chapman had passed through so many fights unscathed that the men had a superstition that he was as invulnerable as the son of Thetis. His hour had come at last, and a bullet pierced the celestial armour of the soldier-priest; but he fought with the rammer of his gun as he fell. He lived to pay the debt he contracted that day. "For time, at last, sets all things even." The victors now held the howitzer, and barred the only way for my escape; but I held in my hand a more potent talisman than Douglas threw into the Saracen ranks.

My faith in the power of a six-shooter was as strong as the Crusader's was in the heart of the Bruce. I darted by the men who were now in possession of the gun, and received no hurt, except getting my face badly scratched by the limb of a tree as I passed. I had left Hoskins, Chapman, and Mountjoy in the hands of the enemy. Their shouts of triumph now rang through the woods; but no further pursuit was made. With a single companion, I stopped at a farmhouse, washed the blood from my face, and started back to get ready for another raid.

In a week I had rallied, and was down in Fairfax stirring up the outposts. Stuart sent me a message, that I might sell another gun for the same price. I had effected more than I had hoped. When the news of my rout reached headquarters at Fairfax Court House, a flaming despatch (which is printed in Moore's *Rebellion Record*) was sent North, announcing that "within two or three days Mosby had lost 150 men, and Gen. Stahel will not let him rest until his band is exterminated." As I had all the time acted on the offensive, it was easy enough for me to get rest by keeping quiet. As I had never had one-half that number of men, of course I could not have lost them. As long as I could keep a thousand men watching on the defensive for every one that I had with me, it was a small matter who got the best in a fight.

The Count of Paris, who was a staff officer in the Union army, in his history of the war, mentions the two affairs on the railroad, and says:

> In Washington itself, Gen. Heintzelman was in command, who, beside the depots, the regiments under instruction, and the artillery in the forts, had under his control several thousand infantry ready to take the field, and Stahel's division of cavalry, numbering 6000 horses, whose only task was to pursue Mosby and the few hundred partisans led by this daring chief.

If Pleasanton had had those 6000 sabres with him a few days after this, on June 9, 1863, in his great cavalry combat with Stuart at Brandy Station, the result might have been different. Hooker had asked for them, but had been refused, on the ground that they could not be spared from the defence of Washington. (See note below).

★★★★★★

Note:— Telegram.

Headquarters, May 30, 1863.

Stahel to Heintzelman:—

We had a hard fight with Mosby this morning, who had

artillery,—the same which was used to destroy the train of cars. We whipped him like the devil, and took his artillery. My forces are still pursuing him. A more full report will follow, hoping the general will be satisfied with this result.

Jul. Stahel, Major-General.

Major-General Stahel reports of the above affair, that:

The train for Bealeton had just passed up, and believing it to have been attacked, he (Col. Mann) immediately went with a detachment of the 5th N.Y. Cavalry, under command of Capt. A. H. Hasbrouck, a detachment of the 1st Vermont, under command of Lieut.-Col. Preston, and a small detachment of the 7th Michigan. The detachment of the 5th New York was sent directly across the country, in order to intercept the Rebels, while the balance of the command went directly to the scene of action. The advance of the 5th New York, led by Lieut. Elmer Barker, came up with the enemy first, and found them with the howitzer posted on a hill, with the cavalry drawn up in line in the rear to support it.

Lieut. Barker, with his small detachment of about 25 men, dashed up the hill, and when within about 50 yards of the gun, received a charge of grape and canister, which killed three (3) and wounded seven (7) of our men, and several horses. The enemy then charged upon us, but were met with a stubborn resistance by the Lieutenant and his men, although the Lieutenant had received two grape-shots in his thigh. We were, however, overpowered and driven back a short distance. Just then Col. Preston of the 1st Vermont (Lieut. Hazleton, with companies H and C, being in advance) came up at a full charge upon their flank, and were received with a discharge from the howitzer of grape and canister. Our men pressed on, however, until they came to a hand-to-hand conflict, when the enemy gradually fell back. We took their howitzer, and they fled in every direction. . . . Our loss was four (4) killed, fifteen (15) wounded, the names of which please find enclosed. We also lost eleven (11) horses killed and several wounded.

★★★★★★

Chapter 12

# On the Road to Gettysburg

*Fight as thy fathers fought,*
*Fall as thy fathers fell!*
*Thy task is taught, thy shroud is wrought;—*
*So—forward—and farewell!*—Praed.

I now turned my attention once more to the troops guarding the line of the Potomac and the defences of Washington. I was afraid that if I continued my attacks on the railroad and in the vicinity of Hooker's camps, the cavalry division of Stahel would be released from doing guard duty, and sent to the front on the Rappahannock. (See note following).

★★★★★★

Note:—In his testimony before the committee on the conduct of the war, Gen. Hooker says, vol. 1, page 162:

> I may here state that while at Fairfax Court House my cavalry was reinforced by that of Maj.-Gen. Stahel. The latter numbered 6100 sabres, and had been engaged in picketing a line from Occoquan River to Goose Creek. This line was concentric to, and a portion of it within, the line held by my army. The force opposed to them was Mosby's guerillas, numbering about 200 (not over thirty men); and, if the reports of the newspapers were to be believed, this whole party was killed two or three times during the winter. From the time I took command of the army of the Potomac there was no evidence that any force of the enemy, other than that above named, was within 100 miles of Washington City; and yet, the planks on the chain bridge were taken up at night during the

greater part of the winter and spring. It was this cavalry force, it will be remembered, I had occasion to ask for, that my cavalry might be strengthened when it was numerically too weak to cope with the superior numbers of the enemy.

★★★★★★

So on June 3, only three days after I had been routed and my howitzer captured near Greenwich, I collected thirty or forty men and started once more for Fairfax. The cavalry down there had enjoyed a season of rest for several weeks. We passed by Fryingpan at night, and slept in a thicket of pines on the Ox road. John Underwood was sent forward with a squad of men to fire on the pickets or patrols. I knew that this would draw out a force in search of us the next morning. Just as I had got in a doze I heard several shots. The men burst out laughing, and said, "That's John Underwood." I had directed him to remain concealed by the roadside to watch for any scouting party of the enemy that might come out in the morning. About sunrise I received a message from him that a body of about fifty cavalry had gone up the road. In an instant we were all in our saddles; but just then Underwood galloped up and informed me that another body had passed on.

"How many do you think there are?"

"About 100," was his answer.

"All the better," I said; "we are in their rear. It is just as easy to whip 100 as 50. Forward, trot!"

The party of the first part got to Fryingpan and halted; we overtook the second party just as we got in sight of the first. They were utterly confounded at seeing a lot of men coming up on their rear, shooting and shouting. They hadn't time to wheel around to meet an attack from behind, but broke and ran away. They were driven pell-mell in a cloud of dust upon the body of cavalry that had halted at Fryingpan, and in turn they communicated the panic to their friends. I came very near being caught here in the same trap that I got in at Warrenton Junction, but managed to get out without loss, beside carrying off a number of prisoners and horses.

Some of my men had chased the fugitives a few hundred yards when they unexpectedly came on a regiment of Federal cavalry drawn up in line just over a hill. I have since ascertained that it was Col. Gray of the 6th Michigan cavalry. He had come out on another road, and hearing the firing at Fryingpan, had formed to receive an attack. If he had followed the example of Major Hammond with the 5th New York, at Warrenton Junction, and charged us when we were in disorder and scattered over the field, that would in all probability have been my last day as a partisan commander. As soon as I heard of this third body of cavalry, which I had not seen, I drew off my men as rapidly as possible, while Col. Gray was waiting to receive us. He managed to catch Dr. Alexander, who was with me. I went off home with my spoil, and it was announced in Washington that I had once more been routed and driven away. A few days after that I caught a Federal surgeon, and set him free on the condition that he would try to secure the release of Alexander. He kept his pledge.

As I have before stated, I had two months before this time received authority from the war department, through Gen. Lee, to raise a command. A good many men had joined me, but a considerable number of them had been captured at different times by raiding parties of the enemy. As it was the third year of the war the soldier element in the country had been pretty well exhausted by conscription, and I was forbidden to receive recruits from this class subject to conscript duty. It was, therefore, very difficult for me to get 60 eligible men, which was the legal standard for organising a company. By this time I had about that number on my muster roll; but at least a third of them were in prison, having been captured at various times by raiding parties of the enemy.

On June 10, 1863, my first company was organised at Rector Crossroads, with James W. Foster as captain, Thomas Turner of Maryland as 1st, William L. Hunter (later of California) as 2nd, and George Whitescarver as 3rd lieutenant. In compliance with law, I had to go through the form of an election. But I really appointed the officers, and told the men to vote for them. This was my rule as long as I had a command, and with two or three exceptions their conduct vindicated my judgment. On the same day that the company was organised I started for the Potomac, as it was my policy to keep up a state of alarm about the capital. I had long meditated crossing the river, but it was not fordable during the spring and winter season. This was but a few weeks after the Battle of Chancellorsville, and there was great fear at the North of a Confederate invasion.

Gen. Lee, (see notes following), was then moving up the Rappahannock on his way to Pennsylvania. I knew that if I only crossed over once, a small army would be detached to protect the border.

Information had reached me that a squadron of Michigan cavalry was at Seneca; and I resolved to attack it. My plan was to cross the river at night, capture the patrols, and surprise the camp about daybreak. (See notes following). Unfortunately, the night was very dark; my guide missed the way, and we did not get over the river until daybreak. I sent Alfred Glasscock, Joe Nelson, and Trunnell ahead, who concealed themselves in the bushes on the canal bank, and seized the patrol as it came along without giving any alarm. When I reached the northern bank they were waiting for me.

The same party then went on up the towpath and captured a canal boat and some mules; while I halted a short time to close up the command. When we got near the bridge over the canal, we met another patrol, that fired and fled. They pulled up the drawbridge behind them; and it took us some minutes to replace it. This delay gave time to the cavalry in camp to saddle up. Before we got in 200 yards of them they retreated rapidly. After crossing a narrow bridge over Seneca Creek, they halted, and held it against a few of my men, who had pursued them. They were armed with carbines, and poured such a hot fire into the men that they started to fall back. Just then I rode up. Some of them were carrying Glasscock away, as he had been severely wounded.

✶✶✶✶✶✶

Note:—The following correspondence between Gen. Pleasanton, chief of cavalry, and Gen. Ingalls, chief quartermaster of the army of the Potomac, which I recently found in the archives of the war department, shows the anxiety at that time to suppress my command. I had never heard of it before I saw it there. It is evident that somebody had hoaxed Gen. Pleasanton, as the whole negotiation was confined to himself and Gen. Ingalls. The fact that he had an unlimited amount of money placed at his disposal for buying me, and did not do it, is conclusive proof that there never had been a chance for it:—

Headquarters Cavalry Corps, June 12, 1863.
Gen. R. Ingalls, Chief Quartermaster:—Your despatch received. Ask the general how much of a bribe he can stand to get Mosby's services. There is a chance for him; and just now he could do valuable service in the way of information, as well as humbugging the enemy. There's no news. The rebels are like the boy the President tells

about who stumped his toe and was too big to cry. Birney is up.

A. Pleasanton, Brigadier-General.

Headquarters Army of the Potomac,<br>June 12, 1863.

Gen. Pleasanton:—If you think your scheme can succeed in regard to Mosby, do not hesitate as to the matter of money. Use your own judgment, and do precisely what you think best for the public interest.

Robert Ingalls,<br>Brigadier-General.

Middleburg, VA., June 10, 1863.

General:—I left our point of rendezvous yesterday for the purpose of making a night attack on two cavalry companies of the enemy on the Maryland shore. Had I succeeded in crossing the river at night, as I expected, I would have had no difficulty in capturing them; but, unfortunately, my guide mistook the road, and, instead of crossing by 11 o'clock at night, I did not get over until after daylight. The enemy (between 80 and 100 strong), being apprised of my movement, were formed to receive me. A charge was ordered, the shock of which the enemy could not resist; and they were driven several miles in confusion, with the loss of seven killed, a considerable number wounded, and 17 prisoners; also 20 odd horses or more. We burned their tents, stores, camp equipage, etc. I regret the loss of two brave officers killed—Capt. Brawner and Lieut. (George H.) Whitescarver. I also had one man wounded.

Respectfully your obedient servant,

John S. Mosby,<br>Major of Partisan Rangers.

Maj.-Gen. J. E. B. Stuart.

Endorsement.

Headquarters Cavalry Division, June 16, 1863.

Respectfully forwarded. In consideration of his brilliant services, I hope the President will promote Maj. Mosby.

J. E. B. Stuart,<br>Major-General.

★★★★★★

After waiting a minute or two for my command to close up, we dashed across the bridge and completely routed the cavalry on the other bank. Frank Stringfellow rode by my side as I led the charge, but we had hardly got over before George Whitescarver was ahead of us. The Michigan men broke and fled, leaving behind 17 prisoners, 30 horses, their colours, four dead and one wounded, beside all their camp equipage and stores. They had formed a line of a crescent shape not more than 50 yards from the bridge, on which they poured a converging fire, but not one of us was touched in going over. I had not gone a hundred yards in pursuit when Foster, who was riding by me, said, as we passed a dead man in the road: "There is one of our boys." He was so begrimed with dust that I did not recognise him. It was Whitescarver. The men were soon recalled.

I was apprehensive that the enemy's cavalry on the river above might come down the towpath and intercept us. Then there was the danger, if I tarried too long in Maryland, that Maj.-Gen. Stahel would be ready to catch me on the Virginia shore, for his camps were only a few miles below. I was accompanied that day by Capt. Brawner, who commanded an independent company, and had come over to Fauquier a few days before. With two or three men he had kept on after I had abandoned the pursuit, and was killed.[1] I returned to Middleburg unmolested, wrote a despatch to Stuart, and forwarded my prisoners. The next day I sent him the captured guidon, by Maj. White of his staff. The raid had all the effect I desired in arousing the fears of the enemy for the safety of the North.

Col. Thompson of the California cavalry battalion, who accompanied Col. Lowell in pursuit of me through Leesburg, recently informed me that when they got to Fairfax on their return they found Gen. Stahel's division prepared for battle. Stahel had sent out scouting parties over the country. I had no positive knowledge of the intention of Gen. Lee to invade the North, but all signs pointed that way. First

---

1. One who was in command at Poolesville, Md., a few miles from Seneca, reports: "About 250 of the enemy's cavalry crossed the Potomac near Muddy Branch at daybreak. The enemy dashed rapidly up the canal, driving in the patrols, and attacked Capt. Deane's company (I) 6th Michigan cavalry, on duty at Seneca locks. Capt. Deane fell back toward Poolesville, forming line three times, and only retreating when nearly surrounded. The enemy followed to within three miles of Poolesville, when he rapidly retired, destroying the camp of Capt. Deane, and recrossing the river at the point where he had crossed. Our loss is four men killed, 16 men missing, one man wounded."

came the news of Milroy's rout by Ewell at Winchester. As I was looking for Stuart every day, I made no more raids that week, but held my men ready to do any work that he wanted. On June 16 Stuart crossed the Rappahannock, and bivouacked near Piedmont station in Fauquier that night. On the same day I went with a few men on a scout in the neighbourhood of Thoroughfare, to find out which way Hooker was moving. I saw from the smoke of his camp fires that he was retiring on Washington as Lee advanced toward the Potomac.

Early on the morning of the 17th I visited Stuart's headquarters at Miss Kitty Shacklett's house. As he was mounted on a very indifferent horse, I gave him a fine sorrel that one of my men had recently captured from a Michigan lieutenant. I told him what I knew about the position of the enemy, and that I was ready to perform any service he wanted. The cavalry moved on to Middleburg, and I met him there again in the afternoon. There were 30 or 40 of my men with me. He had never seen them before, and made some jocular remarks about them as they passed. We had a short conference, and he approved of the expedition on which I was going across the Potomac. There had been so many alarms along the enemy's lines that it was difficult for them to reinforce any one point more strongly than it had been; and I knew that they would now rely on the presence of Hooker's troops for the protection of Maryland.

I did not think they were expecting me to come back to Seneca. My idea was to create a diversion in favour of Gen. Lee, who was marching into the Shenandoah valley, and also to keep him informed of the movement of the enemy. I bade Stuart "goodbye," and told him that he would soon hear from me. He had sent Wickham's brigade down to picket the gap in the Bull Run mountain at Aldie. His duty was to observe the enemy, and mask the movements of the Confederate army. My command turned off three miles above there, and moved again toward Seneca. It was a very hot day, and we had stopped a while to rest under the shade of some trees, and refresh ourselves with buttermilk at the house of a farmer named Gulick. Presently we heard artillery firing over toward Aldie, which indicated a collision of the enemy's cavalry with ours.

In an instant every man was mounted. From a commanding position on the mountain, which we reached in a few minutes, I could see clouds of dust rising on every road, which showed that Hooker was marching for the Potomac. After going a little farther, we captured a number of prisoners, and I immediately sent a despatch to Stuart, with the information I got from them. I could not now get to Seneca without passing through Hooker's infantry, so I concluded to go down on the Little River turnpike, and operate on the line of communication between Pleasanton's cavalry and the general headquarters. I knew I could gather some prizes there, and probably keep Stahel's cavalry from coming to the front, by giving them plenty to do in their rear. So we kept ourselves concealed, like Robin Hood and his merry men, in the green wood until night, and then sallied out in quest of game. After it was dark, we moved to a point about four miles below Aldie, where Pleasanton and Rosser had been fighting, and on the pike leading to Fairfax Court House, near which Hooker's headquarters were established that evening. My command was now inside of Hooker's lines, and environed on all sides by the camps of his different corps. Along the pike a continuous stream of troops, with all the impedimenta of war, poured along.

Taking three men with me—Joe Nelson, Charlie Hall, and Norman Smith—I rode out into the column of Union troops as they passed along. As it was dark, they had no suspicion who we were, although we were all dressed in full Confederate uniform. A man by the name of Birch lived in a house near the roadside, and I discovered three horses standing at his front gate, with a man holding them by their bridles. I was sure that he was an orderly, and that they were officers' horses. We rode up, and asked him to whom they belonged. He replied that they were Maj. Stirling's and Capt. Fisher's, and that they were just from Gen. Hooker's headquarters. I then called him up to me and took him by the collar, and leaning down, whispered in his ear: "You are my prisoner. My name is Mosby." The man, who was an Irishman, understood me to say that he was "Mosby," and indignantly replied, "You are a d—d liar. I am as good a Union man as you are." Just then in the starlight he saw the gleam of a pistol, and had nothing further to say.

In a few minutes the officers came out of the house. I saluted them, and asked which way they were going and where they were from. As we seemed to be in such friendly relations with their orderly, they never suspected our hostile character, and promptly answered that they were from Gen. Hooker's headquarters, and were carrying despatches to Pleasanton. Capt. Fisher was his chief signal officer, going up to establish a signal station at Snicker's gap—if he could get there. By this time my men had dismounted, and as I was talking to Maj. Stirling, Joe Nelson walked up, and, politely extending his hand, asked for his pistol. Charlie Hall, not to be outdone in courtesy by Joe, proposed to relieve Capt. Fisher of his. They both misunderstood what Hall and Nelson meant, and offered to shake hands with them. In an instant the barrels of four glittering revolvers informed them that death was their doom if they refused to be prisoners. Resistance was useless and they surrendered. All now mounted quickly and we left the pike. As we started, both officers burst out laughing. I asked them what they were laughing at. They said they had laughed so much about their people being gobbled up by me that they were now enjoying the joke being turned on themselves.

They were then informed that I knew that they had despatches for Pleasanton, and that they could relieve me of performing a disagreeable duty by handing them over. Maj. Stirling promptly complied. I then went to a farmer's house near by, got a light, and read them.[2] They contained just such information as Gen. Lee wanted, and were the "open sesame" to Hooker's army. I wrote a note to Stuart to go with the despatches, which were sent with the prisoners under charge of Norman Smith. He got to Stuart's headquarters about daybreak. The skies were red that night in every direction with the light of the fires of the Union army. We slept soundly within a mile of Birney's corps at Gum Spring, and in the morning began operations on the pike. We soon got as many fish in our nets as we could haul out, and then returned into the Confederate lines. Stuart was delighted to see me; he had also learned from the captured despatches that a cavalry reconnoissance would be sent to Warrenton the next day. Notice of it was sent to Gen. Hampton, who met and repulsed it.

After a series of indecisive engagements, extending through several days, Pleasanton, finally, on the 21st of June, supported by a force of infantry, drove Stuart back to Ashby's Gap in the Blue Ridge. Having

---

2. Stuart's report of the Gettysburg campaign says: "Maj. Mosby, with his usual daring, penetrated the enemy's lines and caught a staff officer of Gen. Hooker—bearer of despatches to Gen. Pleasanton, commanding United States cavalry near Aldie. These despatches disclosed the fact that Hooker was looking to Aldie with solicitude, and that Pleasanton, with infantry and cavalry, occupied the place; and that a reconnoissance in force of cavalry was meditated toward Warrenton and Culpepper. I immediately despatched to Gen. Hampton, who was coming by way of Warrenton from the direction of Beverly ford, this intelligence, and directed him to meet this advance at Warrenton. The captured despatches also gave the entire number of divisions, from which we could estimate the approximate strength of the enemy's army. I therefore concluded in no event to attack with cavalry alone the enemy at Aldie. . . Hampton met the enemy's advance toward Culpepper and Warrenton, and drove him back without difficulty—a heavy storm and night intervening to aid the enemy's retreat."

effected the object of his reconnoissance, which was to ascertain the position of the Confederate army that was then moving down the Shenandoah Valley, Pleasanton retired on the same night to Aldie, where the 5th Corps was posted, and did not again assume the offensive as long as Hooker remained in Virginia. He stood on the defensive and simply watched and waited. On the next day, Stuart re-established his lines about Middleburg, with his headquarters at Rector's Crossroads, where he kept up communication with Gen. Lee, who was at Berryville. Hill and Longstreet were near there, and Ewell had gone into Maryland.

On the afternoon when Pleasanton followed the Confederate cavalry through Upperville to the mountain, I was with my command on Dulony's farm, about a mile from the pike, as he passed. I determined again to strike at his rear. As we were passing Bull Run mountain by a narrow path that night, one of my men, about the middle of the column, dropped his hat, and stopped to pick it up. It was pitch dark; and, as those in front of him knew nothing about it, they kept on. The men behind him halted. This cut my column in two; and half of it wandered all night in the woods, but never found me. We slept in a drenching rain on the top of the mountain, and started early in the morning. As we were going through Dr. Ewell's farm, I stopped to talk with him; but the men went on. Presently, I saw them halt near a church in the woods; and one of them beckoned to me. I galloped up, and saw a body of about thirty cavalry drawn up not a hundred yards in front of us. I instantly ordered a charge; and, just as we got upon them, they ran away, while a heavy fire was poured into us by a company of infantry concealed in the church. A negro had carried the news of our being on the mountain to Gen. Meade, who had prepared this ambuscade for me.

Three of my men—Charlie Hall, Mountjoy, and Ballard—were wounded; the latter losing a leg. The lieutenant commanding the Federal cavalry was killed. I was not ten steps from the infantry when they fired the volley. We fell back to the mountain; and, no doubt, Gen. Meade thought that I was done for—at least for that day. After taking care of my wounded, I started again for the Little River Pike, which we reached by flanking Gen. Meade. Pretty soon we caught a train of twenty wagons, and proceeded to unhitch the mules. I did not have more than one man to a wagon. The guard to the train rallied, and recaptured some of the animals, and two of my men; but we got away with most of them. That night they were delivered to Stuart's quartermaster. This raid is a fine illustration of the great results that may be achieved by a partisan force co-operating with the movements of an army. My principal aim in these operations was to get information for Stuart, and, by harassing the communications of the Federal army, to neutralize with my small command Stahel's three brigades of cavalry in Fairfax. (See note following).

★★★★★★

> Note:—Gen. Stahel, in a report to the secretary of war, says that on June 21 he received an order from Hooker's headquarters to make a reconnoissance in force to Warrenton and the upper Rappahannock. "In compliance with this order," he says, "I started with my command for Warrenton and the upper Rappahannock. Just as I was about crossing the Rappahannock with two brigades,—one of my brigades being already across,—for the purpose of executing the above orders, and to break up Gen. Lee's communication with Richmond, and which could have been easily effected, as there were but very few troops, and Gen. Lee's rear consisting of their cavalry, with which Gen. Pleasanton was engaged in the upper part of the valley, received the following order from Hooker:
> 
> June 23.
>> Maj.-Gen. Hancock:—Direct Gen. Stahel to return without delay; to dispose his forces so as to catch the party inside our lines, if possible.'
> 
> Another despatch stated that the force was about 100; that they attacked one of our trains on the Aldie road.
>> It was with feelings of bitter regret and disappointment that I received this order, inasmuch as I was just crossing the Rappahannock with three brigades of cavalry and a battery of horse artillery, who were just fresh from camp, etc.... All of Lee's supplies had to pass up between the Rappahannock and Blue Ridge mountains or cross to the Shenandoah valley; and my force was sufficient to have destroyed his entire trains and to cut off Gen. Lee completely from his supplies.... I was compelled by this order to abandon my movement, and restrained from dealing so fatal a blow to the enemy, and return with my whole division to disperse about 100 guerillas who had escaped back out of our lines before I ever received the order to return.

******

It happened that on June 22—the very day we captured the wagon train—Gen. Stahel, in obedience to Hooker's orders, had gone from Fairfax with three cavalry brigades and a battery of artillery, on a reconnoissance to the Rappahannock. On June 23, just as one of his brigades had crossed over the river, and the other two were in the act of crossing, he received an order from Gen. Hooker to return immediately, and to dispose his force so as to catch the party inside his lines that had captured his wagon train. We had got to Stuart's headquarters with Hooker's mules before Stahel got the order. He did not come there to search for them. If he had not been recalled, he might have done much damage on Gen. Lee's line of communication, as it was entirely uncovered. In fact, there was no Confederate force between him and Richmond. When afterward, Gen. Hooker, before the committee on the conduct of the war, criticised the authorities at Washington so severely for keeping this large force to watch my small one, he had forgotten that he had done the same thing himself.[3] In a letter to Stuart, dated June 23, 1863, 5 p.m., Gen. Lee refers with some uneasiness to this expedition of Stahel. He did not know at the time that Stahel had gone back.

In an interview I had with Stuart on my return, we discussed the best route for him to go into Maryland. As I knew all the roads, as well as the location of each corps of the enemy, that were all wide apart, I thought he ought to go through an unguarded gap of the Bull Run mountain, and, cutting his way right through the middle of the Union army, cross the Potomac at Seneca.[4] It was the shortest route he could go into Maryland, and there was a splendid opportunity to destroy Hooker's transportation as he went along, and to cut off communication between Washington and the North.

The plan was at that time perfectly practicable. Hooker was in a defensive attitude, waiting the development of Lee's plans, and only a

---

3. Telegram.

Gainsville, 11 a.m., June 23, 1863.

Stahel to Butterfield, Chief of Staff to Hooker: Your order to return without delay received through Maj.-Gen. Hancock, after midnight; made arrangements at once, and my advance arrived here from Warrenton this morning at 8 o'clock. . . . In accordance with your order, I shall scout the whole country, from Bull Run mountain toward Fairfax Court House, and have ordered the rest of my command and my train to Fairfax, where I shall report personally to you.

4. It now appears from their correspondence that Stuart, Longstreet, and Gen. Lee had already been discussing the feasibility of his going this route.

small portion of the cavalry was necessary to be held in our front to observe the enemy and report their movements to the commanding general. The plan was to leave two brigades of cavalry about Middleburg to do this work, while Stuart, with three brigades, should pass through Hooker's army into Maryland. The brigades selected to be left behind were those of Jones and Beverly H. Robertson, under command of the latter, who happened to be the ranking officer. They numbered over 3000 men, and exceeded in strength the three that Stuart took with him.

As Hancock's corps was holding Hopewell and Thoroughfare gaps, the road that Stuart determined to go was through Glasscock's gap (a few miles south of Thoroughfare) via Haymarket, through Loudoun to Seneca ford on the Potomac. The part assigned to me was to cross the Bull Run at night by the bridle path I had so frequently travelled, and, uniting with Stuart near Gum Spring in Loudoun, take command of his advance guard. Hooker's headquarters were still at Fairfax station, with his army spread out like a fan over Loudoun, Prince William and Fairfax counties, his left being at Thoroughfare, his right at Leesburg, with his centre at Aldie, and Pleasanton's cavalry in front of it. Stuart's plan, of course, contemplated his crossing of the river in advance of Hooker or Lee, and opening communication with Ewell as soon as he was over.

During our interview Gen. Hampton and Fitz Lee came into the room, and soon afterward Stuart started a courier off to Gen. Lee. I have been informed by one of his staff that he rode over to Berryville that day to have a personal interview with the commanding general. Before we parted, he told me that Gen. Lee was very apprehensive that Hooker would steal a march and get into Maryland ahead of him, and asked me to go and find out if any portion of his army was crossing the river. Although I had been almost continuously in the saddle for three days and nights, I agreed to return inside of Hooker's lines. With only two men I crossed the Bull Run again that night, and early the next morning was riding in full Confederate uniform through the Union army.

I soon sent Stuart a despatch that I was certain Hooker's army was not in motion. Proceeding some distance down the pike with my single companion, we had stopped to talk with a citizen, when four lieutenants belonging to the 3rd corps, that was camped near by, walked up to us. There was a drizzling rain, and we had waterproofs thrown over our shoulders. As they were in full view of their camps, they had no suspicion of danger and were without arms. After talking with them for some minutes, they were stunned by a demand for their surrender. I sent them back under guard of one man, with another despatch to Stuart. I then rode on alone down into Fairfax, where I met some of my old acquaintances, who thought when they first saw me that it was my ghost.

Having learned all about the situation of Hooker's army, I started back. I stopped at the house of John I. Coleman to inquire the shortest way to the pike. It was the first time he ever saw me, and, although I showed him my gray uniform and star, he thought I was trying to play a Yankee trick on him, and refused to tell me anything. While we were talking, I heard a noise behind me. Turning around, I saw two mounted men approaching us. When within about fifty yards, they stopped, and began picking cherries from a tree. I drew my pistol, but kept it under my gum cloth, and rode up to them. They never suspected that I was an enemy. I asked them where they were from; they answered that they were on duty with Reynolds' corps that was camped near by at Guilford. They had no arms; so, of course, had to surrender. When Coleman saw this affair, he was more convinced than ever that I was a Yankee dressed up in gray. I had to get to the pike the best way I could. So I tied the heads of my prisoners' horses together with their halters, to keep them from running away, and went on.

It was near sunset when I came in sight of the pike, about four miles below Aldie. There was a wagon train a mile or so in length passing on the road, with a strong cavalry guard, that was carrying supplies to the troops above. I was anxious to get to Stuart that night, and knew that if I waited for the train to pass, it would be dark, and I could not find the mountain path. So I drew my pistol, held it under cover, and told my prisoners that if they spoke a word they would be dead men. I then rode, with them by my side, through a gap in the fence into the pike, right among the Union cavalry. We could not cross over at that point, as the fence on the other side of the road was too high for our horses to leap. We went along for 200 yards, with my prisoners, through the wagon train and cavalry escort, until we got to a road leading away from the pike.

Here we turned off. The gum cloth I had over my shoulders to protect me from the rain, as it did not cover one-third of my body, did not conceal the uniform I wore. I had ridden through the ranks of a column of Union cavalry in broad daylight, with two prisoners, and my elbow had actually struck against one as I passed. In doing so

I had acted on the maxim of Danton—*Audace, toujours audace*. Finding that I could not reach the mountain before night, and fearing to go to sleep in the woods alone with my prisoners, I took their paroles and sent them back to their friends. Of course, I kept their horses. Early the next morning I was again at Stuart's headquarters.[5]

---

5. Stuart's report says: "... I resumed my own position now, at Rector's cross roads, and being in constant communication with the commanding general, had scouts busily employed watching and reporting the enemy's movements, and reporting the same to the commanding general. In this difficult search the fearless and indefatigable Maj. Mosby was particularly active and efficient. His information was always accurate and reliable."

CHAPTER 13

# General Stuart's Raid

Stuart had now received his final instructions from General Lee, authorising him to move into Maryland, around the rear of the enemy and between him and Washington. He was likewise instructed to do them all the damage he could on his way. With his transportation destroyed and communications broken, Hooker would be seriously embarrassed in pursuing General Lee, or probably forced to fall back for supplies, or to defend the capital against this demonstration. In the meantime, while Hooker was thus delayed, the Confederates would have been levying contributions on the farmers in Pennsylvania. His original plan, which was bold in conception and perfectly practicable in execution, was thwarted by an event which he could not control. It was obvious now that Hooker would not *initiate* any movement, but would confine himself to covering the capital and observing his adversary.

It was equally plain that when the Confederate Army made a move west of the Blue Ridge, Hooker would make a corresponding one on the east. It was, therefore, all important for the success of Stuart's movement that the *status quo* of the two armies should be preserved until he could get through Hooker's army to the river, when it would be too late for Hooker to take any step to defeat it. The distance was not more than twenty miles to the Potomac from the point where he would enter Hooker's lines; and this could be got over between sunrise and sundown, as he intended to march in three parallel columns. He knew the country well, and the position of each corps; and it would have been easy enough for him to flank them.

Before Pleasanton could have got ready to follow the blazing meteor, it would have been out of sight. The three brigades that were to accompany Stuart were quietly withdrawn from Pleasanton's front on the evening of June 24, and marched in a southerly direction to their rendezvous at Salem. Those of Jones and Robertson were put in the position they had held about Middleburg, and, of course, were charged with the ordinary duty of cavalry on a post of observation. As Gen. Stuart says in his report:

> Robertson's and Jones's brigades, under command of the former, were left in observation of the enemy, on the usual front (about Middleburg), with full instructions as to following of the enemy, in case of withdrawal, and joining our main army.

An order to a cavalry officer to *observe* an enemy, of course implies that he is to report what he sees; otherwise, there is no use in his observing. Stuart left behind a force of over 3000 cavalry, which was amply sufficient for every purpose. By daybreak, on the morning of the 25th, his column debouched through Glassock's Gap, in the Bull Run, and proceeded towards Haymarket. At the same time I started across by the route I had been travelling for a week, to connect with him at the appointed place. We had stopped at a spring on the mountain side to make our breakfast on some sutlers' stores that had been saved from our captives. Two men had been sent forward on a picket; but they had scarcely got a hundred yards before a volley was fired; and the bullets whistled all around us. We sprang upon our horses; but, as the men did not return, we knew that they must have been killed or captured. General Meade, whose camps were near by, had prepared an ambuscade a second time for me, but I had escaped. (I wonder if he would have called this *bushwhacking*.) We made a *detour* around them, and hurried on to join Stuart; as we could hear his cannon about Haymarket.

It seems that when Stuart got there, he found the roads on which he intended to march that day occupied by Hancock's corps, that had broken up camp that morning, and was moving towards the Potomac. When I got to the Little River Pike, about eight miles below Aldie, which was to be our point of junction, instead of meeting him we struck the head of Hancock's column. His divisions were marching on every road. I spent the day and night riding about among them, and with great difficulty extricated myself from the dilemma in which I was placed. I could not find out where Stuart was, nor he where I was; for Hancock was between us. So I retraced my steps and went on to Pennsylvania through the Shenandoah Valley, passing General Robertson's command, that was quietly resting in Ashby's and Snicker's Gaps, in the Blue Ridge, after the enemy retired on the 26th.

Pleasanton that day had moved by his flank, across General Robertson's front, to Leesburg, to cover the crossing of Hooker's army. Why he should have halted and remained idle three days in the gaps of the Blue Ridge in Virginia after both armies had marched into Pennsylvania is a mystery that has never been satisfactorily explained. If there were any sound military reasons for his staying there *three* days, there were equally as sound ones for his not leaving at all. His proper position was on General Lee's flank, next to the enemy, in order to protect his rear and to keep him informed of their movement.

If General Robertson had then in obedience to General Lee's and Stuart's instructions, promptly followed the enemy along the base of South Mountain through Boonesboro, the Confederate cavalry might easily have reached Gettysburg in advance of the Federal troops. In this event, there would not have been the accidental collision of armies. General Lee would have fought a defensive battle, and Gettysburg might have been to Southern hearts something more than "*a glorious field of grief.*" Even as it was, Stuart's movement around his rear had so confused General Meade, that his army was more scattered than ours, and two of his corps in the first day's fight, were caught *in delicto* and crushed. He was looking for Lee on the Susquehanna, when in fact he was concentrating on Gettysburg.

On account of Hancock's unexpected movement, Stuart had been compelled to make a wider circuit than he had intended, and did not cross the Potomac until the night of the twenty-seventh, the day after Hooker got over. He thence moved northerly towards the Susquehanna, to put himself on Ewell's flank in accordance with the instructions of General Lee. But owing to the derangement of his plans by the advance of the Union army, without General Robertson having given him notice of it, Ewell had been recalled, and Stuart did not join the army until July the second, at Gettysburg, when the battle was raging. But Robertson's command had not even then come up.

This movement of Stuart's around the rear of Hooker's army has been condemned by General Long, the military secretary and biographer of General Lee, as having been undertaken either "from misapprehension of his instructions, or love of the *éclat* of a bold raid" (which, of course, implies disobedience of orders); (see note following), and General Longstreet says that as he was leaving the Blue Ridge, he instructed Stuart to follow him down the Valley, and cross the Potomac at Shepherdstown, but that Stuart replied that he had discretionary powers from General Lee where to cross the Potomac.

★★★★★★

Note:—In the *Memoirs of General Lee*, General Long says: "Previous to the passage of the Potomac, General Stuart was instructed to make the movements of the cavalry correspond with those of the Federal army, so that he might be in position to observe and report all important information. In the performance of this duty Stuart had never failed, and probably his great confidence in him made Lee less specific in his instructions than he would otherwise have been. But on this occasion either from the misapprehension of instructions or the love of the éclat of a bold raid, Stuart, instead of maintaining his appropriate position between the armies, placed himself on the right flank of the enemy, where his communication with Lee was effectually severed. This greatly embarrassed the movements of General Lee, and eventually forced him to an engagement under disadvantageous circumstances."

In the *Century Magazine*, General Longstreet, in his article on Gettysburg, says: "When Hill with his troops and well-supplied trains had passed my rear, I was ordered to withdraw from the Blue Ridge, pass over to the west of the Shenandoah and to follow the movements of the other troops, only to cross the Potomac at Williamsport. I ordered Gen. Stuart, whom I considered under my command, to occupy the gaps with a part of his cavalry and to follow with his main force on my right, to cross the Potomac at Shepherdstown, and move on my right flank. Upon giving him this order, he informed me that he had authority from Gen. Lee to occupy the gaps with a part of his cavalry, and to follow the Federal army with the remainder.

At the same time he expressed his purpose of crossing the river east of the Blue Ridge and trying to make way around the right of the Federal army; so I moved my troops independent of the cavalry, following my orders, crossed at Williamsport, come up with A. P. Hill in Maryland, and we moved on thence to Chambersburg.".... "On the 30th of June we turned our faces toward our enemy and marched upon Gettysburg. The third corp, under Hill, moved out first, and my command followed. We then found ourselves in a very unusual condition: we were almost in the immediate presence of the enemy with our cavalry gone. Stuart was undertaking another wild ride around the Federal army. We knew nothing of Meade's movements further than the report my scout had made. We did not know, except by surmises, when or where to expect to find Meade, nor whether he was lying in wait or advancing." Gen. Longstreet will find it difficult to reconcile what he now says were his orders to the cavalry with his letter to Stuart, or the following one to Gen. Lee:

Headquarters, June 22, 1863, 7.30 p.m.

Gen. R. E. Lee,
Comdg., &c.
General:—Yours of 4 O'C. this afternoon is rec'd. I have forwarded your letters to Gen. Stuart with the suggestion that he pass *by the enemy's rear*, if he thinks that he may get through. We have nothing of the enemy today.
Most respectfully,   J. Longstreet,
Lt.-Genl., Comdg

So it appears that it was Gen. Longstreet who suggested to Stuart the idea of "another wild ride around the Federal army."

★★★★★★

When this charge was made against Stuart, both the critics were viewing his movement in the light of the disaster to our arms at Gettysburg, and it was more agreeable to put the blame of it on a dead man than a living one. General Long, who had access to the Confederate archives, may plead the blindness with which he is afflicted as an excuse for his error, and I have no doubt that General Longstreet has forgotten that his own letter to Stuart contradicts his statement.

Gen. Lee made two reports of this campaign; one written in July, 1863, a few weeks after the battle; and a more detailed one in January, 1864. There is a slight colour of truth in the imputation cast upon Stuart that Gen. Lee intended to censure him in his report. But this is owing to a false interpretation given to it by persons who have construed a single sentence literally, and not in connection with others that qualify and explain it. (See note following). Gen. Lee does say: "It was expected that as soon as the Federal army should cross the Potomac, Gen. Stuart would give notice of its movements, and nothing having been heard from him since our entrance into Maryland, it was inferred that the enemy had not yet left Virginia. Orders were therefore issued to move on Harrisburg."

★★★★★★

Note:—General Lee says:

In the meantime, the progress of Ewell, who was already in Maryland with Jenkin's cavalry, advanced into Pennsylvania as far as Chambersburg, rendered it necessary that the rest of the army should be within supporting distance, and Hill having reached the Valley, Longstreet was withdrawn to the west side of the Shenandoah, and the two corps encamped near Berryville.

General Stuart was directed to hold the mountain-passes with part of his command *as long as the enemy remained south of the Potomac*, and with the *remainder* to cross into Maryland and place himself on the right of General Ewell. Upon the suggestion of the former officer, that he could damage the enemy and delay his passage of the river by getting in his rear, he was authorized to do so, and it was left to his discretion whether to enter Maryland east or west of the Blue Ridge; but he was instructed to lose no time in placing his command on the right of our column as soon as he perceived the enemy moving northward.

The expedition of General Early to York was designed in part to prepare for this undertaking, by breaking the railroad between Baltimore and Harrisburg, and seizing the bridge over the Susquehanna at Wrightsville.

The advance against Harrisburg was arrested by intelligence received from a scout on the night of the 28th, to the effect that the army of General Hooker had crossed the Potomac and was approaching the mountains. In the absence of the cavalry it was impossible to ascertain his intentions; but to deter him from advancing farther west and intercepting our communications with Virginia, it was determined to concentrate the army east of the mountains.

The movement of the army preceding the Battle of Gettysburg had been much embarrassed by the absence of the cavalry. As soon as it was known that the enemy had crossed into Maryland, orders were sent to the brigades of (B. H.) Robertson and (Wm. E.) Jones, which had been left to guard the passes of the Blue Ridge, to rejoin the army *without delay*, and it was expected that General Stuart, with the *remainder* of his command, would soon arrive. In the exercise of the discretion given him when Longstreet and Hill marched into Maryland, General Stuart determined to pass around the rear of the Federal army, with three brigades, and cross the Potomac between it and Washington, believing that by that route he would be able to place himself on our right flank in time to keep us properly advised of the enemy's movements. He marched from Salem on the night of June 24th, intending to pass west of Centreville, but found the enemy's forces so distributed as to render that route impracticable.

Adhering to his original plan, he was forced to make a wide detour through Buckland and Brentsville, and crossed the Occoquan at Wolf Run Shoals on the morning of the 27th. Continuing his march through Fairfax Court House and Drainesville, he arrived at the Potomac below the mouth of Seneca Creek in the evening. He found the river much swollen by the recent rains, but after great exertion gained the Maryland shore, before midnight, with his whole command. He now ascertained that the whole Federal army, which he had discovered to be drawing towards the Potomac, had crossed the day before, and was moving towards Fredericktown, thus interposing itself between him and our forces.

Robertson's and Jones's brigades arrived on July 3d, and were stationed upon our right flank. The severe loss sustained by the army, and the reduction of its ammunition, rendered another attempt to dislodge the enemy inadvisable, and it was therefore determined upon to withdraw.

★★★★★★

Now if all that Gen. Lee says in his report about Stuart's cavalry is read, together *as a whole*, it is apparent that in the sentence above quoted, he uses *Stuart's* name not in a personal sense, but descriptive of his cavalry corps, for in another place he says that Stuart had been directed to divide his cavalry, leaving a portion to watch the enemy in front of the mountain passes in Virginia, and "with the *remainder* to cross into Maryland and place himself on the right of Gen. Ewell," who was marching on Harrisburg.[1]

Clearly Gen. Lee did not intend to involve himself in the contradiction of saying that he expected Stuart *personally* to perform at the same time the double duty of watching Hooker along the Potomac, and guarding Ewell's flank on the Susquehanna.[2] Gen. Lee in thus referring to Stuart was somewhat careless and inaccurate in his language, as he was when, in describing the battle of Gettysburg, he said that Robertson's command *arrived* on July 3rd, when, in fact, it never got nearer than Cashtown, some eight miles from the battle-field. But Gen. Lee is explicit in saying, *in his report*, that he gave Stuart full authority to make the movement around the enemy's rear. Among the Confederate archives in Washington, I have at last found in Gen. Lee's confidential letter-book his final instructions to Stuart, which have never been published, which must set this controverted question at rest forever. At the time when they were written, Gen. Lee's headquarters were at Berryville. They are dated June 23, 1863, 5 p.m.

In them Gen. Lee presents to Stuart the alternative of crossing the Potomac west of the Blue Ridge at Shepherdstown and moving over to Frederick, Md., or, *"you will, however, be able to judge whether you can pass around their army without hindrance, doing them all the damage you can, and cross the river east of the mountains. In either case, after crossing the river, you must move on and feel the right of Ewell's troops, collecting information, provisions, etc."* In a letter to Stuart dated June 22, he had said:

> If you find that he is moving northward, and that two brigades can guard the Blue Ridge and take care of your rear, you can move with the other three into Maryland and take position on General Ewell's right, place yourself in communication with

---

1. Stuart has been criticised for carrying into our lines a train of one hundred and twenty-five wagons, which he captured in Maryland, with supplies for Hooker, on account of the delay it produced in joining Gen. Lee. But the expedition has been condemned, not as an independent raid, but because it is said that it deprived Gen. Lee of his cavalry, which ought to have given him notice of Hooker's advance into Pennsylvania. But as Gen. Lee actually received notice of it on the very night that Stuart crossed the Potomac, it is hard to see what harm was done by taking the wagons with him. And I have shown that Stuart left with Gen. Lee sufficient cavalry to do the work of guarding his flank and observing the enemy.

2. So far as keeping Gen. Lee informed of Hooker's movements is concerned, it was immaterial whether Stuart crossed east or west of the Ridge. In either event he would have been separated from Gen. Lee and unable to watch the line of the Potomac. Stuart was *ordered* to take three brigades to the Susquehanna and to leave two behind him to watch Hooker. He was simply given discretion as to the point of crossing the Potomac. He is not responsible for the division of his command.

him, guard his flank and keep him informed of the enemy's movements, and collect all the supplies you can for the use of the army. One column of General Ewell's army will probably move towards the Susquehanna by the Emmetsburg route, another by Chambersburg.

The intention of General Lee clearly was that Stuart with one portion of the cavalry was to guard Ewell's flank and give him information of the enemy. The other was to be left [3] behind, as he says in his report, "to hold the mountain passes *as long as the enemy remained south of the Potomac.*" To suppose that Gen. Lee intended them to remain there after the enemy had gone is to suppose that he was not only unfit to command an army, but even a corporal's guard. It is clear that he intended the two brigades under Robertson to perform the same service for the column of Longstreet and Hill (with whom he had his headquarters) as Stuart was to do for Ewell, who was separated from him.

When these two corps crossed the Potomac on the 25th, *he knew* that Stuart had not crossed *west* of the Ridge in advance of them. He would not have committed the blunder of marching all his infantry into Pennsylvania knowing that all his cavalry was in Virginia. He must, therefore, have expected for Stuart to cross the Potomac on the same day to the *east* of the Ridge; which he would have done but for Hancock's movement. Some have contended that his anxious inquiries for Stuart when he got to Chambersburg prove that he did not know which way he had gone. They only show that he did not know where Stuart was *at that time*. As Stuart had been directed to open communication, as soon as he got into Pennsylvania, with Ewell, and had not been able to do so on account of the Federal army getting between them, Gen. Lee, not having heard from him, very naturally felt a great deal of solicitude for his safety.

If Gen. Lee had not thought that he would cross the Potomac somewhere on the same day that he did, he would have waited and sent for him. But again, Gen. Lee would not assume the responsibility

---

3. On June 22, 1863, 3.30 p.m. Gen. Lee, writing from Berryville, Va., to Ewell, who was then about Hagerstown, Md., says: "My letter of today, authorizing you to move toward the Susquehanna, I hope has reached you ere this. I have also directed Gen. Stuart, should the enemy have so far retired from his front as to permit of the departure of a portion of the cavalry, to march with three brigades across the Potomac, and place himself on your right and in communication with you, keep *you advised of the movements of the enemy*, and assist in collecting supplies for the army. I have not heard from him since." As Stuart was not ubiquitous, Gen. Lee must have relied on the cavalry left behind to do for him what he intended that Stuart should do for Ewell.

of authorizing Stuart to go around Hooker's rear unless the movement had the approval of Gen. Longstreet, whose headquarters were at Millwood, not far from Berryville. Gen. Lee's instructions to Stuart were therefore sent through Longstreet. In a letter to Stuart, Longstreet not only approves of Stuart's going into Maryland around the rear of the enemy, but *opposes* his going the other route through the Shenandoah Valley, on the ground that it would disclose their plans to the enemy. In concluding his letter he says:

> N.B.—I think that your passage of the Potomac by our rear at the present moment will in a measure disclose our plans. You had better not leave us, therefore, unless you can take the proposed route in rear of the enemy.

By "*our rear*" Longstreet meant through the Shenandoah Valley. The reasons he gave Stuart were conclusive in favour of the course he took. It was Gen. Lee's policy to detain Hooker as long as possible in Virginia. But if Stuart passed to the west of the Ridge and crossed the Potomac at Shepherdstown, he would be discovered by the signal stations of the enemy on Maryland heights. This would indicate, of course, that the infantry was to follow him. On the contrary, Hooker would interpret a movement around his rear as nothing more than a cavalry *raid*, and it would be a mask to conceal Lee's designs. It was no fault of Stuart's that he was unable to execute his plan.

The Count of Paris says that it was impracticable from the first, and differed in its condition from his other operations of this kind, because they were undertaken while the armies were both stationary. Now, at the time when Stuart resolved on going into Maryland by this route, both armies were as stationary as when he rode around McClellan on the Chickahominy; and Hooker was waiting for the Confederates to move. But it could not be expected for Hooker to stand still while his adversary was in motion. Now it so happened that the corps of Longstreet and Hill moved from Berryville on June 24, towards the Potomac, which they crossed the next day, Hill at Shepherdstown, and Longstreet at Williamsport.[4] Their route of march was in plain view of Maryland Heights, and the news was immediately telegraphed from

---
4. Telegram.

> Maryland Heights, June 24, 1863.
> H. W. Halleck, General-in-Chief:—Longstreet's corps, which camped last between Berryville and Charlestown, is today in motion and before 6 O.C. this morning commenced crossing by the ford one mile below Shepherdstown to Sharpsburg.
> Gen. Tyler, Brigadier-General.

there by General Tyler. This set the whole of Hooker's army in motion, on the morning of the 25th, for the Potomac. About the time, therefore, that Stuart's column appeared on the eastern side of Bull Run, on the morning of the 25th, Hancock broke up camp and started on the same road that Stuart intended to march. Hancock was ahead of him, and had the right of way. Gen. Longstreet had urged Stuart to go that route, for fear that if he went through the Shenandoah Valley, the plans of the commanding general would be disclosed to the enemy.

I am unable to understand why he could not foresee that the march of all the Confederate infantry in full view of the enemy would have the same effect. If the corps of Longstreet and Hill had delayed a single day in leaving Berryville, Stuart would have landed on the north bank of the Potomac on the night of the 25th. Hooker would then have been utterly confounded. Before he could have made up his mind what to do, the Confederate cavalry would have been watering their horses in the Susquehanna, and all the communications between Washington and the North would have been broken. But now to return to the cavalry which Stuart, under Gen. Lee's orders, had left in front of the enemy in Virginia, as he says, "*to observe his movements, and follow him in case of withdrawal.*" Of course, this duty could not be discharged without keeping in sight of the enemy.

But instead of following, they fell back in an opposite direction, and gave no information to Gen. Lee and no trouble to the enemy. Gen. Lee says that on the night of the 28th he heard through a scout that had come in that Hooker was over the river, and was moving north. He is mistaken as to the date, as there is a letter of his to Gen. Ewell, dated Chambersburg, June 28th, 7.30 a.m., which says:

> I wrote you *last night*, stating that Gen. Hooker was reported to have crossed the Potomac, and is advancing by way of Middletown,—the head of his column being at that point in Frederick County, Md.

He directs Ewell to move to Gettysburg, which had become to him what Quatre Bras was to Wellington, when he learned that Napoleon was over the Sombre. In his report of the campaign, Gen. Lee says that as soon as it was known that the enemy had crossed into Maryland, orders were sent to Gen. Robertson to rejoin the army "*without delay.*" The very fact that Gen. Lee had to send back for this cavalry shows that it was in the wrong place, and where he did not intend it to be. In his instructions to Stuart, when leaving, he had said:

Give instructions to the commander of the brigades left behind, to watch the flank and rear of the army, and (in event of the enemy leaving their front) retire from the mountains west of the Shenandoah, leaving sufficient pickets to guard the passes, bringing everything clean along the valley, close upon the rear of the army.

It is clear that the instructions to Gen. Robertson were to leave Virginia when the enemy left; for how could he otherwise "*watch the flank and rear*" of the Confederate army, and be "*close upon*" it. Gen. Robertson[5] says that during the time he was lying in the gaps of the Virginia mountains, after the enemy had crossed the river, he was in daily communication by couriers with Gen. Lee's headquarters[6] Then so much the worse if he did not inform him that the enemy had disappeared from his front. The inquiry is now naturally suggested, *What did he communicate?*

Again he says, "He (Gen. Lee) was fully aware of my position and the specific duty I was then performing." But what that specific duty was no one knows. If Gen. Lee ordered him to remain there unemployed, then he could blame no one but himself for the want of cavalry, and the responsibility would rest on him[7] But the fact that

---

5. See his letter of Dec. 27, 1877, in *Phila. Times*.
6. Stuart's report says: "I submitted to the commanding general the plan of leaving a brigade or so in my present front, and passing through Hopewell, or some other gap in the Bull Run Mountain, attain the enemy's rear, passing between his main body and Washington, cross into Maryland, joining our army north of the Potomac. The commanding general wrote to me, authorizing this move if I deemed it practicable, and also what instructions should be given the officer left in command of the two brigades left in front of the enemy. He also notified me that one column should move via Gettysburg and the other *via* Carlisle towards the Susquehanna, and directed me, after crossing, to proceed with all dispatch to join the right (Early) of the army in Pennsylvania.
"Robertson's and Jones's brigades, under command of the former, were left in observation of the enemy on the usual front, *with full instructions as to following up the enemy in case of withdrawal and rejoining our main army*." This report was read by Gen. Lee and not one word of dissent by him is endorsed on it. It bears his initials in pencil, *R. E. L.,* in his own handwriting.
7. Gen. Robertson says that when he received Gen. Lee's order he was at Ashby's Gap in the Blue Ridge in Fauquier County. Jones's brigade was twelve miles farther north, at Snicker's Gap in Loudoun, and joined him at Berryville. Stuart had placed them about fifteen miles to the front of the Gaps at Middleburg to watch the enemy. After he left, they retired to the mountain and rendered Gen. Lee no more service while there than if they had been west of the Mississippi. There are reports of their operations on file from all the brigade and regimental commanders of the cavalry in this campaign *except Gen. Robertson*, who, at his own request, was relieved of his command as soon as he returned to Virginia.

Gen. Lee sent for him to join the army as soon as he heard that the enemy was advancing north, is proof that he never intended him to stay in Virginia after they had gone. Gen. Lee had issued orders from Chambersburg for the concentration of his army at Gettysburg, and as he says, sent back for Robertson's command to join the army *without delay.*

When the order was read, Gen. Robertson marched his two brigades that night to Berryville, which is west of the mountain, on a route almost parallel and in an opposite direction from Gettysburg, which is east of it.

On June 30, he continued his westerly and circuitous march to Martinsburg, and on July 1, the day of the battle, crossed the Potomac at Williamsport. If he had crossed at Shepherdstown and gone to Boonesboro, he might easily have reached Gettysburg after receiving Gen. Lee's order on the morning of July 1, when it was held by Buford with only two brigades of cavalry. Gen. Meade had sent off most of his cavalry in search of Stuart. It was this diversion created by Stuart that saved Gen. Lee's communications from attack. Buford was too weak to assume the offensive. On June 24, when Gen. Lee moved with Longstreet and Hill down the Shenandoah Valley, he left Gen. Robertson's command between him and the enemy. On July 3, Gen. Robertson had so manoeuvred that *Gen. Lee had got between him and the enemy.* Stuart had ridden around Gen. Hooker while Gen. Robertson rode around Gen. Lee. *Sic itur ad astra.*

Since the above was written, I have found in the archives of the war office a copy of Stuart's orders to Gen. Robertson when leaving Virginia; but he does not appear to have been in the least governed by them. They confirm all I have said as to the duty required of the cavalry that were left under his command. Through abundant caution Stuart repeated them to Gen. Jones. He was instructed to watch the enemy and report their movements through a line of relay couriers to Gen. Longstreet; and when the enemy withdrew, to harass his rear and impede his march, and follow on the right of our army. There seems to have been no effort made to execute these orders; for both Gens. Lee and Longstreet say that no intelligence having been received through the cavalry of Hooker's crossing the Potomac, it was supposed that he was still south of it; while Pleasanton says that he never had a skirmish in retiring.

The fact that Pleasanton's cavalry corps reached Leesburg by noon of the 26th shows that they must have left Gen. Robertson's front at

Aldie early that morning. In a despatch [8] from Leesburg to Hooker's headquarters dated June 26, 12.45 p.m., he significantly says that all is *quiet* towards the Blue Ridge, and that only a few cavalry videttes were seen about Middleburg, and none on the Snickersville Pike. If his flank and rear had been harassed, all would not have been *quiet*. Again, Gen. Robertson was directed to keep his command on the right of the army and in contact with the enemy when they left, in order that he might keep the commanding general informed of their movements.

But when Gen. Lee had sent an order for him to come on and join the army, as there could be no reason for his remaining any longer in Virginia after the enemy had left, he actually followed on the *left* and crossed the Potomac at Williamsport. Gen. Lee's *right* flank was thus left exposed to the enemy's cavalry, but fortunately they had nearly all been sent in search of Stuart. If the pressure of the column of three thousand cavalry with two batteries under Robertson had been brought to bear on the flank of the Union army, its advance into Pennsylvania would have been less rapid, and Meade could not have spared two-thirds of his cavalry to send after Stuart to embarrass his march. If the force of cavalry which Stuart left behind him had promptly moved in obedience to his orders on the 26th to place itself in its proper position on the right of the army, then it could easily have occupied Gettysburg in advance of the enemy. It did nothing of the kind, but quietly rested three days at Ashby's Gap to learn through Gen. Lee where the enemy had gone. The professed historians of the war make no mention of these facts. *Stuart is dead*: "O! for one hour of Dundee."

Headquarters, June, 22, 1863.

Major-General J. E. B. Stuart,
Commanding Cavalry.
General:—I have just received your note of 7.45 this morning to General Longstreet. I judge the efforts of the enemy yesterday were to arrest our progress and ascertain our whereabouts.

---

8. Telegram.

Leesburg, (Va.), 12.45 p.m. June 26, 1863.
Major-Gen. Butterfield, Headquarters, A.P. Have just arrived. One division is covering the flank from Aldie to this place by way of Mount Gilead. Three brigades of Second division are covering the three roads from Aldie and Gum Springs. *All quiet towards the Blue Ridge. Very few cavalry pickets seen near Middleburg this morning. None in the Snicker's Gap pike.*     A. Pleasanton, Major-General

Perhaps he is satisfied. Do you know where he is and what he is doing? I fear he will steal a march on us and get across the Potomac before we are aware. If you find that he is moving northward, and that two brigades can guard the Blue Ridge and take care of your rear, you can move with the other three into Maryland and take position on General Ewell's right, place yourself in communication with him, guard his flank, and keep him informed of the enemy's movements, and collect all the supplies you can for the use of the army.

One column of General Ewell's army will probably move towards the Susquehanna by the Emmetsburg route, another by Chambersburg. Accounts from him last night state that there was no enemy west of Fredericktown. A cavalry force (about one hundred) guarded the Monocacy Bridge, which was barricaded. You will, of course, take charge of Jenkins' brigade and give him necessary instructions. All supplies taken in Maryland must be by authorised staff-officers, for their respective departments, by no one else. They will be paid for or receipts for the same given to the owners. I will send you a general order on this subject, which I wish you to see is strictly complied with.

I am, very respectfully, your obedient servant,

R. E. Lee, General.

Headquarters, Millwood, June 22, 1863, 7 p.m.
Maj.-Gen'l J. E. B. Stuart,
Comdg Cavalry.
General:—Gen. Lee has enclosed to me this letter for you, to be forwarded to you, provided you can be spared from my front, and provided I think that you can move across the Potomac without disclosing our plans. He speaks of your leaving *via* Hopewell Gap and passing by the rear of the enemy. If you can get through by that route, I think that you will be less likely to indicate what our plans are, than if you should cross by passing to our rear. I forward the letter of instructions with these suggestions.

Please advise me of the condition of affairs before you leave, and order Genl. Hampton—whom I suppose you will leave here in command—to report to me at Millwood either by letter or in person, as may be most agreeable to him.

Most respectfully,

J. Longstreet,
Lt.-Genl.

*N.B.* I think that your passage of the Potomac by our rear at the present moment will, in a measure, disclose our plans. You had better not leave us, therefore, unless you can take the proposed route in rear of the enemy.

J. Longstreet,
Lt.-Genl.

Headquarters, Army of North Virginia,
June 23, 1863, 5 p.m.

Major-General J. E. B. Stuart,
Commanding Cavalry.

General:—Your notes of 9 and 10.30 a.m. today have just been received. As regards the purchase of tobacco for your men, supposing that Confederate money not be taken, I am willing for your commissaries or quartermasters to purchase this tobacco and let the men get it from them; but I can have nothing seized by the men.

If General Hooker's army remains inactive, you can leave two brigades to watch him and withdraw with the three others; but should he not appear to be moving northward, I think you had better withdraw this side of the mountain tomorrow night, cross at Shepherdstown next day and move over to Fredericktown.

You will, however, be able to judge whether you can pass around their army without hindrance, doing them all the damage you can, and cross the river east of the mountains. In either case, after crossing the river, you must move on and feel the right of Ewell's troops, collecting information, provisions, etc.

Give instructions to the commander of the brigades left behind, to watch the flank and rear of the army and (in event of the enemy leaving their front) retire from the mountains west of the Shenandoah, leaving sufficient pickets to guard the passes, and bringing everything clean along the Valley, closing upon the rear of the army.

As regards the movements of the two brigades of the enemy moving towards Warrenton, the commander of the brigades to be left in the mountains must do what he can to counteract them; but I think the sooner you cross into Maryland, after tomorrow, the better.

The movements of Ewell's corps are as stated in my former letter. Hill's first division will reach the Potomac today, and Longstreet will follow tomorrow.

Be watchful and circumspect in all your movements.

I am, very respectfully and truly yours,

R. E. Lee,
General

Confidential.

Hd. Qrs. Cav'y Div.: Army of N. Va.,
June 24, 1863.

Brig.-Gen'l B. H. Robertson, Com'dg Cavalry:

General:—Your own and Gen'l Jones's brigades will cover the front of Ashby's and Snicker's Gaps; yourself, as senior officer, being in command.

Your object will be to watch the enemy, deceive him as to our designs, and harass his rear if you find he is retiring. Be always on the alert, let nothing escape your observation, and miss no opportunity which offers to damage the enemy.

After the enemy has moved beyond your reach, leave sufficient pickets in the mountains, and withdraw to the west side of the Shenandoah, and place a strong and reliable picket to watch the enemy at Harper's Ferry, cross the Potomac, and follow the army, keeping on its right and rear.

As long as the enemy remains in your front in force, unless otherwise ordered by Gen'l R. E. Lee, Lt.-Gen'l Longstreet, or myself, hold the gaps with a line of pickets reaching across the Shenandoah by Charlestown to the Potomac.

If, in the contingency mentioned, you withdraw, sweep the valley clear of what pertains to the army, and cross the Potomac at the different points crossed by it.

You will instruct General Jones from time to time as the movements progress or events may require, and report anything of importance to Lieut.-Gen'l Longstreet, with whose position you will communicate by relays through Charlestown.

I send instructions for Gen'l Jones which please read. Avail yourself of every means in your power to increase the efficiency of your command, and keep it up to the highest number possible. Particular attention will be paid to shoeing horses, and to marching off of the turnpikes.

In case of an advance of the enemy, you will offer such resistance as will be justifiable to check him and discover his intentions; and, if possible, you will prevent him from gaining possession of the gaps.

In case of a move by the enemy upon Warrenton, you will counteract it as much as you can compatible with previous instructions.

You will have with the two brigades two batteries of horse artillery.

    Very respectfully your obl. servt.

J. E. B. Stuart,<br>Major Gen'l Com'dg.

Do not change your present line of pickets until daylight tomorrow morning unless compelled to do so.

CHAPTER 14

# Stuart's Cavalry

Soon after the outbreak of war in the spring of 1861 the First Regiment of Virginia Cavalry was organised with J. E. B. Stuart as colonel. He was then just twenty-eight years of age, a native of Virginia and a graduate of West Point. As lieutenant of cavalry he had had some experience in Indian warfare in the West in which he had been wounded; and in the raid of John Brown on the United States arsenal at Harper's Ferry had acted as *aide* to Colonel (afterwards General) Robert E. Lee.

The First Virginia Cavalry was attached to the command of General Joseph E. Johnston in the Shenandoah valley and assigned to the duty of watching Patterson, who had crossed the Potomac and was threatening the Southern army, then at Winchester. I was a private in a company of cavalry called the Washington Mounted Rifles, which was commanded by Capt. William E. Jones, an officer who some years before had retired from the United States army, and gave the company the name of his old regiment. Jones was a graduate of West Point and had been a comrade of Stonewall Jackson's while there. He has often entertained me in his tent at night with anecdotes of that eccentric genius. No man in the South was better qualified to mould the wild element he controlled into soldiers. His authority was exercised mildly but firmly, and to the lessons of duty and obedience he taught me I acknowledge that I am largely indebted for whatever success I may afterwards have had as a commander.

I first saw Stuart in the month of July, 1861, at a village called Bunker Hill on the pike leading from Winchester to Martinsburg, where Patterson was camped. His regiment was stationed there to observe the movements of the Union army. His personal appearance bore the stamp of his military character, the fire, the dash, the energy and physical endurance that seemed able to defy all natural laws. Simultaneously with the movement of McDowell against Beauregard, began Patterson's demonstration to keep Johnston at Winchester. It was, however, too feeble to have any effect except to neutralize his own forces. The plan of the Southern generals was to avoid a battle in the valley and concentrate their armies at Manassas. The duty was assigned to Stuart's cavalry of masking the march of Johnston to Manassas and at the same time watching Patterson. General Scott had ordered him to feel the enemy strongly and not to allow him to escape to Manassas to reinforce Beauregard. Patterson replied in the most confident tone that he was holding Johnston.

After the battle had been won by the Confederates, in reply to Scott's criticism upon him for not having engaged them, Patterson comforted him with the assurance that if he had done so, Scott would have had to mourn the defeat of two armies instead of one. The records show that at that time Patterson had about 18,000 men and Johnston about 10,000.

On the 15th of July, Patterson advanced and drove us with artillery from our camp at Bunker Hill. Stuart had none to reply with. All of us thought a battle at Winchester was imminent. Patterson had one regiment of the regular besides some volunteer cavalry from Philadelphia, but made no use of them. He never sent his cavalry outside his infantry lines, and their only service was to add to the pomp and circumstance of war on reviews and parades. He stayed one day at Bunker Hill, and then, thinking he had done enough in driving us away, turned off squarely to the left and marched down to Charlestown. He had not been in twelve miles of our army, and this was the way he executed General Scott's order to feel it strongly.

Stuart still hung so close on his flanks that he occasionally let a shell drop among us. As soon as the movement to Charlestown was developed, Johnston received intelligence of it through Stuart. He saw then that Patterson did not intend an attack, and got ready to join Beauregard. The Union general went into camp at Charlestown while the Confederate folded his tent like the Arab and quietly stole away. Stuart spread a curtain of cavalry between the opposing armies which so effectually concealed the movement of Johnston, that Patterson never suspected it until it had been accomplished. The telegraphic correspondence at that time between Generals Scott and Patterson now reads like an extract from the transactions of the Pickwick Club.

On July 13th, Scott telegraphs to Patterson: "Make demonstrations to detain Johnston in the valley."

July 14th, Patterson replies: "Will advance tomorrow. Unless I can rout shall be careful not to set him in full retreat toward Strasburg." He seemed to be afraid of frightening Johnston so much that he would run away.

Again, Scott telegraphs to Patterson: "Do not let the enemy amuse and delay you with a small force in front whilst he reinforces the junction with his main body." This shows that General Scott, who was in Washington, had the sagacity to discern what we were likely to do.

On July 18th, General Scott says to him: "I have been certainly expecting you to beat the enemy. If not, to hear that you had felt him strongly, or, at least, had occupied him by threats, and demonstrations." At that time Patterson was twenty miles distant from Johnston and never got any closer. This was all the feeling he did.

On the same day Patterson replies: "The enemy has stolen no march on me. I have kept him actively employed, and by threats and reconnoissances in force caused him to be reinforced." At that time, Johnston was marching to Manassas, and Stuart's cavalry were watching the smoke as it curled from the Union camps at Charlestown.

Again, on July 18th, in order to make General Scott feel perfectly secure, Patterson tells him: "I have succeeded, in accordance with the wishes of the General-in-Chief, in keeping Johnston's force at Winchester. A reconnoissance in force on Tuesday caused him to be largely reinforced from Strasburg." And on July 21st, when the junction of the two armies had been effected, and the great battle was raging at Manassas, he telegraphs to Scott: "Johnston left Millwood yesterday to operate on McDowell's right and to turn through Loudoun on me."

As Patterson was haunted by the idea that Johnston was after him, although he had marched in an opposite direction, he concluded to retreat to Harper's Ferry. The success of Johnston's strategy in eluding Patterson and cheating him into the belief that he was still in the valley, is due to the vigilance of Stuart and his activity and skill in the management of cavalry. The Northern General never discovered how badly he had been fooled until the day of the battle, when he was too far away to give any assistance. But Stuart was not satisfied with the work he had done. After the infantry had been transferred to the railroad east of the Blue Ridge, he left a single company as a veil in front of Patterson and joined the army at Manassas on the evening before the battle. We had been almost continuously in the saddle for a week, and I have a vivid remembrance of the faces of the men—bronzed with sun and dust from the long march. The two armies were in such close contact that all knew there would be a battle on the morrow. Patterson was safe in the valley.

When he was before the committee on the Conduct of the War to give his reasons for not advancing on Johnston at Winchester, he filed a paper containing the following statement: "Among the regiments there was one of Kentucky riflemen armed with heavy bowie knives; they refused to take more than one round of cartridges. They proposed to place themselves in the bushes for assault." Of course, no prudent commander would lead men where they would be disembowelled by an enemy hidden in the bushes. Perhaps General Patterson was imitating the example of Othello, and trying to captivate Congressmen, as the Moor did the ear of Desdemona, with tales of

*The cannibals that do each other eat;*
*The anthropophagi, and men whose heads*
*Do grow beneath their shoulders.*

On the night before the battle, the raw troops were excited by every noise, and the picket firing was incessant. We slept soundly in our bivouac in the pines, and early in the morning were awakened by the reveille that called us to arms. As the sun rose, the rattle of musketry began along Bull Run, and soon from one end of the line to the other there was a continuous roar of small arms and artillery.

War loses a great deal of its romance after a soldier has seen his first battle. I have a more vivid recollection of the first than the last one I was in. It is a classical maxim that it is sweet and becoming to die for one's country; but whoever has seen the horrors of a battle-field feels that it is far sweeter to live for it. The Confederate generals had expected a battle on our right; as a fact, our left wing was turned, and the battle was mostly fought by Johnston's troops, who, having come up the day before, had been held in reserve. Stuart's regiment having just arrived, had not been sent on the outposts, and hence is in no way responsible for the surprise. In the crisis of the battle, when Jackson with his brigade was standing like a stone wall against the advancing host, he called for Stuart's cavalry to support him. Stuart sent one squadron to Jackson's right, under the Major, who did nothing (I was with him), while with six companies he came up on Jackson's left, just in time to charge and rout the Ellsworth Zouaves. Their general, in his report, says that he was never able to rally them during the fight.

This cavalry charge had an important effect upon the fortunes of the day, as it delayed the enemy, and gave time for troops to come to the relief of Jackson, who was then hard pressed by superior numbers. Stuart afterward, with a battery of artillery, led the turning movement that caused the rout, and associated the stream of Bull Run with the most memorable panic in history. Shortly after the battle, all the cavalry of the army was organised into a brigade, with Stuart in command. Jones was also promoted to be colonel of the regiment, and Fitz Lee became lieutenant-colonel.

From this time until the army evacuated Manassas, in the spring of 1862, the cavalry was almost exclusively engaged in outpost duty. McClellan kept close to the fortifications around Washington while he was organising the army of the Potomac, and his cavalry rarely ventured beyond his infantry pickets. No field was open for brilliant exploits; but the discipline and experience of a life on the outpost soon converted the Confederate volunteers into veterans.

Without intending any disparagement, I may say that the habits and education of Northern men had not been such as to adapt them readily to the cavalry service, without a process of drilling; while, on the contrary, the Southern youth, who, like the ancient Persians, had been taught from his cradle "to ride, to shoot, and speak the truth," leaped into his saddle, almost a cavalryman from his birth. The Cossacks, who came from their native wilds on the Don to break the power of Napoleon, had no other training in war than the habits of nomadic life; and in the same school were bred the Parthian horsemen who drove to despair the legions of Crassus and Antony.

I must also say that the Confederate authorities made but slight use of the advantage they enjoyed in the early periods of the war, for creating a fine body of cavalry; and that little wisdom was shown in the use of what they did have. It would have been far better military policy, during the first winter of the war, to have saved the cavalry as McClellan did, either to lead the advance or cover the retreat in the spring campaign. It was largely consumed in work which the infantry might have done, without imposing much additional hardships on them, as the proportion of cavalry was so small. When the Southern army retired, in March, 1862, three-fourths of the horses had been broken down by the hard work of the winter, and the men had been furloughed to go home for fresh ones. The Confederate government did not furnish horses for the cavalry, but paid the men forty cents a day for the use of them.

This vicious policy was the source of continual depletion of the cavalry. Stuart's old regiment,—the First Virginia Cavalry,—of which I was adjutant, with at least 800 men on its muster-rolls, did not have 150 for duty on the morning we broke up winter quarters on Bull Run. If the cavalry brigade had been cantoned on the border, in the rich counties of Fauquier and Loudoun, the ranks would have been full, and their granaries would not have been left as forage for the enemy.

The Confederate army fell back leisurely from the front of Washington, and rested some weeks on the Rappahannock, waiting the development of McClellan's plans. Stuart's cavalry was the rear-guard. Sumner pushed forward with a division along the Orange and Alexandria railroad, to make a demonstration and cover McClellan's operations in another direction. He rather overdid the thing. On reaching our picket line on Cedar Run, he made a grand display by deploying his whole force in an open field. I happened to be on the picket line that day, and told Col. Jones that it was only a feint to deceive us. We retired, and the enemy occupied our camping-ground that night.

The next morning Stuart was at Bealeton station; and our skirmishers were engaged with the enemy, who was advancing towards the Rappahannock. My own regiment had just taken position on the railroad, when I rode up to Stuart, with whom I had become pretty well acquainted. Since we had left the line of Bull Run, I had several times returned on scouts for him. He said to me, "I want to find out whether this is McClellan's army or only a feint."

I replied, "I will go and find out for you." I immediately started towards the rear of the enemy's column with two or three men, and reached a point some distance behind it about the time they were shelling our cavalry they had driven over the river. I saw that the enemy was only making a demonstration, and rode nearly all night to get back to Stuart. When I got to the river, we came very near being shot by our own pickets, who mistook us for the enemy. I found Stuart with Gen. Ewell, anxiously waiting to hear from me, or for the enemy to cross the river.

I have not been so fortunate as to have a poet to do for me on this occasion what Longfellow did for the midnight ride of Paul Revere. There was a drizzling rain and a dense fog; it was impossible to see what the enemy were doing. I remember Stuart's joy and surprise when I told him that they were falling back from the river. In the rapture of the moment he told me that I could get any reward I wanted for what I had done. The only reward I asked was the opportunity to do the same thing again.[1] In ten minutes the cavalry had crossed the river and was capturing prisoners. Nothing had been left before us but a screen of cavalry, which was quickly brushed away. It now became evident that McClellan would move down the Potomac and operate against Richmond from a new base and on another line.

This was the first cavalry reconnoissance that had ever been made to the rear of the enemy, and was considered as something remarkable at that time; at a later period they were very common. Soon after this, Stuart's cavalry was transferred from the line of the Rappahannock with the rest of Johnston's army, to confront McClellan on the Peninsula. I dined with Gen. Lee at his headquarters, near Petersburg, about six weeks before the surrender. He told me then that he had been opposed to Gen. Johnston's withdrawing to the Peninsula, and had written to him while he was on the Rapidan, advising him to move back towards the Potomac. He thought that if he had done this, McClellan would have been recalled to the defence of Washington. He further said that, instead of falling back from Yorktown to Richmond, Gen. Johnston should have made a stand with his whole army, instead of a part of it, on the narrow isthmus at Williamsburg.

Just before we reached Williamsburg, news came of the passage of the conscription law, which preserved all the regimental organisations as they were. The men were held in the ranks, but allowed to elect their company officers; and these in turn elected field officers. It is hard to reconcile democracy with military principles; and, consequently, many of the best officers were dropped. Such was the fate of my colonel. The staff officers, not being elected, were supposed to hold over without reappointment. I immediately handed my resignation as adjutant to the new colonel,—Fitz Lee,—*who accepted it.*

The conscription law at first produced some dissatisfaction among the men, as most of them had served twelve months without a furlough; but this soon subsided. All acquiesced in what was regarded as imperious necessity. The loss of our positions in the First Virginia Cavalry resulted in a benefit both to Jones and myself. Through the influence of Stonewall Jackson, Jones was made a brigadier-general, and soon after the death of Ashby was given the command of his brigade. Stuart invited me to come to his headquarters and act as a scout for him. In this way I began my career as a partisan, which now, when I recall it through the mist of years, seems as unreal as the lives of the *paladins.*

---

1. See Stuart's report to Gen. Johnston.

I wish it to be understood that a scout is not a spy who goes in disguise, but a soldier in arms and uniform who reconnoitres either inside or outside an enemy's line. Such a life is full of adventure, excitement, and romance. Stuart was not only an educated, but a heaven-born soldier, whose natural genius had not been stifled by red tape and the narrow rules of the schools.

The history of the war furnishes no better type of the American soldier; as a chief of cavalry he is without a peer. He cared little for formulas, and knew when to follow and when to disregard precedents. He was the first to see that the European methods of employing cavalry were not adapted to the conditions of modern war.[2] His inventive genius discovered new ways of making cavalry useful, that had never been dreamed of by the regular professors of the science. I will now give some illustrations of his originality and the fertility of his resources. When McClellan was lying in the swamps of the Chickahominy, the infantry lines of the two armies were so close together that cavalry operations in their front were impracticable.

One morning, when Stuart's headquarters were near Richmond, he invited me to breakfast with him, and at the table asked me to take two or three men and find out whether McClellan was fortifying on the Totopotomoy Creek. I had been inactive for some time, and this was just the opportunity I wanted. I started, but was diverted from the route I had been directed to go by there being a flag of truce on the road. I did not want to return without accomplishing something, so I turned north and made a wide detour by Hanover Court House. Although I was then engaged in the business of breaking idols, I had not lost all reverence for antiquity. I stopped a while to muse in the old brick building where Patrick Henry made his first speech at the bar, and pleaded the cause of the people against the parsons. In order to understand the enterprise on which I was going, a geographical description of the country and situation of the armies is necessary.

The Battle of Fair Oaks or Seven Pines had been fought, and the army of the Potomac was lying on the Peninsula between the James and Pamunkey rivers, and astraddle of the Chickahominy, which meanders between them and finally empties into the James. McClellan's right wing rested on the Pamunkey, with his base at the White House and his line of supply by the York River Railroad. His left extended to

---

2. That infantry armed with repeating rifles and fixed ammunition would have destroyed the squadrons of Murat at Eylou and Mount Tabor before they ever got close enough to use their sabres.

within a few miles of the James. The Totopotomoy Creek flows into the Pamunkey. I got down in the enemy's lines on the Totopotomoy and ascertained that six or eight miles of McClellan's front was a mere shroud of cavalry pickets that covered his line of communication with his depot at the White House. Of course, as he had no infantry on his right there would be no fortifications there. The idea immediately occurred to me that here was a grand opportunity for Stuart to strike a blow. It is now clear why General Lee wanted to get information about the enemy's fortifying the Totopotomoy.

About three weeks after that he called Jackson from the valley, who struck McClellan on this very ground. I was chased away from there and came out just behind a regiment of Union cavalry going on a scout. They very little thought that I was coming back so soon. I hastened to Stuart's headquarters to give him the information. Everybody there was in high glee. News had just come of Jackson's victories over Fremont and Shields: Cross Keyes and Port Republic had been inscribed on his banners. It was a hot day in June, and Stuart was sitting under the shade of a tree, and I lay down on the grass to tell him what I had learned. After giving him the information, I remarked, that as the cavalry was idle, he could find on the Pamunkey something for them to do.

A blow on this weak point would greatly alarm McClellan for the safety of his supplies, and compel him to detach heavily from his front to guard them. After I got through, he said to me, "Write down what you have told me." I went to his adjutant's office and wrote it down hurriedly; but, not attaching much importance to it, did not sign the writing. When I brought the paper to Stuart he had his horse ready to mount. He called my attention to the omission, and I went back and signed it. He started off at a gallop with a single courier to General Lee's headquarters. He returned that afternoon, and orders were immediately issued for a part of the cavalry to get ready to march.

General Lee's instructions to Stuart, directing, or rather authorizing, the expedition, are dated June 11, which shows how soon he started after my return, which was on the 10th.[3] With about 1200

---

[3] Von Borcke, a Prussian on Stuart's staff, in his *Memoirs*, says that he and Stuart rode alone at night five miles, inside the enemy's lines on the Chickahominy, to the house of an Irishman, which Stuart had appointed as a rendezvous to meet a spy. The spy not appearing, he says that he and Stuart waited for him till daylight, and then rode to his house, just as the reveille sounded in the Yankee camps, only 400 paces distant. Such rides, he says, were habitual with Stuart, and, of course, Von Borcke always went with him. He adds: "The object of this excursion soon, (continued next page),

cavalry and two pieces of artillery, on the morning of June 12, Stuart left Richmond, moving in a northerly direction, to create the impression that he was going to reinforce Jackson. That night we bivouacked within a few miles of Hanover Court House. During his absence his adjutant was left in charge of his headquarters. I was present when he started. The adjutant asked him how long he would be gone. Stuart's answer was, "It may be for years, and it may be forever." Taking leave of his staff had suggested the parting from Erin and Kathleen Mavourneen.

There were many surmises as to his destination; but I never doubted for a moment where we were going. Early the next morning Stuart sent me on in advance with a few men to Hanover Court House, and I then saw that my idea of a raid on McClellan's lines was about to be realized. When we got within a few hundred yards of the village, a squadron of cavalry was discovered there, and I sent a man back to inform Stuart of it, so that he might send a regiment round to cut off their retreat. He ordered the First Virginia Cavalry to go; but the enemy, suspecting that there was a stronger force than they could see, withdrew too soon to be caught.

The column then pushed rapidly towards the camp of Union cavalry at Old Church. At that place Captain Royall was stationed with two squadrons of the 5th U.S. Regular Cavalry. There was a running fight of several miles with the pickets, and finally we met Captain Royall, who came out with his whole command to reinforce the outpost. He had no suspicion of the number he was attacking, and as soon as he came in sight, Stuart ordered the front squadron of the 9th Virginia cavalry to charge. Royall was wounded and routed. On our side, Captain Latané was killed. We could not stay to give him even the hasty burial that the hero received who died on the ramparts of Corunna. This was left for female hands to do. The scene has been preserved on canvas by a Virginia artist. As Royall's command had

---

appeared. Our cavalry force received orders to provide themselves with rations for three days, and on the 12th we commenced that ride round the army of McClellan which attracted so much attention even in Europe." The Baron Munchausen, who was a countryman of Von Borcke's, never invented a purer fiction. Tradition says that King Alfred went, disguised as a harper, into the court of the Danes; he was, however, acting as a spy, and did not go to meet one. There is not a soldier of the army of Northern Virginia who does not know that neither Stuart nor any other Confederate general ever did such a thing. Stuart employed scouts and spies to get information for him; but they reported to him at his headquarters; he never went either inside or outside the enemy's lines to meet them.

been scattered, we soon had possession of his camp, and were feasting on the good things we found in it. Nearly everybody forgot—many never knew—the danger we were in.

A mile or so on our left was an impassable river—not more than six miles to the right were McClellan's headquarters, with Fitz John Porter's corps and the reserve division of cavalry camped near us. Here was the turning-point of the expedition. Stuart was as jolly as anybody; but his head was always level in critical moments—even in the midst of fun. There was a short conference between him and the Lees, who were the colonels of the two Virginia regiments. I was sitting on my horse, buckling on a pistol I had just captured, within a few feet of them and heard all that passed. Stuart was for pushing on to the York River Railroad, which was still nine miles off. Lee, of the 9th (son of General R. E. Lee), was in favour of it, but Fitz Lee was opposed. Stuart had no idea of turning back, and determined to go on and strike McClellan in his rear. In the conception and execution of this bold enterprise he showed the genius and the intrepid spirit that took the plunge of the Rubicon.

Just as he gave the command, "Forward!" he turned to me, and said, "Mosby, I want you to ride some distance ahead." I replied: "Very well. But you must give me a guide; I don't know the road." He then ordered two cavalrymen who were familiar with the country to go with me; and I started on towards Tunstall's station. I was on a slow horse; and I remember that I had not gone very far before Stuart sent one of his staff to tell me to go faster and increase the distance between us. It was important that we should reach the railroad before dark, or reinforcements could be sent there. So I went on with my two men at a trot.[4]

Stuart's biographer, without so intending, has made a statement which if true would rob him of all the glory of the enterprise. He says that after reaching Old Church, Stuart kept on because it was safer than to go back by the route he had come. The road to Hanover Court House was open; and it would not have been possible for the enemy to have closed it against him for several hours. The fight with Royall was near his camp, and did not last five minutes; it took only a

---

[4]. Stuart's report contained recommendations of a number who had been with him for promotion. He said: "Captains W. D. Farley and J. S. Mosby, without commission, have established a claim for position which a grateful country will not, I trust, disregard. Their distinguished services run far back towards the beginning of the war, and present a shining record of daring and usefulness."

few minutes to destroy it. If he had intended to return by Hanover, he would have left pickets behind him to keep the way open. But he did nothing of the kind. He took no more account of his rear than Cortez did when he burned his ships, and marched to the capital of the Aztec kings. The route of the two squadrons of cavalry was, in itself, an insignificant result as compared with the magnitude of the preparation. At this point, he had simply broken through McClellan's picket line, but had not gained his rear. To have returned after doing this and no more, would have been very much like the labour of a mountain and the birth of a mouse.

The fight and capture of Royall's camp at Old Church occurred about two o'clock p.m., on June 13. The nearest camps were three or four miles off. Major Williams reports that he came on the ground with 380 of the 6th cavalry at 3.30 p.m., about one hour after the rear of Stuart's cavalry had passed on towards Tunstall's. This one hour would of itself have been amply sufficient to allow Stuart's return unmolested before the arrival of that force. It will hardly be contended that 380 men of any cavalry the world ever saw could have stopped Stuart with 1200 men and two pieces of artillery. The 5th U.S. cavalry came on the ground about five o'clock; and Gen. Cook (who was Stuart's father-in-law), with the rest of his cavalry division, Warren's brigade of infantry, and a battery of artillery, reached there after dark. It is very difficult, therefore, to see what there was to prevent Stuart from returning if he had so desired. In all, there were two brigades of cavalry, one of infantry, and a battery of artillery sent in pursuit of him.

Gen. Emory, who led the advance, says that he followed on Stuart's track, and reached Tunstall's at two o'clock that night, where he found Gen. Reynolds, who had come up with a brigade of infantry on the cars about twelve o'clock. Reynolds says that our rear guard had left there about two hours before he arrived. At Tunstall's, Gen. Emory says he lost Stuart's trail, and set every squadron he had to hunting for it, and did not succeed in finding it until eight o'clock the next morning. As Stuart had left Tunstall's on the plain country road on which he had been marching all day, and on which Gen. Emory had followed him, it seems strange that 1200 cavalry, with two pieces of artillery, should have left no track behind them. Gen. Warren says that *"the moon was shining brightly, making any kind of movement for ourselves or the enemy as easy as in daylight."*

General Cook, with the rest of the cavalry, and infantry, and artillery, arrived about 9 o'clock the next morning. General Emory then moved forward in pursuit with infantry, cavalry, and artillery. Warren says: "*It was impossible for the infantry to overtake him [Stuart], and as the cavalry did not move without us, it was impossible for them to overtake him.*" And Fitz John Porter regrets, "*That when General Cook did pursue he should have tied his legs with the infantry command.*"

Perhaps General Cook was acting on the maxim that recommends us to *build a bridge of gold for a retreating foe*. But then it can hardly be said that Stuart was retreating. As there were six cavalry regiments—including all the regulars—on our track, with a battery of artillery, it is hard to see the use they had for infantry, except as a brake to keep them from going too fast. The pursuit was from beginning to end a comedy of errors. The infantry could not have expected to overtake us, whereas, if we had attempted to return by the same route we came, then they might have intercepted us by remaining where they were.

Stuart was reduced to the alternative of returning home by the road along the Pamunkey, or the one up James River. If he took the latter, then a slight extension of McClellan's left flank would have barred his way. It could hardly have been imagined that we were going down to capture Fort Monroe, or that Stuart's cavalry were amphibious animals that could cross the York and James rivers without pontoons. Only the cavalry on McClellan's right was in the pursuit. He had an abundance on his left to block our way, and they had twenty-four hours' notice of our coming. Now to return to my narrative of Stuart's march. As I was jogging along with my two companions, a mile or two ahead of the column, I came upon a well-filled sutler's wagon at a cross-roads, of which I took possession by right of discovery.

At the same time, about a mile off to my left, I could see the masts of several vessels riding at anchor in the river. I sent one of the men back to tell Stuart to hurry on. The sutler was too rich a prize to abandon, so I left the other man in charge of him and his wagon and hurried on. Just as I turned a bend of the road, I came plump upon another sutler, and a cavalry vidette was by him. They were so shocked by the apparition that they surrendered as quietly as the coon did to Captain Scott. Tunstall's Station was now in full view a half a mile off. I was all alone. Just then a bugle sounded. I saw about a squadron of cavalry drawn up in line, near the railroad.[5] I knew that the head of our column must be close by, and my horse was too tired to run, so I just drew my sabre and waved it in the air. They knew from this that support was near me. In a few seconds our advance guard under

---

5. 11th Pennsylvania.

Lieutenant Robbins appeared in sight, and the squadron in front of me vanished from view. Robbins captured the depot with the guard without firing a shot. Stuart soon rode up.

Just then a train of cars came in sight, and as we had no implements with which to pull up a rail, a number of logs were put on the track. When the engineer got near us, he saw that he was in a hornet's nest, and with a full head of steam dashed on under a heavy fire, knocked the logs off the track, and carried the news to the White House below. General Ingalls, who was in command of the depot there, says that he had received a telegram from General McClellan's headquarters, telling him of the attack on Royall's camp and warning him of danger. As soon then as the telegraph line was broken, which was about sunset on the 13th, it was notice to McClellan that we were in his rear and on his line of communication.

There was now but one route by which we could return, and that was up James River. Yet he made no signs of a movement to prevent it, and the only evidence that he knew of our presence is a telegram to Stanton on the next day—dated 11 a.m., June 14th, saying that a body of cavalry had passed around his right and that he had sent cavalry in pursuit to punish them. Before reaching Tunstall's, Stuart sent a squadron to burn the transports in the river and a wagon train that was loading from them. The small guard fled at the approach of our cavalry, while the schooners and wagons disappeared in smoke. As some evidence of the consternation produced by this sudden irruption, I will mention the fact, that after we left Old Church, a sergeant with twenty-five men of the United States regular cavalry followed on under a flag of truce and surrendered to our *rear-guard*. They supposed they were cut off and surrounded. The Jeff Davis legion was the rearguard, and these were the only enemies they saw.

The despatch to Stanton shows the bewildered state of McClellan's mind. At the time he was writing it we were lying on the banks of the Chickahominy, building a bridge to cross on. To have caught us, it was not necessary to pursue at all; all that he had to do was to spread his wings. We halted at Tunstall's long enough for the column to close up. Our march was slow, the artillery horses had broken down, and we were encumbered with a large number of prisoners on foot, and of course we could march no faster than they did. After dark the column moved down through New Kent towards the Chickahominy. On the road were large encampments of army wagons. Many a sutler was ruined that night; with sad hearts they fell into line with the prisoners, and saw their wagons, with their contents, vanish in flames. The heavens were lurid with the light reflected from the burning trains, and our track was as brilliant as the tail of a comet.

The Count of Paris, who was on McClellan's staff, thus describes Stuart's march: "But night had come, and the fires kindled by his hand flashing above the forest were so many signals which drew the Federals on his track." Now, the Count of Paris evidently means that the glowing sky ought to have been a guide to the Federal generals as the pillar of fire was to Moses. As a fact, the only pursuers we saw were those who came after us to surrender under a flag of truce. Stuart halted three hours at Baltimore Store, only five miles from Tunstall's. At twelve o'clock he started again for a ford of the Chickahominy, which was eight miles distant, and reached it about daylight.

That summer night was a carnival of fun I can never forget. Nobody thought of danger or of sleep, when champagne bottles were bursting, and Rhine wine was flowing in copious streams. All had perfect confidence in their leader. In the riot among the sutlers' stores "grim-visaged war had smoothed his wrinkled front," and Mars resigned his sceptre to the jolly god. The discipline of soldiers for a while gave way to the wild revelry of the crew of Comus. During all of this time General Emory was a few miles off, at Tunstall's Station, hunting our tracks in the sand with a lighted candle. Stuart had expected to ford the Chickahominy; but when we got there, it was found overflowing from the recent rains, and impassable. Up to this point our progress had been as easy as the descent to Avernus; but now, to get over the river, *hic labor, hic opus est*.

He was fortunate in having two guides, Christian and Frayser, who lived in the neighbourhood, and knew all the roads and fords on the river. Christian knew of a bridge, or rather, where a bridge had been, about a mile below the ford, and the column was immediately headed for it. But it had been destroyed, and nothing was left but some of the piles standing in the water. He was again fortunate in having two men, Burke and Hagan, who knew something about bridge-building. Near by were the remains of an old warehouse, out of which they built a bridge. It was marvellous with what rapidity the structure grew; in a few hours it was finished—it seemed almost by magic. It was not as good a bridge as Cæsar threw over the Rhine, but it was good enough for our purpose. While the men were at work upon it, Stuart was lying down on the bank of the stream, in the gayest humour I ever saw him, laughing at the prank he had played on McClellan.

As I was a believer in the Napoleonic maxim of making *war support war*, I had foraged extensively during the night, and from the sutlers' stores spread a feast that Epicurus might have envied. During all the long hours that we lay on the bank of the river waiting for the bridge, no enemy appeared in sight. That was a mystery nobody could understand. There was some apprehension that McClellan was allowing us to cross over in order to entrap us in the forks of the Chickahominy. When, at last, about two o'clock, the cavalry, artillery, prisoners and captured horses and mules were all over, and fire had been set to the bridge, some of Rush's lancers came on a hill and took a farewell look at us. They came, and saw, and went away, taking as their only trophy a drunken Dutchman we had left on the road. General Emory received news of the crossing eight miles off at Baltimore Store. Our escape over the river was immediately reported to him. In his official report, he says that we crossed the Chickahominy at daylight and that we left faster than we came.

Now, I am unable to see the evidence of any particular haste in the march: in fact, it seems to have been conducted very leisurely. About one o'clock p.m., on the 13th, we captured Royall's camp at Old Church; about sunset we reached Tunstall's, nine miles distant, and at daylight on the 14th got to a point on the Chickahominy twelve miles from there, where we stayed until noon. So if we had been pursued at the rate of a mile an hour, we would have been overtaken.

But the danger was not over when we were over the Chickahominy. We were still thirty-five miles from Richmond and in the rear of McClellan's army, which was five or six miles above us. It was necessary to pass through swamps where the horses sunk to their saddle girths, and when we emerged from these, we had to go for twenty miles on a road in full view of the enemy's gunboats on one side of us in the James River, and McClellan's army within a few miles on the other. Nothing would have been easier than for him to have thrown a division of infantry as well as cavalry across our path. Then nothing could have saved us except such a miracle as destroyed Pharaoh and his host.

Stuart, apprehending a movement on McClellan's left, had sent a messenger early in the morning to General Lee requesting him to make a diversion in his favour. But we were out of danger before he had time to do it. After getting through the swamp the command halted in Charles City for several hours to give rest to the men and horses. Stuart then turned over the command to Fitz Lee, as we were then in comparative safety, and with two men rode on to General Lee's headquarters, which he reached about daybreak the next morning. During the night march I was in advance of the column, but saw nothing in the path except occasionally a negro who would dart across it going into the Union lines. Early in the morning, just as I got in sight of Richmond, I met Stuart returning to the command. Although he had been in the saddle two days and nights without sleep, he was as gay as a lark and showed no signs of weariness. He had a right to be proud; for he had performed a feat that to this day has no parallel in the annals of war. I said to him, "This will make you a major-general." He said, "No, I don't think I can be a major-general until we have 10,000 cavalry." But in six weeks he had that rank.

This expedition, in which Stuart had ridden around McClellan in a circle of a radius of ten miles, created almost as much astonishment in Richmond and even in Europe as if he had dropped from the clouds, and made him the hero of the army. It had an electric effect on the morale of the Confederate troops and excited their enthusiasm to a high pitch. Always after that the sight of Stuart on the field was like

*A blast of that dread horn*
*On Fontarabian echoes borne.*

McClellan attempts in his report to belittle it, by saying that in this affair Stuart's cavalry did nothing but gain a little *éclat*; but with more truth it might be said that by it he lost a good deal. His staff officer, the Count of Paris, says, in reference to these operations of our cavalry:

> They had, in point of fact, created a great commotion, shaken the confidence of the North in McClellan, and made the first experiment in those great cavalry expeditions which subsequently played so novel and so important a part during the war.

At midnight, on June 14, at the very hour when we were marching along his left flank, McClellan telegraphed to Stanton, "All quiet in every direction; the stampede of last night has passed away." In his telegram six hours before, he had said that we ran away from an infantry force, at Tunstall's, that he had sent after us. The fact was that we left that place long before the infantry arrived there, and never heard of it until long after we left. Gen. Reynolds says he never saw us. The stampede that McClellan talks about was not in *our* ranks. The Count of Paris again says:

> As soon as he (Stuart) was known to be at Tunstall's, McClellan had divined his purpose, and despatched Averill to intercept him.

I have made a diligent examination of the archives of the war, but have been unable to find any authority for this statement. The despatches of the general-in-chief, the corps, division, brigade, and regimental commanders, in reference to this *raid*, have all been published, besides the report of Col. Clitz, who was ordered to investigate the conduct of those who were charged with the pursuit. They all relate to the operations on McClellan's right, and there is perfect silence as to any attempt to intercept us on his left, or any order to do so. Averill, who was stationed with the cavalry on the left flank, is nowhere mentioned, and there is no report from him.

After we crossed the Chickahominy we were in a *cul de sac*, formed by the junction of that river with the James. Yet we never saw an enemy in that vicinity, although they must or ought to have had twenty-four hours' notice that we were coming, as the army headquarters were connected with each corps by both telegraph lines and signal stations.

As McClellan was very much criticised for permitting Stuart to escape, if it had been due to the failure of Averill or anyone else to execute his orders, he would have put the blame where it belonged. McClellan's conduct on this occasion has always been unaccountable to me, and the only explanation I have ever seen of it is in the report of Gen. Pleasanton, who soon after that became his chief of cavalry. Pleasanton says:

> McClellan dreaded the rebel cavalry, and supposed that by placing his army on a peninsula, with a deep river on each side, he was safe from that arm of the enemy; but the humiliation on the Chickahominy, of having a few thousand of the enemy's cavalry ride completely around his army, and the ignominious retreat to Harrison's Landing, are additional instances in support of the maxim '*that a general who disregards the rules of war finds himself overwhelmed by the consequences of such neglect, when the crisis of battle follows.*'[6]

At that time Pleasanton was commanding the 2nd U.S. Cavalry. The telegraph line at Tunstall's was repaired soon after Reynolds arrived, on the night of the 13th; and it is impossible to believe that he and Ingalls did not inform the general-in-chief which way we had

---

6. This was written by Pleasanton after the war. He does not seem to have felt the humiliation of Stuart's ride around him to Chambersburg, when he, as chief of cavalry of the army of the Potomac, was charged with the duty of pursuing him.

gone. Stuart then had no choice of routes, but was confined to the road up James River, or not to return at all. This raid is unique, and distinguished from all others on either side during the war, on account of the narrow limits in which the cavalry was compelled to operate. From the time when he broke through McClellan's line on his right until he had passed around him on his left Stuart was enclosed by three unfordable rivers, over one of which he had to build a bridge to cross. During the whole operation the cavalry never drew a sabre except at the first picket post they encountered. But it was something more than a mere raid on McClellan's communications; it was, in fact, a *reconnoissance* in force to ascertain the exact location of the different corps of his army, and the prelude to the great battles that began ten days afterwards, in which Jackson's flank was covered by Stuart's cavalry. (See note following)

※※※※※※

Note:—General Lee's congratulatory order is as follows:
      Headquarters Department of Northern Va.,
General Orders, No. 74.      June 23, 1862.
The commanding general announces with great satisfaction to the army the brilliant exploit of Brigadier-General J. E. B. Stuart, with part of the troops under his command. This gallant officer, with portions of the 1st, 4th, and 9th Virginia Cavalry, a part of the Jeff Davis Legion, with whom were the Boykin Rangers, and a section of the Stuart Horse Artillery, on the 13th, 14th, and 15th of June, made a reconnoissance between the Pamunkey and the Chickahominy rivers, and succeeded in passing around the rear of the whole of the Union army, routing the enemy in a series of skirmishes, taking a number of prisoners, and destroying and capturing stores to a large amount.
Having most successfully accomplished its object, the expedition recrossed the Chickahominy almost in the presence of the enemy, with the same coolness and address that marked every step of its progress, and with the loss of but one man, the lamented Latané, of the 9th Virginia Cavalry, who fell bravely leading a successful charge against a superior force of the enemy. In announcing the signal success to the army, the general commanding takes great pleasure in expressing his admiration of the courage and skill so conspicuously exhibited throughout by the general and the officers and men under his command.

In addition to the officers honourably mentioned in the report of the expedition, the conduct of the following privates has received the special commendation of their respective commanders: Private Thomas D. Clapp, Co. D, 1st Virginia Cavalry, and J. S. Mosby, serving in the same regiment; privates Ashton, Brent, R. Herring, F. Herring, and F. Coleman, Co. E, 9th Virginia Cavalry.

By command of

R. H. Chieton, A.A.G.                                         General Lee.

In General McClellan's posthumous book there is a private letter of his, dated June 15th, 10.45 p.m., in which he says: "I then gave orders to Averill for a surprise party tomorrow, to repay Secesh for his raid of day before yesterday." So the surprise party was not ordered until Stuart had got back to camp.

******

The seven days' battles were fought behind entrenchments, and in swamps which afforded no opportunity for the use of cavalry except in guarding the flanks of the infantry and the minor operations of outpost duty. When they were over, the cavalry had a short respite from labour. I never could rest inactive; and so I asked Stuart to let me take a party of men to northern Virginia.

Gen. Pope had then just assumed command of that department. He had a long line of communications to guard; and his scattered army corps offered fine opportunities for partisan war. The wiser policy of concentration had not then been adopted by the Federal generals. Stuart was recruiting his cavalry, and was not willing to spare any for detached service; but gave me a letter of introduction to Gen. Jackson, who had been sent up to Gordonsville to observe Pope. He sent him by me a copy of Napoleon's maxims, which had just been published in Richmond. Stuart wanted Jackson to furnish a detail of cavalry to go with me behind Pope, who had just published the fact to the world that he intended to leave his rear to take care of itself. With a single companion, and full of enthusiasm, I started on my mission to Jackson. I concluded to take the cars at Beaver Dam and go on in advance to his headquarters and wait there for my horse to be led on.

I was sitting in the depot, and my companion had hardly got out of sight, when a regiment of Union cavalry rode up, and put an attachment upon my person. They had ridden all night from Fredericksburg to capture the train which was due in a few minutes. I was chagrined, not only at being a prisoner, but because my cherished hopes were now disappointed. The regiment fronted into a line to wait for the cars; and they placed me in the front rank. I called to an officer, and protested against being put where I would be shot by the guard on the train. For some reason, the commanding officer gave orders to leave; perhaps it was because he was as much opposed to being shot as I was. The train soon afterwards arrived; and I do not think there were any soldiers on it. That night, I slept on the floor of the guard-house at Fredericksburg; on the next day the *cartel* for the exchange of prisoners was agreed on.

My imprisonment lasted ten days; and I confess that I rather enjoyed my visit to Washington. I kept up my habits as a scout, and collected a large budget of information. The steamer on which I came back lay four days in Hampton Roads, and then proceeded up James River. When we first arrived there I noticed a large number of transports, with troops on board, lying near Newport News, and learned that they belonged to Burnside's corps just arrived from North Carolina. Here, now, was a problem for me to solve. Where were they going? to reinforce Pope or McClellan? I set about to find out. If they went to Pope it meant the withdrawal of McClellan. The captain of the steamer promised me to find out their destination. A few hours before we left, I observed them all coming down and passing out by Fort Monroe. When the captain returned from on shore, he told me that the transports were going up the Potomac. This settled the question; the Peninsula campaign was over.

About ten o'clock in the morning we reached the point on James River where the commissioners had met. I knew that it would take several hours to complete the exchange and every minute then was precious. I whispered to the Confederate commissioner—Judge Culd—that I had important news for General Lee and he let me go immediately. I started off with a haversack full of lemons I had bought at Fort Monroe to walk twelve miles to headquarters on a hot day in August. I trudged on several hours weary and footsore, until completely exhausted I had fallen down on the roadside. While lying there a horseman of the Hampton Legion came riding by, and I stopped him and explained my condition and anxiety to see General Lee. He dismounted, put me on his horse, took me to his camp near by, and, getting a horse for himself, went with me to the general's headquarters. I wish that I knew his name that I might record it with the praise that is due to his generous deed.

The first one I met at headquarters, with a good deal of the insolence of office, told me that I could not see the general. I tried to explain that I did not come to ask a favour, but to bring him important information. Another one of the staff standing by told me to wait a moment. He stepped into the adjoining room and soon called me in. I now found myself for the first time in the presence of the great commander of the Army of Northern Virginia. He was alone and poring over some maps on the table, and no doubt planning a new campaign.

Although his manner was gentle and kind, I felt for him an awe and veneration which I have never felt for any other man. He was then the foremost man in all the world, and I almost imagined that I saw one of the Homeric heroes before me. With some embarrassment I told what I had learned about Burnside's troops. He listened attentively, and after I was through called to a staff officer to have a man ready to take a despatch to General Jackson. At that time communication was kept up between them by a line of relay couriers. They were afraid to trust the telegraph that had been tampered with by raiding parties from Fredericksburg. Jackson received the despatch that night informing him that Burnside was on his way to Pope, and hastened to strike him at Cedar Mountain before reinforcements could arrive. Pope says:

> This battle was fought at a distance of more than one hundred miles from Richmond, only five days after General McClellan received his orders to withdraw and five days before he had commenced to do so, or had embarked a man.

When the Army of the Potomac was being withdrawn from the front of Richmond, Gen. Lee began to transfer his own to the line of the Rapidan. Stuart, with his staff, came ahead by rail and left Fitz Lee to bring on the cavalry division. I joined him on the evening of August 17th, and that night we rode to a place called Vidiersville in Orange County, where we expected to find the cavalry. It had not, however, come up, and Stuart sent his adjutant to look for it, and the rest of us—five in number—unsaddled our horses and lay down to sleep on the porch of a house by the roadside. We were outside our picket lines and in a mile or so of the enemy on the river, but did not think there was much risk in spending the night there.

About sunrise the next morning a young man named Gibson, who had been a fellow-prisoner with me in the Old Capitol, woke me up and said that he heard the tramp of cavalry down the road. We saddled quickly, and started to see what it was, but first woke Stuart up. As Fitz Lee was due, we supposed it was our own cavalry, but there was a chance that it might be the enemy, and we did not want to be again caught napping. After going about two hundred yards, we saw through the morning mist a body of cavalry that had stopped at a house to search it. We halted, but could not tell who they were. Presently two officers rode forward and began firing on us. This convinced me that they were no friends of mine, and as neither one of us had a pistol or a sabre, I am not ashamed to say that we turned and ran away with the Yankee cavalry close after us.

The firing saved Stuart. He had walked out into the yard bareheaded, and when he heard it, mounted his horse and leaped over the fence, and escaped through the backyard with one of his *aides* just as Gibson and I passed by at full speed. The cavalry stopped the pursuit to pick up Stuart's hat and cloak and the nice patent-leather haversack I had brought from Washington, which we had left on the porch. It was a scouting party General Pope had sent out. They had caught Stuart's adjutant during the night and found on him a letter from General Lee, disclosing the fact that he would cross the river to attack Pope on the 20th. So Pope, on the 18th, issued orders to withdraw beyond the line of the Rappahannock; he had already received information through a spy that our whole army was assembling in his front and was about retreating anyway. If the cavalry had not stopped at the house they would have caught us all asleep.

Von Borcke, a Prussian officer on Stuart's staff, who published a mass of fables, under the title of "Memoirs of the Confederate War," gives an account of this affair, in which he represents himself as playing a most heroic part. As Gibson and I were between him and the enemy, and running with all our might, it is hard to discover any heroism in anybody. Von Borcke's horse ran faster than ours, and that was the only distinction he won. The chase was soon over, and we returned immediately to look over the ground. Just as Stuart got in sight of the house, he saw the enemy going off in triumph with his hat and cloak. In two days the armies were again confronting each other on the Rappahannock; on the morning of the 22nd the Confederate column began a movement up the river to turn Pope's right. Jackson's corps was just in rear of the cavalry. When we got to Waterloo bridge, where we crossed, Stuart galloped by, and said to me, laughing, as he passed, "I am going after my hat."

I had no idea then that what he said would come true. He had heard that Pope had his wagon trains parked at Catlett's, on the Orange and Alexandria Railroad, and was going after them. Pope's headquarters were ten or twelve miles distant, at Rappahannock Station. Stuart had with him about 1500 cavalry and two pieces of artillery. We passed around to Pope's rear unobserved, and got to Catlett's just after dark. A picket post on the road was captured without any alarm, and the guards with the trains had no suspicion of our presence until we rode into their camp.

General Pope unjustly censures them. Considering the surprise, I think they did remarkably well. It was no fault of theirs that Stuart had got to the rear of their army without being discovered. It was the duty of their cavalry on the front to watch him, and tell them he was coming. Fortunately for Pope, the most terrific storm I ever saw came up before we reached Catlett's. But for that, nearly the whole of the transportation of his army would have been destroyed. The night was pitch dark and the rain fell in torrents. Flashes of lightning would often illuminate the scene, and peals of thunder seemed to roll from pole to pole. Stuart halted about half a mile from the station, and sent the First and Fifth Virginia cavalry to destroy a large park of wagons whose camp-fires could be seen.

I went along with my old regiment. We had to cross a railroad embankment and a ditch, of which the men knew nothing until they tumbled into it. Most of them scrambled out, and got into the camp on the other side. It was defended by the Bucktails, who, under cover of the wagons and the darkness, poured a hot fire into us. All that we could see was the flashes from their guns. The animals became frightened, and increased the noise and confusion of the fight. The shooting and shouting of the men, the braying of the mules, the glare of the lightning and roll of the thunder, made it seem like all Pandemonium had broken loose.

But cavalry, in a fight against invisible infantry, is defenceless. We left the camp with little or no damage to ourselves or the enemy. Other detachments were more successful in burning wagons and making captures. A party was sent to burn the railroad bridge over Cedar Run; but in such a storm they might just as well have tried to burn the creek. It happened that not far from Catlett's we met a negro in the road, who recognised Stuart as an old acquaintance, and offered to conduct him to Pope's headquarter wagons. The Ninth Virginia cavalry was sent with the guide after them. A festive party of quartermasters and commissaries was captured there, together with Pope's money-chest, despatch book, and correspondence, and also his wardrobe, including *his hat* and ostrich plume. Stuart was now revenged—he had swapped hats with Pope.

The material results of the expedition were not what had been expected. The storm of that night—which caused a rise of six feet in the river—was the salvation of Pope. The *raid* had, however, a demoralising effect on the army whose communication had been so audaciously assailed. Von Borcke, as usual, relates prodigies he performed that were never surpassed by Amadis of Gaul. He says that he was detailed by Stuart to capture Pope, and tells how he entered his tent shortly after he had left. Now Pope had never been on the spot; his headquarters were then fifteen miles from there; and Stuart knew that a general commanding an army does not sleep with his wagon trains. We returned the next morning by the same route we came, but never saw an enemy. It would be a natural question to ask—what was Pope doing with his cavalry? In the storm and darkness we had failed to cut the telegraph wire, so Pope kept up communication with Washington. At five o'clock p.m. that day—when Stuart's cavalry was in the rear and within a few miles of Catlett's, he told Halleck, "*The enemy has made no attempt today to cross the river.*"

At nine o'clock that night, when we were plundering his headquarter trains, he tells Halleck a heavy force had crossed the river that day, and asked him to send up a brigade to guard the bridge over Cedar Run. But for the providential rain the bridge would have then been burning, and Halleck would have been saved the trouble of sending infantry to protect it. Pope had no idea where we were. Fifteen minutes later, he tells Halleck, that he must either fall back behind Cedar Run, or cross the Rappahannock at daybreak the next morning and assail the rear of the Confederate army. Halleck advised the latter movement. Pope said the rise of the river that night that swept away his bridges prevented his crossing. Here Providence stepped in again and saved him. If the "*stars in their courses fought against Sisera,*" so did the floods against Robert E. Lee in this campaign.

At that time Jackson and Longstreet were in front of Pope, and Stuart was behind him. A week after this he was defeated, when we were no stronger and he had received at least 25,000 reinforcements from McClellan. But General Pope had left out an important factor in his calculation,—and that was Stonewall Jackson. He had already thrown one of his brigades over the river at Sulphur Springs, but the storm arrested the passage of the others. If General Pope had attempted such a movement as he indicated to Halleck, General Lee would not have interfered with it but let him go on. Jackson and Stuart would then have swept down the north bank of the river in his rear, and General Pope would have found himself in the condition of a fly in an exhausted receiver. This would have saved Jackson the long flank march he afterwards made to Manassas without involving his separation from Longstreet. Speaking of the raid on Catlett's, General Pope says:

> At the time this cavalry force attacked Catlett's—and it certainly was not more than three hundred strong—our whole army trains were parked at that place, and were guarded by not less than 1500 infantry and five companies of cavalry. The success of this small party of the enemy, although very trifling and attended with but very little damage, was most *disgraceful* to the force that had been left in charge of the trains.

It was certainly not the fault of the troops guarding the trains that they had no notice that we were coming; and I think he has greatly exaggerated their number.

On the 25th, Jackson, having gone higher up the river, crossed the Rappahannock four miles above Waterloo Bridge, which was held by Sigel's Corps and Buford's Cavalry. The Black Horse Company [7] acted as his escort, and the Second Virginia Cavalry led the advance. The signal stations near the rivers reported this movement immediately to Gen. Pope. An officer in the army under Pope, who had been a classmate of Jackson's at West Point, thus speaks of the great hero and his wonderful march:

> In that devotion which men yield to monarchs of the battle-field; in that glow of pride which men share with the great chieftain whose powers have created chances and directed results,—the soldier subjects under Napoleon Bonaparte were closely allied in enthusiasm, in worship, and in admiration with the soldier citizens under Stonewall Jackson.
>
> The sun sank down; the stars appeared; the night sped on till nearly twelve, when Jackson's advance had approached within one mile of Salem, where, as his weary column sank down to rest, McDowell received the message that Pope believed the enemy was marching for the *Shenandoah Valley by way of Front Royal and Luray.*

---

7. Commanded by Capt. A. D. Payne.

On the mathematical principle that parallel lines meet in infinity, Jackson might have reached the valley by the route he had travelled. His camp that night was in Pope's rear, and in twelve miles of McDowell, who was occupying Warrenton. But Gen. Pope was bewildered, and appeared to have no suspicion of where he was going. At daylight no reveille sounded in the Confederate camps; but Jackson moved silently on, and turned to the east. After his column had passed out of sight of the signal stations, Gen. Pope seemed to lose entirely the touch of it; but the "lost *Pleiad*" kept on its way. A competent general would have struck Jackson's flank with a cavalry reconnoissance on his first day's march. I do not know whether the failure to do so was the fault of the chief of cavalry or the commander-in-chief.

On the 26th, before daylight, Stuart's cavalry corps crossed the Rappahannock and followed the route Jackson had taken the day before, until it got to Salem, and then turned to the right. About four o'clock p.m., we overtook Gen. Jackson at Gainesville; having marched all day around the flank and rear of the Federal army without seeing an enemy. We were now within about seven miles of Manassas Junction. On the same day, Longstreet followed on Jackson's track. While all this was going on in his rear, Gen. Pope's attention had been attracted by some Confederate batteries that kept up a fire in his front. His army remained motionless. Its very tranquillity at last became oppressive; some feared that it was the awful stillness that precedes the storm; that he was imitating Napoleon at Austerlitz, and allowing one wing of our army to be extended in order to pierce its centre and destroy it.

About six o'clock on the afternoon of the 26th, the advance of Jackson's column, under Col. Munford, struck the Orange & Alexandria Railroad at Bristoe Station, nine miles from Pope's headquarters, which were at Warrenton Junction. The small guard was surprised and captured; they had no more expectation of seeing Stonewall Jackson than Hamlet's ghost. Just then a train came up, and ran the gauntlet under fire, that carried the astounding news to Manassas, five miles off. From there it was telegraphed to Washington. Two more trains came along in a few minutes, that had just left headquarters, and were caught. Stuart was then sent on with a force of infantry and cavalry to capture Manassas, which, with all its immense stores, fell into his hands. Twenty thousand Confederate troops were now behind Gen. Pope; and Longstreet was marching around his flank; but his army still faced the other way. As Gen. Jackson says, "My command was now in the rear of Gen. Pope's army, separating it from the Federal capital and base of supplies."

This march of Jackson's I regard as one of the most wonderful things ever achieved in war. Gen. Pope says that it "was plainly seen and promptly reported to Gen. Halleck," but that so confidently did he rely on troops promised from Washington being in position to oppose Jackson that it gave him no uneasiness. That it gave Gen. Pope no uneasiness, I think is due to the fact that *he knew nothing about it*. It certainly would have given Napoleon or Wellington a good deal of uneasiness to have had Stonewall Jackson with 20,000 men in his rear and in nine miles of his headquarters. Now, it seems to me that his knowledge of what Jackson was doing cannot be reconciled with fidelity to his government, and his contemporaneous despatches and conduct. *They* can only be explained on the theory of his ignorance of the movement, or his *co-operation* with Jackson.

The night before he had told McDowell that he believed the Confederate troops had gone to the Shenandoah valley. Jackson, I know, did marvellous things; but Gen. Pope could hardly have thought he could march an army east and west at the same time. If he knew that Jackson was going to Manassas, he could not have believed that he had gone to the valley. Admitting that he thought Franklin's corps was at Manassas to meet him, he would be a curious commander-in-chief not to inquire if it was or not to give his subordinate warning of the enemy's approach, in order that he might get ready to fight, or burn his stores and run away. If he had even called the telegraph operators at Bristoe and Manassas, they could have told him that there were just enough troops there to get caught, and that they knew nothing of Jackson's coming. He tells McDowell, *after* Jackson got to Bristoe, that the enemy's cavalry have interrupted communication with Manassas, and orders a single regiment to go down on the cars to repair the damage. Did he think one regiment could drive Stonewall Jackson away?

The next morning Halleck sends up a brigade to Manassas, that was almost annihilated,—its commander killed, and the train captured on which they came. If Halleck had known he was sending them into the jaws of death, he would have incurred a criminal responsibility. All of General Pope's orders and despatches at the time have been published; there is not a hint in any of them that he knew of Jackson's movement around him. The first time he suspected it was when the telegraph wire was cut, and he had to stop talking with Halleck. Three hours after that, McDowell telegraphs to Pope that an *intelligent* negro had just come in and reported that Jackson had passed through Thoroughfare Gap that day. Pope's answer shows that this news was a revelation and a surprise to him.

At that time Jackson's men, after a march of over fifty miles in two days, were eating his rations in sight of the blazing bridges and railroad trains at Manassas. The next day a cavalry reconnoissance under Buford was ordered to Salem, to ascertain the truth of the negro's statement. If it had been sent two days earlier it might have done some good. But Pope did not wait to hear from Buford, but changed front and hastened towards Manassas to recover his communications. Buford returned with his broken-down cavalry to Warrenton that night, but Pope's whole army had gone. During that day Jackson's wearied soldiers were resting and refreshing themselves from their abundant spoils. At night Jackson marched away towards Thoroughfare to unite with Longstreet. The supplies that he could not transport were burned. Pope's army with the railroad broken was now in a starving condition.[8] To lead Pope astray, A. P. Hill's division was sent a roundabout way by Centreville and rejoined Jackson the next day at Sudley.

The reason that Jackson left Manassas was that Stuart had captured a despatch showing that Pope was concentrating his army on that point. General Jackson says: "General Stuart kept me advised of the movements of the enemy." In a despatch to Fitz John Porter on the evening of the 27th, Pope ordered him to be at Bristoe at daylight the next morning to bag Jackson who was then five miles off. General Pope says that Jackson made a mistake in leaving Manassas before he got there. If Jackson went there to be caught it was. If Pope had reached the place at daylight he would have found nothing but a rearguard of Stuart's cavalry. He has censured Porter for not getting there in time to bag Jackson. Pope himself arrived about noon. It happened that the evening before I rode off to a farmer's house to get some supper and slept under a tree in the yard. The next morning I returned to the Junction thinking our army was still there. I found the place deserted and as silent as the cities of the plain.

So, if General Pope and Fitz John Porter had come at that time they might have caught *me*, that is, if their horses were faster than mine. Pope was deceived by Jackson's stratagem and marched off to Centreville to find him. Every step he took in that direction carried him farther from Jackson. He seemed to be groping in the dark. Instead of marching his infantry off in the morning on a fool's errand

---

8. See his despatch to Halleck.

to Manassas in search of Jackson he ought first to have felt the enemy with his cavalry, and then manoeuvred his army so as to intercept his junction with Longstreet. Pope did exactly the reverse.

On the evening of the 28th, Longstreet drove Ricketts' division from Thoroughfare and the head of his column bivouacked in about six miles of Jackson. During the fight I rode with Stuart towards the Gap.

As Ricketts was then between him and Longstreet, Stuart sent a despatch by a trusty messenger urging him to press on to the support of Jackson.

I do not think any other commander ever performed such a feat, or extricated himself from such perils as environed Jackson on this expedition. His success was largely due to Stuart's cavalry, who were the eyes of the army, that brought him quick intelligence of the enemy, and as the Count of Paris says, "screened all Jackson's movements as with an impenetrable veil." On the morning of the 29th, in a despatch to Porter and McDowell, Gen. Pope says:

> The indications are that the whole force of the enemy is moving in this direction at a pace that will bring them here by *tomorrow* night or *next* morning.

His cavalry could not then have informed him of the result of the combat between Longstreet and Ricketts on the afternoon before; for it was impossible for him to believe that the man who was called the war-horse of the Southern Army would take two days to march six miles with the thunders of battle rolling in his ears. General Pope does not seem to have recovered his mental equilibrium when he wrote his report, for he says, in one place:

> Every indication during the night of the 29th and up to 10 o'clock on the morning of the 30th pointed to the *retreat* of the enemy from our front.
>
> During the whole night of the 29th and the morning of the 30th the *advance* of the main army under Lee was arriving on the field to reinforce Jackson.

That is, the arrival of 30,000 fresh Confederate troops on the field was a sign to Gen. Pope that they were running away.

No one can study this campaign without being struck by the marked difference between the commanders of the two armies in the employment of their cavalry. A distinguished general who served under Pope says:

> That judicious use of cavalry by which Jackson covered his front, concealed his movements, discovered his enemies, and succeeded in his raids, had not at that period been generally appreciated by Federal commanders, and was almost entirely neglected by Pope.

I cannot close this account of the part borne by Stuart's cavalry in this campaign without some reference to the use that has been made of his report of it by the partisans of General Pope, and the criticism it has borne from the friends of General Porter. It is remarkable that both parties should agree in the construction put upon it, and that so clearly a wrong one. One side refers to it to prove the assertion of General Pope:

> I believe—in fact I am positive—that at five o'clock on the afternoon of the 29th General Porter had in his front no considerable body of the enemy. I believed then—as I am very sure now—that it was easily practicable for him to have turned the right flank of Jackson and to have fallen on his rear: and if he had done so, we should have gained a decisive victory over the army under Jackson before he could have been joined by any of the forces of Longstreet, etc.

He further says that about sunset of the 29th the advance of Longstreet began to arrive on the field. The essence of the controversy is the time of Longstreet's arrival. Could Porter have reached Gainesville, the objective point on which he and Longstreet marched that day, in time to have executed the order of 4.30 p.m. of the 29th to turn the Confederate flank? While the order does not specify Jackson's, but says the enemy's flank, it clearly referred to Jackson, for General Pope asserted that Longstreet was not then on the field and could not arrive before the next day. As Porter and Longstreet had camped the night before about the same distance from that place, and as Porter,[9] owing to contradictory orders, had marched twice the distance that Longstreet did, the presumption is that the latter arrived there first.

To my mind Stuart is a conclusive witness for Porter. Yet one critic (General Cox) argues that there was no obstruction but Stuart's cav-

---

9. Porter's corps camped at Bristoe the night of the 28th. About 6 o'clock on the morning of the 29th he was ordered by Pope to Centreville. When he got near Bull Run he was ordered to countermarch to Gainesville.

alry between Porter and Jackson, and an author of a defence of Porter (General George H. Gordon) calls his report a romance. Stuart says that General Lee arrived at Gainesville on the morning of the 29th with Longstreet's corps; that he passed his cavalry through Longstreet's column and placed it on his flank; that during the day his videttes reported the approach of Porter's corps; and that he sent notice of it to General Lee, who ordered infantry and artillery to his support. He adds that in the meantime he kept his cavalry dragging brush to raise a dust, and that the ruse had the desired effect of deceiving Porter. As Stuart was recovering Longstreet's flank he would be close to it. Now the object he had in dragging the brush was to deceive Porter as to the force with which he was in immediate contact. His saying that Porter was deceived by it was the mere expression of his opinion—not the statement of a fact. Stuart's object was to gain time enough for Longstreet (not Jackson) to readjust his line to meet a threatened attack on his flank. That was all. If Porter saw a heavy cloud of dust rising in the road before him, he could not tell, without halting his column and reconnoitring, what created it. But the delay involved in doing this was all that Stuart wanted.

Longstreet had been in the same dilemma at Salem two days before; when he reached there he met Buford's cavalry. If he had known that nothing else was in front of him, he would have brushed them away with a few skirmishers without losing a minute on his march. But he halted his column, he says, and was detained an hour before he could find out what it was. Pope was deceived by a few shells the Confederates threw at him across the Rappahannock into the belief that our army was in his front when in fact it was in his rear. The divine genius has never yet appeared in war that could always at a glance detect every stratagem and see through every mask. "He who wars," says Napier, "walks in a mist through which the keenest eye cannot always discern the right path."

★★★★★★

The Military Society of Massachusetts has published a volume of papers on the Fitz John Porter case, which contains a letter from Gen. B. H. Robertson to Gen. Porter, in which he says: "There was no cavalry in that direction (Manassas Junction) *but mine*, which was held there the remainder of the day."
"I have no knowledge of bushes having been dragged by cavalry to create the impression of large forces coming, or for any

purpose. Had these directions been given, the order would naturally have been transmitted through me. I heard no order on that subject."

And Gen. Porter says, "There was no dragging of brush, nor such a project thought of, although Gen. Stuart so states in his report. Gen. Pope harps on it." The conclusion suggested is that the statement contained in Stuart's report is false, because *Robertson had never heard of it.*

"*There are more things in heaven and earth than were ever dreamt of in your philosophy, Horatio!*" Now, Gen. Robertson is mistaken in saying that we had no cavalry in the direction from which Porter approached *but his*; Stuart was there in person with a part of Fitz Lee's brigade. Gen. Rosser, who was then a colonel in Lee's brigade, says: "When Stuart joined me he notified me that the enemy was moving on our right flank, and ordered me to move my command up and down the dusty road, and to drag brush, and thus create a heavy dust, as though troops were in motion. I kept this up at least four or five hours." Robertson was relieved by Stuart of his command immediately after the battle, and sent back to a camp of instruction.

As Gen. Porter was not inside the Confederate lines that day, it is hard to understand how he could know that the brush was not dragged to raise a dust to deceive him, or that nothing of the sort was thought of. I am glad that he has been relieved of an unjust sentence; but I am not willing to be silent now, when "young Harry Percy's spur is cold," and see his reputation sacrificed to save Gen. Porter's.

# Reminiscences by the Surgeon of Mosby's Command

# Contents

| | |
|---|---|
| Preface | 167 |
| Meeting with Mosby | 171 |
| Officers and Men Eager to Join the Partisan Command | 177 |
| Mosby Wounded | 183 |
| The Wounded Chief | 189 |
| Inconsistencies of Patriotism | 194 |
| Major Blaizor's Expedition, Defeat and Capture | 200 |
| Successful Pursuit of the Enemy | 205 |
| Escape on the House Top | 212 |
| A Desperate Attempt at Rescue | 219 |
| Mosby's Return to the Command | 223 |
| Union Men and Quakers | 228 |
| Mosby's Successful Ambush | 236 |
| First News of the Fall of Richmond and Surrender of Lee | 242 |
| The Work Still Goes Bravely on | 248 |
| The Chief Excluded from Parole | 254 |
| A Flag of Truce | 260 |
| A Negro Slave's Conception of a Yankee | 266 |
| A Cruel Order Countermanded | 270 |

| | |
|---|---|
| Colonel Chapman Mistaken for Mosby | 275 |
| Description of the General and his Surgeon | 281 |
| Return from Winchester | 286 |
| The Curtain Falls upon the Last Act | 291 |
| Sketches of Prison Life by a Guerrilla | 296 |

# Preface

These papers were written more than a dozen years after the last eight thousand Confederate muskets had been stacked at Appomattox. It was only at the request of esteemed army comrades, whose memory seemed to linger yet, with the cold ashes of long extinguished camp-fires, that they were written at all. These thoughts were transmitted to paper under the pressure of extraordinary and exacting professional labours. The opinions and sentiments expressed, are the shadows and reflections, of uncommon events and startling scenes. Many years afterwards, an accomplished physician and an estimable gentleman, Dr. J. B. Brewster, of Plymouth, Massachusetts, read these papers. He advised and recommended their publication.

Whilst in his possession for examination, he submitted them to a severe test of merit. They were placed in the hands of the Rev. Frederick N. Knapp, of Plymouth. This distinguished scholar, philanthropist, and patriot, was a warm personal friend of the illustrious General Grant and the lamented Lincoln. He had held a high position on the National Sanitary Commission during the war. It would not be reasonable to anticipate for the literary labours of a partisan Major of medicine, a very flattering criticism from such an exalted source.

This excellent man, noted alike for high literary attainments, pure patriotism, and exalted Christian virtues, generously tendered his valuable services "to review these papers for the press." He was suddenly removed by death, and called to his reward before he completed his task. His valuable suggestions, however, have been carefully observed. Many "passages which might have given pain or annoyance" have been omitted.

The following criticism from this distinguished son of Massachusetts needs no extended explanation:

Plymouth, Mass., July 16, 1888.

My Dear Doctor—I have looked over with care *The Reminiscences of the War by the Surgeon, of Mosby's Command.* They are of great interest and value. They should be published after some passages which might give pain or annoyance, perhaps, are cut out.

They present details of the war such as I have not elsewhere seen. They evidently are an honest transcript of the feelings and impressions of a clear-headed, earnest Confederate, who was by Mosby's side during those most trying days, including the days of the surrender. The generous tone in which the writer gives his impressions of the cordial greeting and kind fellowship of the Union generals at the time of the surrender of the Confederate army, is admirable. So also is the graphic setting forth, previously, of what a Yankee stood for in the eyes of the South. The tribute to Lincoln, coming from the source it did, is full of pathos. Whatever is exaggerated or severe in any of these papers can readily be accepted, as a most natural fruit of the circumstances under which these experiences were obtained. What is caustic in tone can now cause no ill feeling, or lead to reproach. It portrays what was, not what is. We want facts just as they were. These papers admit us to a most interesting gallery, where we may see drawn, with a bold, if sometimes dashing hand, pictures of the war as seen by a Confederate officer.

I would with pleasure, if it should be desired, assist in reviewing these papers for the press.

Yours, truly,

Frederick N. Knapp.
Dr. J. E. Brewster.

In answer to a letter recalling the papers, after the death of Mr. Knapp, the following from Dr. Brewster was received:

Plymouth, February 9, 1889.

Dr. A. Monteiro:

Dear Doctor—I received your note of January 24th, and thank you for the kindness expressed. In your brief correspondence, you have read correctly the character of Mr. Knapp. He was, as you have said, "a noble patriot and philanthropist." Our whole community mourns him as a dear friend gone. I return the papers, as you requested, and regret deeply that the opportunity was not afforded Mr. Knapp to have assisted you in their publication. Death only has prevented. He was very much interested, and very anxious to have them given to the public. Now, dear doctor, let me assure you of my very great regard for yourself, and that I shall ever consider your acquaintance as the pleasantest souvenir of my trip South.

Very truly yours,

J. B. Brewster.

Chapter 1

# Meeting with Mosby

The gallant sons of the South had gathered around their last stronghold—the devoted city of Petersburg. The long drawn-out legions of General Grant, that persistent, stubborn child of fortune, encircled the withered remnant of what was once the invincible Army of Northern Virginia. (To the heart of a Confederate veteran, what memories cluster around that name! ) Like a starved lion within the inexorable folds of an anaconda, that skeleton band of heroes resisted the contracting lines of overwhelming numbers with a heroism and courage that the ghost of Leonidas, after the lapse of two thousand years, might gracefully inscribe over the graves of his three hundred Spartans that defended the pass at Thermopylae. The eventful summer of 1864 was drawing to a gloomy autumn, with the fast declining hopes of all true sons of the South, those devoted though daring and doomed followers of our immortal Lee.

A three-months' storm, both day and night, of shot and shell had poured into the Confederate lines an incessant fire that would convert Milton's description of hell into a paradise when compared with the defences of Petersburg in the summer of 1864. It was late in the month of October, while on duty as surgeon of the Twenty-sixth Virginia regiment, Wise's brigade, I was ordered to take charge of a train of wounded men and transport them to the hospitals at Richmond. This mutilated cargo of suffering humanity had to be removed under the fire of the enemy's guns. So closely were their lines drawn upon us that our hospital flags were saluted with blazing artillery and our trains of wounded serenaded with screaming shells.

On my return from Richmond, when the train stopped at Chester for fuel and water, I stepped off to make a hasty call on two old comrades at that post. I was accosted by a gentleman of decidedly striking appearance. He was dressed in the usual Confederate uniform of a cavalry officer with the rank of colonel. There was something about this officer's appearance that would attract the attention of the most indifferent observer. I could trace something like a familiar expression, particularly of his eyes, recalling scenes or emotions long since past, but not entirely forgotten. He wore a rough, unkempt beard that imparted a wild yet care-worn expression to his otherwise animated and somewhat fierce physiognomy. A very grim smile, that recalled reminiscences of a long past era, and a warm, cordial grasp of the hand, convinced me at once that I had accidentally stumbled upon an old acquaintance in disguise.

Fourteen years before this interview, I had formed the acquaintance and friendship of a youthful student at the University of Virginia. At that time, though my junior by several years, he had already made a considerable reputation in the-active line of hostile encounters with his fellow-students and the overbearing civil authorities of the town of Charlottesville. As we were attached to different schools at the university, we were not so constantly thrown together as if belonging to the same class. My young friend was a student of the law class, whilst my studies were those of the medical department. I must confess that there was nothing very remarkable about this young limb of the law during his school days, with the exception of a well-marked ruling passion to fight on all possible occasions.

The feud ever existing between the university students and the citizens of the town of Charlottesville was once ignited into a full blaze of hostility by an overbearing civil officer, with a sort of despotic disposition, attempting to arrest my young friend for whistling on the public highway. The town constable, in the role of petty tyrant, issued an order that forbade students to whistle on the streets of the good town of Charlottesville. Like most high-spirited young gentlemen, my youthful friend claimed the right to whistle. The despotic officer was a man of powerful and gigantic physique, and attempted by violent means to execute his anti-whistling decree. The student, though in stature a mere child, seized the club of the official Goliah, wrenched it from his hand, and belaboured the giant until he yelled aloud for help, to save him from the ferocity of his Lilliputian adversary.

The *unequal* contest was speedily brought to a termination by the united force of the corporate authorities, whose combined powers succeeded in arresting and imprisoning this diminutive, though daring and belligerent student. A long and tedious trial followed this adventure, and my young friend was meantime confined within the sombre walls of that dread abode, the Albemarle jail. I visited him often during his incarceration, and generally found him busily engaged in sounding the unfathomable mysteries of Coke, Blackstone, Vattel, and other brain-defying absurdities of legal lore. I yet believe that he acquired more real knowledge of that mystical nonsense called law within the prisoner's cell than he would have accomplished within the more airy and pleasant precincts of the lecture-room.

Of all my university friends and acquaintances this youthful prisoner would have been the last one I would have selected with the least expectation that the world would ever hear from him again. Many bright and promising sons of Virginia matriculated at her favourite institution of learning at the session of 1850-'51; yet no name out of five hundred students of that session has been more admired for dauntless courage, or absurdly damned for political treason, than that of my youthful and belligerent friend. The lapse of fourteen years had changed the smooth-faced, beardless boy of seventeen summers to the war-scarred and hard-featured veteran soldier of thirty-one. I could yet trace a likeness of the boy in the bronzed face of the grim-visaged leader.

"Have you forgotten me?" he enquired, with as pleasant smile as could illumine such a face as his. The sound of his voice and a certain manner that even the rough hand of time and ghastly scenes of carnage could not change, brought up with the magic of thought a living picture of the youthful prisoner. Time had indeed changed the stripling student of law into the already famous partisan leader and guerrilla chief, John S. Mosby. That was the first time I had seen him since our college days; and I now discovered that the name so distinguished for daring, intrepidity, cunning, and dauntless courage belonged to the insignificant boy who was arrested and tried for beating old George Slaughter, the gigantic town constable of Charlottesville, with his own club. The partisan chief informed me that he was then on his way to General Lee's headquarters with important information; that he was anxious to return to his command with as little delay as possible, and asked me if I would be willing to go up and act as surgeon of his battalion. If I would consent, he proposed to go with me to the army headquarters and make all necessary arrangements for my assignment.

I was glad of an opportunity to satisfy a very reasonable curiosity in regard to that peculiar mode of warfare and the causes of such extraordinary military success as my friend had accomplished. I at once consented to serve him as surgeon. With a painful experience of military red tape, running through a period of three years in the field, I had strong reasons to doubt the ability of Colonel Mosby, or any other man, to overcome the Rip Van Winkle tendency of chronic habit. I had on more than one occasion lost many months in consummating what common sense, without red tape, could have accomplished in as many hours. He who has passed through the circumlocution offices of the medical, quartermaster, or commissary departments of an army, will never forget his disappointments and his acute disgust for official authority, engendered by a uniform failure to accomplish the smallest object with the most lavish expenditure of time.

With a strong doubt of Colonel Mosby's ability to have me transferred to the partisan battalion, I yet hoped for his success. We proceeded by the train to Petersburg. When we arrived at my hospital, above the city, I ordered my horse to be saddled for Colonel Mosby, borrowed Dr. Edmund Mason's horse for my own use, and we rode directly to the headquarters of the Army of Northern Virginia. General Lee was with his staff occupying a house on the plank road several miles west of Petersburg. Ten minutes' ride brought us to the door of the great Confederate chief. His care-worn features, stern, earnest, manly, and sad expression, for the first time in three eventful years of war, weakened my hopes in the final success of our cause.

I shall never forget the earnest look, and the warm, almost affectionate greeting the partisan chief and the Confederate surgeon received from this big-hearted Christian soldier. I have never looked into such eyes as his. His great soul was tortured by doubt verging upon despair. In the face of the dire peril that hung like a funeral pall over the fair land he loved so well, there was a deep meaning in his steady gaze that I have never seen in any other eyes than his. It has been poetically said that the eye is the window of the soul. In the dark gloom that foreshadowed the dissolution of our country, kindled with a blaze that even brightened the gloom of despair, I looked through a dazzling and beautiful window into the most magnificent soul that ever gave immortality to man.

The noble and stately chief sat alone, in a small, plain room, surrounded by maps and papers. As we entered he arose with majestic mien, advanced, and cordially grasped our hands. With few but earnest words the partisan leader detailed the startling achievements of his gallant clan in Northern Virginia. Mosby, at that period of the war, with his eight hundred rangers, commanded all of Northern Virginia not occupied by the enemy. I had never known until this interview between the rough rider and his great commander, how important was the little band known as the Forty-Third battalion of Virginia Cavalry to the general welfare of the Confederate cause.

The idol of the army thanked the brave partisan for the great services he had rendered, and told him that the army was under obligations to him for signal and efficient work in holding at bay large bodies of the enemy, and for the capture of valuable supplies, so essential to our suffering troops. The colonel, in his usual curt and snappish manner, said: "General, I want my friend here assigned to my command. I have only an assistant surgeon; I am entitled to a surgeon. He is an old friend, and I want him with me."

"It will give me pleasure to assist you in any way," replied General Lee; "but I have no control over this matter more than to request the Medical Director, Dr. Guild, to grant your wish if possible."

With this short interview I left the presence of this great soldier and pure Christian never to look into his manly face again. A short gallop carried us to the Appomattox river. We crossed on a pontoon bridge to the headquarters of the Medical Director of the Army of Northern Virginia. We dismounted and entered the tent of Dr. Lafayette Guild. The distinguished head of the medical department of the field was fast asleep. Whether the soporific condition of the medical director could be ascribed to brain exhaustion, fatigue, or the proverbial effect of the atmosphere of the county of Chesterfield I know not, but it was with some difficulty that I aroused him, and introduced Colonel Mosby. The partisan chief, being a man of few words and remarkable quickness of thought and action, promptly, positively and bluntly stated the object of his visit, and asked that his friend be assigned to duty with his battalion. "I am very sorry to disappoint you," said the sleepy medical director, "but I cannot make any changes now in the Medical Department of the army."

At this abrupt and unexpected refusal the colonel made as gallant a charge upon the great head of the Medical Department of the Army of Northern Virginia as he had ever made upon the Yankees. He seemed to lose all control of his temper, and dashed into the sleepy representative of martial physic. The doctor was aroused and wide awake in less time than it takes me to write this sentence.

"This is infamous red tape," said the irate colonel. "This is the devil's work in all military matters. This red tape is the halter of stupidity and indolence that has strangled General Lee and starved the armies of the South. I shall not submit to it. You shall at once grant what I ask, or I will get an order from the Secretary of War this very night and have it delivered in the morning."

The sudden, snappish and galvanic manner in which the above, "or words to that effect," were discharged, aroused the doctor to as wakeful a condition as his phlegmatic nature would admit. Turning to me he asked: "Doctor, what Colonel Mosby is this, anyhow?" On being informed that he was in the presence of the renowned partisan leader of Northern Virginia, with an air of surprise he reached out his hand to Mosby, apologised for not recognising him before, and expressed pleasure in making his acquaintance. He hurriedly assured him that his wish should be immediately complied with. The colonel grinned a ghastly grin, and told the military medicine man that he had at last adopted the proper method of dispatching important business, and galloped off with the promise that I should surely hear from him next morning.

CHAPTER 2

# Officers and Men Eager to Join the Partisan Command

The visit of Colonel Mosby to the medical department of Wise's brigade aroused all the latent curiosity of that command. Many were the questions asked by officers and men regarding the purpose of his visit. A rumour sprang up that Mosby was recruiting to fill the wasted companies of his battalion. The peculiar fascinations of partisan life, added to the brilliant record he had already made as an independent leader, his daring adventures and successful raids, mingled with a charming spirit of romance and the capture of dazzling spoils, excited the strongest emotions and kindled the liveliest ambition in the hearts of the old soldiers of the regular service.

Officers and enlisted men crowded my tent anxiously and earnestly requesting that they be transferred to the free-and-easy battalion of partisan rangers. Many commissioned officers expressed their willingness to join Mosby as private soldiers. I had the good fortune to make many friends in the old brigade, and when the rumour ripened into the fact that I was preparing to leave that old heroic band forever, many of the rough, bronzed faces around me were moistened by honest tears that had neither hypocrisy nor selfishness in them. I never shall forget the emotions excited by this final parting.

Men accustomed to the presence of death in its most hideous and revolting forms; veteran soldiers who were ever in readiness to die in defence of their country; brave souls that only a few weeks before had fearlessly looked down into the very cannon's mouth in that saturnalia of death at the murderous crater; sun-burnt, weather-beaten and battle-scarred heroes of the war, whose eyes brightened at the gleam of the bayonet charge, who never faltered in deadliest shock of battle, shed tears at the final parting with a comrade and a friend. I have not forgotten you, my brave companions of the blood-marked battlefield, and never shall forget you.

Many sons of old Virginia, 'tis sadly true, have been wrapped in the gloomy folds of the old Confederate blanket, and buried in obscure and shallow graves; but such souls as the true Confederate soldier carried into battle, cannot die, neither can they be wrapped in the army blanket nor buried in a shallow grave. The truly great men of the war have mingled their dust with mother earth all the way from Gettysburg to Chickamauga, while fate has decreed the cheap humanity of the survivor and the conqueror, to revel in ill-gotten wealth at home and abroad, even amidst the despotic, rotten and corrupt kingdoms of the Old World. The brave defenders of their country's honour fell in battle, while the coarse, cheap pets of prostituted fame carouse with kings and take lessons in republican liberty from the jewelled hand of royal despotism. Time alone will place the monarch and the peasant, the hero and the despot, the sage and the sot, on the same eternal plane of everlasting equity

*Weighed in the balance, hero dust*
*Is vile as vulgar clay;*
*Thy scales, Mortality, are just*
*To all who pass away.*

It is difficult for people unaccustomed to camp life to understand how the grotesque and the beautiful, the sublime and the ludicrous, are so intimately blended in a soldier's life. My friend, Dr. Wm. Hoskins, was the surgeon of the Fifty-ninth Virginia regiment. He placed over my tent a rough board, on which appeared the attractive inscription, "Recruiting Office for Mosby's Battalion." This cunning display of poetical wit on the part of my friend Hoskins brought all kinds of military candidates to my quarters. Commissioned officers of high rank were willing to exchange their commissions for a place in the ranks of the partisan battalion; wounded and invalid soldiers crawled out of their hospital tents and tendered their services; old veterans of a hundred fights hobbled around with one leg or one arm, declaring they could follow Mosby, and begging to be transferred to him. While the impression that I was a recruiting officer continued, Donnybrook fair was a well-disciplined place, and even Bedlam a quiet abode, compared with the scenes around the medical department of Wise's brigade.

Earnest and repeated denial of the rumour failed to convince the zealous applicants that I was not a recruiting officer for the distinguished partisan chief. Much to the disappointment of my friend, Dr. Hoskins, who seemed to enjoy his fun in proportion to my perplexity, a courier delivered my order from the Secretary of War, to "Report without delay to Colonel J. S. Mosby for duty." The anxious candidates for partisan honours became convinced, and seemed, though slowly, to comprehend the situation when the order from the War Department was made known to them, though a few, like doubting Thomas, insisted on seeing and handling the paper itself.

This order severed me forever from the gallant band of heroes known as Wise's brigade. To the reader unacquainted with medico-military matters, it would be extremely difficult to convey in language the aggregate stupidity attending the cruel meanderings of the medical department of an army. From the cerebrum to the caudal appendix of this department, individual egotism and general imbecility prevail. "May the angels and ministers of grace" watch and defend a brave army against the diabolical machinery of organic military medicine. It is sadly disgusting in civil life to witness professional men without brains, secure behind fortifications of the time-honoured idiocy called professional etiquette, show their contempt for human right and human life.

But these creatures are powerless in private practice, and succeed in their imposture only through the ignorance of their unlucky patrons. Unfortunately, in military medicine, the fool and the charlatan is powerful if he has procured a commission through the pusillanimous influence of nepotism. The uncles, the sisters, and the aunts of a medical association, like those of a military association, have been known to raise contemptible imposters to places of great power and responsibility.

With a singleness of purpose I served the Southern cause, and a fidelity of which I am not ashamed even in these days of reconstruction. From its bright incipiency to its gloomy close, I guarded as best I could every avenue through which danger or damage could approach our ill-fated government. With a deep interest in my own department, I worked earnestly in behalf of the wounded and the sick. After years of the best thought I am capable of bestowing upon this interesting subject, I am forced by the irresistible logic of facts to declare that of all the causes that conspire to increase and intensify the cruelties of war, without excepting the numerous diseases and injuries, the multiform miseries of idiopathic, contagious or infectious disorders, a drunken, mal-administration of the medical department constitutes the most dire affliction that can befall an army in the field.

The veiled prophet of Khorassan was less cruel to his unhappy and deluded followers than were the executive methods of Confederate medicine to the sick and wounded soldiers of our unfortunate army. The chief duties of this department seemed to be clerical: To keep books; to order the largest number of wounded men to be transported the greatest possible distances by the roughest modes of transportation; to refuse all needed supplies to the surgeons in the field; to encourage all medical officers to be as cruel and severe to the sick and wounded as possible; to prevent the examining boards from discharging maimed, crippled, or consumptive soldiers; to avoid by strict care the appointment of intelligent or qualified surgeons to positions of responsibility, were the chief functions of the surgeon-general's office.

Should a surgeon be so indiscreet as to manifest any human feeling or sympathy for the sick or wounded under his care, he would surely be reprimanded for the kindness of his heart. To please the head of the department, surgeons must be cruel, stern, severe; and, above all things, stupid, submissive and sycophantic. To manifest the smallest degree of intelligence, or exhibit any sympathy at all, or display the least kindness of heart toward a suffering soldier, would surely incur the displeasure of all the prominent officers of the Medical Department of the army.

No surgeon was promoted, or even respected, if he was not both stupid and despotic. Ignorance and presumption, as a rule, with blood relations in power, were the chief factors of promotion or of obtaining soft positions in the army, and more particularly in the medical wing of the military service. The circumstances that environed my application for a surgeon's commission were amusing, if not ludicrous. I procured certificates of scientific qualifications and moral character from the purest, ablest, and most distinguished medical men and officers in the army and in civil life. Among the prominent names in my profession were those of Professors James L. Cabell and John Staige Davies, of the University of Virginia, my preceptors and friends.

These testimonials were presented to the executive head of the medical department, to enable me to procure permission to be examined by a board of *distinguished Southern experts*. I was not more surprised than disgusted when the great Mogul in authority told me, without blushing, that the names I presented, though known to the scientific people of two continents, were *unknown to him!* He insisted that I should present certificates from people of his acquaintance. The contempt and disgust inspired by this incident increased my determination to succeed. I made a diligent search for such unknown creatures as were likely to enjoy the friendship of a great man.

Through the kindness of my ever-valued friend, Dr. James Beale, of Richmond, my research was rewarded by the discovery of two obscure medical students One had been a pupil in my office; the other was of worse than doubtful reputation, but both were favourites with the office that represented the big end of the medical department. I easily procured the signatures of these unknown stripplings, and soon discovered they were far more influential with the ruling power than were the distinguished names before presented. Strange as it may seem to the civilized reader, the autographs of these pet boys, like the tear of the penitent criminal found by the Peri, gained admittance to the august tribunal of medical qualification. I had often before the war been catechised by very distinguished professors, and always succeeded in impressing them with a belief that I was proficient in the healing art. I now had to face a very different tribunal.

A real Confederate examining board is a very different body of men from the faculties of the University of Virginia and the Jefferson Medical College of Philadelphia. These learned Southern experts held certain doctrines and fine-drawn theories that no other people held. The first proposition that startled me was the differential diagnosis between a Confederate soldier and any other soldier from a surgical standpoint. I knew of several intellectual peculiarities of the Confederate soldier that no other soldier possessed. One was that he would receive Confederate money for his services—an act that no other sane individual would commit—but that his physical being differed from that of other men, and that he demanded a different system of medical and surgical treatment than other people, I was not prepared to admit. My examination was not difficult but peculiar.

I recognised one member of the board of examiners as a classmate. I had spent many months with him in the lecture-room of the university. As a medical student he was dignified and silent. He rarely condescended to answer any question addressed to him in class. He left that institution of learning without a diploma, but his father possessed cash, and a voyage to the city of Paris no doubt gave him a passport to an elevated position in the medical department of our new government.

Another member was eccentric. He died by suicide soon after the war. One other member owed his promotion to nepotism—a very common disease at that time. A fourth member was very drunk. He died in that way soon after my examination. The fifth and last member was a scientific gentleman and thoroughly qualified for the responsible position he occupied. The only peculiarity of disposition that marked these learned and privileged gentlemen was the punctuality they displayed in drawing their salaries in Confederate money, and in writing quaint essays on diseases incident to the Confederate soldier and gun-shot wounds of the *human intellect* generally. I enjoyed the rare good fortune of reading several curious productions of this sort before my examination, and it is probable my *good luck* and success in passing this comical ordeal may be ascribed to that accident. One of these professional sages held that gun-shot wounds of the lung should be treated, *a la Dr. Sangrado*, by copious blood-letting. His opponent held an opposite *doctrine*. This very question confronted me: I could not please one of my tormentors without offending the other.

I was compelled to hedge on common sense to escape defeat, and answered boldly that, "to the best of my knowledge and belief, both methods had been eminently successful in Chinese surgery, and that if both gentlemen happened to be present on any battlefield where I was on duty (a very improbable hypothesis, as government pets are cautious animals,) I would, by their authority, treat all traumatic affections of the Confederate lung both ways." This answer pleased the scientific jury, and I was acquitted of professional heresy and commissioned to kill, *secundum artem*, and to draw from the Confederate treasury one hundred and sixty-two dollars per month in a sort of *infidel* currency that knew not a redeemer.

## Chapter 3

# Mosby Wounded

With the aid of my assistant surgeon, Dr. Bristow and faithful hospital steward, Dr. Leigh, a carefully prepared report of all the sick and wounded of the regiment, for the period of one month, was duly rendered the surgeon-general. My friend, Colonel Tabb, one of the bravest and most chivalrous officers of the army, requested me to delay my departure a few days and accompany him to Richmond, where he anticipated a matrimonial union with one of the fairest daughters of the Confederate capital. I promised to gratify my brave comrade and witness that most interesting and happy event of human life—the union of two hearts that love. I fulfilled the promise and witnessed the marriage of the knightly groom and the beautiful bride.

Only fourteen years, (as at 1890), have swept with dark and funereal wing over that bright and joyous scene—the beautiful flower faded and died; the young wife has been sleeping for years in the grave, and the noble husband has followed her to that dark abode! This officer was as insensible to fear as the heroic Frenchman, Marshal Ney. If Napoleon could designate his great lieutenant—amidst thousands of dauntless veterans—as *"the bravest of the brave,"* surely that distinguished honour could be worn as meritoriously and as gracefully by my warm-hearted friend and gallant comrade, Colonel Tabb.

Before taking my departure from the regular service, I visited, amongst other officers, the statesman and soldier who bequeathed a name to the old brigade. General H.A. Wise occupied a small wooden house near the western suburbs of Petersburg. I found this representative specimen of Virginia's genius engaged in a very animated discussion of the probable results of the war with his old friend, Mr. Parker, from the county of Accomac. Mr. Parker exhibited the same fiery vehemence in discussion so characteristic of General Wise. It was amusing and entertaining to witness these two active and impetuous old gentlemen wrestle in playful controversy. It was an intellectual gladiatorial encounter. They were old friends, and indulged in the widest latitudes of freedom with each other, and were well matched in wit, quickness of thought, and sarcasm.

Their rapid and sharp criticisms of the imaginary faults and frailties of each other constituted one of the most interesting exhibitions I have ever enjoyed. Rapid and brilliant scintillations of wit would snap and flash from one to the other like sparks of electric fluid from the poles of a strong galvanic battery. After silently awaiting a pause in the storm of words that played upon the auditorial nerves like the music of a nail factory, I informed General Wise that I had been ordered to report to Mosby, and must leave his brigade. The old gentleman had been tuned to concert pitch by the boisterous encounter with his verbose companion. Abruptly turning upon me, with that inimitable mimic expression of displeasure and anger that only General Wise could assume, he asked if I was in earnest. "Are you going to leave the Twenty-Sixth regiment, sir; my brigade, sir? Do you know that Mosby fights under the black flag, sir? Do you desire to be captured and hung, sir?" and, with that peculiar shake of the head and clenching of teeth so characteristic of the man, with increased emphasis, he repeated:

"Will be hung, sir; hung by the neck like a dog, sir; hung to a tree, sir, as certain as you leave my brigade, sir, and join that band of pirates. 'The worst part is, that you will deserve to suffer, sir, for leaving my poor Twenty-Sixth regiment, sir." (This was the general's pet regiment.) "I shall not object to your going, sir, if you had rather be hung than remain in my brigade. Go, sir; go, go; we can bear your loss as well as you can stand hanging."

While delivering himself of these soothing expressions, so consoling to a retiring comrade, the general was busily engaged in pulling off one of his boots. Impressed with the idea that the old hero was "troubled with corns," that may have contributed somewhat to his accustomed irritability of temper, I was not surprised at this manoeuvre, but there was something ludicrous in his gesture and gait as he awkwardly advanced to me, boot in hand, and quietly requested that I would take off one of my boots and try his on. I asked a reason for this singular proceeding.

"You see, my boots are nearly worn out," was the reply, "and I can't get another pair; there is no good leather in the Confederacy, and I can't wear bull's hide. If my boot fits you, I want you to send me the best pair you capture from the d——d Yankees; try them on; and I don't want you to wait for a second capture; send me the first you get, for they will hang you before you get another choice. I am an old man; I know more than you do about black flags; they will hang you, sir; hang you. Send me the boots before they catch you."

I confess this prophetic language did not increase my relish for the new field of service before me. I had already been informed that the chaplain of Mosby's command had been hung to a tree for no other offense than praying for the partisan battalion. I had no cause to expect more leniency than the unfortunate young preacher had received. If the pious non-combatant was hung for ministering to the diseased Confederate soul, what plea for mercy could be sustained in behalf of the less godly surgeon, whose art only ministered to the rebel body? But, with unshaken confidence in the truth of the saying, that "catching comes before hanging," I bade an affectionate *adieu* to the fiery old general and his staff, with the promise that I would not forget his boots should a Yankee of the proper size, with boots of the proper make, be captured before my time came, according to his prophesy, to be hung.

At this period of the war no commissioned officer or soldier could walk the streets of any city in Virginia without being arrested, unless protected by a pass or order, signed by officers of high rank. I have sometimes thought that, if half the men on conscript duty had been in active service in the field, the result of the war would have been different; and it is possible that Washington, and not Appomattox, would have seen its termination. The last few years of the desperate and unequal struggle found the Army of Northern Virginia growing weaker and smaller, while the home guards and conscript forces grew larger and stronger every year. This department of the service was becoming more popular as the struggle became warmer and more desperate. The streets of our cities were filled with guards, whose only or chief duty seemed to be to keep out of the army themselves and put every invalid and wounded veteran back into the ranks again.

To see able-bodied loafers, musket in hand, on every street corner and on every sidewalk, while lame, crippled soldiers were performing active duty in the field, became one of the most unpromising and revolting phenomena of the closing scenes of the war. The home guards and conscript bureaus became the refuge of safety and comfort for the favourites and pets of authority; young and green lieutenants could save their reputations and their innocent bodies by this ingenious military contrivance; and the soft sons, nephews and cousins of all the *rear action* officials in power sought shelter and ease in these pleasant and safe bombproof establishments.

On leaving Petersburg *en route* to Mosby's command, no sooner had I stepped from the railway train in Richmond, than one of these vigilant conscript-hunters, noticing my uniform, worn and dusty, at once believed me to be one of the old veterans of the field who should not be permitted to enjoy the freedom, or the luxuries of a city even for a moment. He promptly advanced, dropped the butt of his musket heavily upon the pavement, and, with the characteristic whining twang of the chronic guard, not easily forgotten but impossible to describe with the pen, said: "Ha-lt! pa-ss!" at the same time extending his hand to receive whatever paper authority I might be fortunate enough to possess.

I presented my order, from the Secretary of War to report to Colonel J. S Mosby. At this, the potent engine of belligerent authority, with musket attachment, informed me that he could not read (like a true and candid disciple of Dr. Dabney's creed). He gruffly ordered me to read my own passport for him. It did not occur to this vigilant watchman on the outposts of Southern liberty, that I could deceive him at pleasure by reading from imagination instead of the paper before me.

I read the order as it was written, and also the name of the highest officer of the military department of the government, as my authority for travelling by the most speedy and direct route, in obedience to the high command of the yet powerful Confederate rule, from the regular army to the partisan command. On hearing the order read, a rapid change came over the spirit of my newly made and inquisitive acquaintance. He suddenly changed his tone of authority, and expressed a strong desire to exchange places with me. He said he had heard so much of Mosby, and his men lived so well and made so much money, that, if I had no objection to taking his place and his musket, he would be very glad to take mine, and promised faithfully that he would not desert, but do his duty like a man. With the firm belief that he would get rich on partisan spoils in a very short time, he begged me to take him with me if I would not exchange places with him. So popular was the partisan band at this period of the war, that an unsophisticated guard could be easily seduced from duty by its charm of novelty and romance, with the spice of avarice attached.

This ignorant guard had heard marvellous stories about the immense wealth captured by Mosby. He told of certain Yankee pay masters being captured and relieved of millions at a single raid. His eyes moistened with emotion as he related to me the bright pecuniary prospects for us both, if I would only agree to take him with me, and even went far enough to promise I should be a partner in his expected spoils if I would comply with his very reasonable request.

I have related this simple incident to elucidate the general sentiment of the army regarding the prospective pleasures and profits of the guerrilla service.

After remaining only one day in Richmond, to procure proper equipments of partisan life, I proceeded directly to the county of Albemarle. On arriving at Charlottesville, I learned that my new leader had returned to his command the day following my last interview with him at Petersburg; had been seriously, if not mortally, wounded, and would be conveyed to his father's house near Lynchburg, if not captured by the enemy. I remained in Charlottesville that night, and heard it rumoured that he was dead and his body had been sent to McIvor depot, near the home of his father. Before the departure of the evening train for Lynchburg another rumour came that he was not dead, but seriously wounded. I proceeded at once to McIvor depot, and there learned that my friend was at his father's, a short distance from the depot. I was glad to find him in much better condition than I had cause to expect. He was cheerful, though in considerable pain. This was the seventh wound he had received from the enemy.

Though feeble from haemorrhage he was able to give me a graphic and interesting account of his adventures since our recent parting. Two days after leaving my camp near Petersburg, he was skirmishing with a large force of the enemy at Rector's cross-roads, in Fauquier county. At night he rode in company with two of his men to the house of Mr. Lud. Lake, only three miles from the enemy's camp. While at supper a strong force of the enemy surrounded the house and fired on him through the windows. One bullet entered his left side below the heart, and passing around his body, lodged under the skin on the right side. He fell to the floor, yet retained presence of mind sufficient to take off his jacket, with the mark of his rank upon it, and conceal it under a small bed before the assassins entered the room.

A Federal officer, followed by a number of men, rushed in upon the wounded colonel. The officer examined the wound carefully, and saying it was mortal, asked his name and command. The colonel feebly replied that his name was Wilson, and that he was a lieutenant of the Sixth Virginia cavalry. The appreciative murderer, with true military *sang froid*, said to Mr. Lud. Lake, "Have him decently buried; he seems to be a brave soldier." While the gallant colonel was pretending to be much worse than he really was, and the Yankee major delivered himself of a sympathetic eulogy over what he supposed to be a dying soldier, his followers were busily engaged in relieving the victim of his boots. They also found his overcoat and hat. With this capture of personal property, they departed, without suspecting the importance of the unknown officer they had robbed and left, as they supposed, to die. No sooner had the unwelcome visitors left his presence than the brave colonel arose from the floor, notwithstanding his great loss of blood, and ordered Mr. Lud. Lake to furnish some sort of transportation immediately.

He knew that certain papers and dispatches contained in the pocket of his overcoat would betray him, whenever they were examined at the enemy's camp. His suspicions were well founded. Mr. Lake unfortunately had no other mode of removing the wounded colonel than a clumsy ox-cart, and two untrained calves to pull it. This quaint apparatus for "rapid transit" was soon ready, and the colonel removed several miles in a forest and carefully concealed himself with leaves and brush. A few hours after he effected his exodus from the unlucky precincts of old Lud. Lake, the entire country was closely scoured by Yankee cavalry. Papers in the pockets of the stolen overcoat, had revealed the fact that the wounded officer was no other than the renowned partisan chief. Every house was searched, and every citizen threatened with immediate death, if any were so hardened in sin or lost in iniquity, as to aid in the concealment of the dreaded guerrilla.

This active search was kept up several days. Herod's endeavour to discover the young child was not more energetic. Every well, icehouse, barnyard, and chicken coop, was examined in vain. Sharp, experienced officers and lynx-eyed enlisted men explored every hole, cavern and corner of sufficient capacity to conceal a medium sized rebel. They cast anxious glances under every bed and looked up every chimney, yet no wounded colonel did they find.

While this scrutinising investigation of field, forest and domicile progressed, Mosby rested quietly under his pile of leaves and brushwood. When the excitement of the human hunt subsided, the cunning chief emerged from his hiding place, and by the aid of an ambulance made good his escape to Gordonsville.

Chapter 4

# The Wounded Chief

I remained with my new commander until he was sufficiently improved to leave his chamber. The wound he had received was a severe one. Exhaustion from haemorrhage, with attendant inflammation and symptomatic fever, left him in a feeble and prostrated condition. His strong will and cheerful disposition resisted successfully the results of serious injury.

After the dull routine of camp life and the tiresome monotony of regular service, it was exceedingly interesting to hear from the lips of the great raider, a lively recital of his many "hair-breadth 'scapes" and daring encounters with the enemy. His description of the capture of General Stoughton made a lasting impression. I remember well the manner and zest with which he related this most remarkable incident of the war. There is something so wild and desperate in piercing the very heart of a large army, with a squad of twelve men, to capture a general in his camp, surrounded by his videttes, pickets and guard, that it reads more like the creation of fiction, than the historic realities of military life. I doubt that either ancient or modern warfare has produced a leader that combined the rare strategy and extraordinary courage requisite to plan and execute such an enterprise as Mosby consummated in the capture of General Stoughton.

His narrative was, that he selected twelve good men, and advanced cautiously through the darkness of a stormy night upon the enemy's first line of pickets. He captured them without difficulty and carried them with him. He then made prisoners of the second and third lines of pickets. They were now more than he could well guard. He then proceeded alone to the house where the general slept. The guard at the door was captured and disarmed, and ordered to act as guide to General Stoughton's room. With a pistol bearing upon his head, the prisoner slowly and reluctantly obeyed. He found the general asleep and shook him several times before he was aroused. He seemed to be only halfway conscious, and probably supposed the raider to be one of his own men. With a gruff voice and an ugly epithet, he ordered the intruder to leave and not disturb him again. Knowing that his name was not entirely devoid of interest or significance to a live Yankee, he asked the general in a rather loud tone if he had heard of Mosby? The talisrnanic name seemed to get the attention of the drowsy officer. Turning suddenly, he asked, with some interest, "Have you caught the d——d rascal?"

"No," said the chief; "but he has caught you! My name is Mosby, and you are my prisoner."

It is not reasonable to suppose that any man since the melancholy event of man's first fall, has ever been more surprised or shocked than was this general, when informed that he was Mosby's prisoner.

He was ordered to rise, dress and follow his captor. He seemed to be so reluctant and slow to obey, that the stimulus of a pistol presented to his face convinced him at once that disobedience was synonymous with death while Mosby was at one end of the pistol and he was at the other. The general and his pickets were all brought out safely and sent to Gordonsville, under guard. Compared with this adventure the boasted exploits of the old knights in the days of chivalry, pale into utter insignificance.

In the month of May, in the ever-memorable year 1862, the brave and lamented Stuart won military renown by one of the most daring adventures ever made by a small body of cavalry. This accomplished and brilliant officer performed the daring feat of leading his followers entirely around one of the largest and best equipped armies of ancient or modem times. When McClellan, with nearly two hundred thousand men, held the Confederate capital as with the grip of a giant—when the dismal sound of the alarm bells of the doomed city of Richmond carried dismay and despair into the hearts of the truest and bravest men that ever marched with steady step to the music of death—this heroic band cut its way through dense masses of the enemy's columns, severing the great body of the army from its base of supplies.

This was considered at the time one of the most wonderful achievements of modern warfare; and indeed just so long as supernatural courage is admired by mankind, will ever mark a brilliant page in the annals of history. Without detracting by comparison, from the well-earned fame of the glorious Stuart, I may ask that a flower from the garland that encircles his heroic brow, be permitted to adorn the chaplet of a much younger Confederate soldier—one who, without rank or command at that time, but acting only as a scout, had alone blazed the way for this wonderful exploit. This indomitable scout proposed the method and guided the raid, that gave such great *éclat* to the distinguished cavalry general. Mosby's consummate skill, great presence of mind, and absolute courage ministered in no small degree to Stuart's success in this perilous enterprise.

When memory bears our fancy back into the dark period of the war; when we are permitted to view through the lens of the imagination, the storm-cloud of despair, mingled with hope, that lowered for four long years like a funereal pall over our loved country; when we take a retrospective view of the dazzling flashes of heroism and self-sacrifice that gave for a brief period a silver lining to that sombre cloud, the few bright spots shine forth with a vivid glare, like a green oasis in the sandy and parched desert, falls upon the visions of the weary Arab and his faithful camel; when the fever of prejudice and the present paroxysm of injustice, gives place to reason—we may expect history to speak the truth, and render justice to the purity, manhood and patriotism of Lee; the stern faith, Christian integrity and wonderful genius of Jackson; the beautiful chivalry of Stuart, and the incomparable skill, dash, and courage of Mosby.

*Let fate do her worst, there is something of joy:*
*Sweet dreams of the past that she cannot destroy;*
*We may break, we may ruin the vase, if we will,*
*But the fragrance of roses will cling 'round it still.*

Virginia will never forget such sons, let cheap humanity whine and fret as it may. The carping outlaws of nature and the desecrators of our household gods may cast the slime of their own foul natures against the bright jewels of Virginia's crown, but the halo of true glory, that enshrines their noble deeds will illumine and expose the contemptible malice and dastardly meanness, of the coarse traducer and cowardly calumniator.

He who risks his life with the almost absolute certainty of death, in defence of his country, cannot be a bad man, or a traitor. Of the four bright names I have written, two yielded up their great souls on the field of their country's honour. They died with their harness on in the discharge of an almost sacred duty. No country can demand a more priceless gift offering than Virginia placed on the altar of liberty, in the blood of her Jackson and her Stuart. The great and pure-minded Lee, survived the dissolution of his cause for only a brief period of time. He could not live after his country died. When the Virginia that gave Washington to the world and many States and statesmen to the Union was maimed, divided, robbed, and reduced to Military District No. 1, by the reckless conqueror; when the liberty her Washington had won was lost forever, the greatest military genius our continent has known, laid down his unstained life. His big heart was broken by the shock. With the exception of Cincinnatus, our Washington offers to history the only example of refusing absolute power. The example of Lee has no parallel: A great leader, so benign in victory, so sublime in defeat, who could pause, with mingled charity and philanthropy, amid the ghastly carnage of the battlefield, and when the sun of hope went down, he placed the last gift offering—a broken heart—upon the blasted altar of his country's honour.

Only one of this heroic quartet lives, (1890). Mosby, whose remarkable military achievements makes a conspicuous chapter in Virginia's history, survives the desperate, unequal conflict of arms, that yielded so curious a conglomeration of glory and of shame. He bears on his person many honourable scars received in defence of his country; yet his good record and manly service, his unquestioned patriotism and self-sacrifices, protect him not, against the infamous calumnies of political assailants. He may well feel proud that the same high spirit and chivalry that won for him a splendid reputation in war, also bequeathed him a manly independence in time of peace. History has often borne testimony, that the most contemptible and faithless members of the human race have been found amongst the politicians of every age. Strange as it may seem to the honest reader, this brave soldier and patriotic Virginian has been persistently charged with political treason to his State and the people he loved so well and defended with such conspicuous heroism; and still more strange, the charges against him have been preferred by bombproof political demagogues who skulked to the rear when "red battle stamped her foot," and when their old mother Virginia most needed the aid of her true children.

The mercenary, who sold beer, speculated in bread, acted the part of quartermaster, and robbed the soldier of his clothing, his money and his food during the war, now, with bronzed brow and monumental cheek, steps nimbly to the front, to assail Mosby for want of patriotism. Such men must have an alloy of zinc and copper in their nature sufficient to mould at least one twenty-four pound brass howitzer.

From many recent disclosures in high political circles, it is reasonable to conclude that of such chemical elements are the average politicians constructed. From Titus Gates, who was flogged at the cart's tail through the streets of London, to Secretary Belknap, who was kicked out of Grant's Cabinet for what common people call stealing, the world has no good cause to praise the professional politician. Thomas Paine, a politician of no mean ability, deliberately insulted mankind by an unprovoked assault upon the unstained character of Washington and the holy creed of Christ.

The modern political blasphemer, true to the oblique instincts of his vicious nature, feeds upon the reputations of good men with the voracious avidity that a hungry hyena seeks a new-made grave. With an experience of many years, and a contact with good and bad men, with great men in small places and small men in great places, with honest and dishonest men, with detestable hypocrites and pure patriots, with men of unquestioned truth and with the most notorious liars, I write with the conviction of certainty, that Virginia can claim no truer son or braver soldier, nor has she ever given birth to a more honest and faithful man than John Singleton Mosby. In this narrative of war incidents, mingled with such thoughts as the stirring events of the time inspired, I am anxious to avoid misleading the reader. No man differs from the political views of my distinguished military leader more widely than does the writer.

But the man who knows Mosby and can doubt his honour, his patriotism, or his courage, must possess an obliquity of thought that reflects doubtful credit upon his own intellect. Will any sane member of society question the sincerity or integrity of the martyr while the ligatures that bound him. to the stake were cutting into his living tissues and the fierce flames scorching his quivering flesh? Can any man, *not a politician*, doubt the honour or the patriotism of Regulus, as every revolution of his cylinder of death, thrust torturing spikes into his body? When such questions can be answered in the affirmative with truth, then, and only then, can an intelligent mind receive the revolting doctrine that the heroes that suffered most and made the greatest sacrifices for their country are traitors to its cause.

CHAPTER 5

# Inconsistencies of Patriotism

One week from, the day I took charge of my wounded commander he expressed some impatience to take the saddle again and lead his gallant followers to the front. I advised him to bear philosophically the necessary delay; that it would yet be many weeks before he could with safety return to duty. His convalescence was sufficiently advanced for me to leave him. He gave me letters of introduction to his friends in Fauquier county and the officers of his command. I left him in the care of his family and departed for the stirring scenes of partisan strife. One of the difficulties that awaited me in preparing for the new service was the scarcity of horses sufficiently fleet for that peculiar and precarious warfare. The class of animals used in the regular service were unfit for the extra-hazardous risks of guerrilla life.

The safety and efficiency of the ranger depended much upon the fleetness of his horse. All the best animals within the limits of the Southern Confederacy had been stolen, captured, or pressed into service by the ubiquitous quartermaster, or the more active and indefatigable horse-thief. At this advanced and unpleasant stage of hostilities every farmer who possessed any property worth stealing would be sure to hide it. Provisions of every kind were concealed in garrets and cellars or buried in unfrequented fields. Horses, mules and cattle were often picketed out in forests, or immured in subterranean recesses and ice-houses.

All the patriotism of the South was in the army, and very little, if any of it, could be found with the home-staying male inhabitants. The true test of patriotism was not found in the father who would freely give up his youthful sons as food for villainous gunpowder, but in the man who would surrender his property for the common cause. I have known many instances of parents sending young sons to battle, where grim death awaited them, without pausing to consider the priceless value of patriotic blood.

That fluid was indeed the only cheap commodity during the strained excitement of war, and it flowed as free as water from the mountains to the sea. But who amidst the insane saturnalia of war, can forget the false reasoning and bitter opposition made: by the parents (who had given their young sons to slaughter) when the dire distress of their country demanded *pecuniary aid* in the way of slaves or other property in behalf of the government? The stern law of necessity justified the government in its merciless demands on human life. Young boys—mere children—were driven into the ranks of battle and sacrificed without a murmur of remonstrance. Life was cheap and blood was valueless. Let humanity blush!

When a horse or mule was pressed into service, a bullock taken to feed the hungry and starving soldiers, or a slave temporarily taken to aid in the construction of earthworks, or fortifications to protect the bodies of living men against the murderous storm, of shell and shot, a great cry went up, a spirit of complaint was heard throughout the land, wildly proclaiming that the government had no right to take the property of the people. At this period of the war, human life was the cheapest commodity in the Southern Confederacy, not excepting its irredeemable currency itself. That uncertain chimera had at least a constructive value, while Southern life had none.

Notwithstanding the abnormal love for property and money that marked this unhappy period, and so often outweighed the love of country, we had some noble exceptions to the general rule. I found one man, a plain, unpretending and *honest* farmer in the county of Albemarle. This man possessed a liberal disposition, a good conscience, and moderate means. His kindness and generosity I shall not soon forget. Mr. Adam Via, the "good Samaritan," lived near the village of Batesville, a hamlet not distinguished for its liberality or bigness of heart. Like many Virginians of the remote past, he had a well-developed attachment for fast horses, and was noted for keeping the best stock in his section of the county. In looking over the long list of my friends and acquaintances in my old neighbourhood, it occurred to me that if any farmer in that portion of the Piedmont region had a horse fast enough to help a partisan ranger out of a hard place, Mr. Via was certainly the man.

Mosby had informed me that it was neither proper nor safe to engage in his peculiar methods of warfare with an indifferent steed.

On leaving the railway train at North Garden depot I proceeded at once to Mr. Via's house, a distance of five miles. I found the kind and hospitable gentleman at home. He seemed to be exceedingly glad to meet his old family physician again, and I was equally well pleased to find my old patient enjoying excellent health and cheerful spirits. I soon told him that I was *en route* to Mosby's command, and was in quest of a suitable horse for that wild service, and desired him to furnish me with the best animal in his stables. I knew full well that the hard experiences of the war had made most men grasping and mercenary in proportion to the uncertainty of the struggle, and fully expected my old friend would place a high price upon the horse. My pecuniary resources at this time could not be considered in a very robust condition.

I had only a few months before this visit paid the sum of $162 (one month's salary) for one small jug of butter-milk, when Confederate money was not so depressed as at the time of this interview. I was prepared to learn that the price of an extra good horse would ascend to the vicinity of $50,000, if not higher. I confess to as much surprise as pleasure when my generous friend said he had the very horse I needed—a beautiful black, the fleetest horse in his county, and could leap the highest fence on his farm. It was his favourite horse; he would not sell him at any price, and he did not think it right to take a soldier's money, so he would not sell.

But as I had saved the lives of his two boys before the war, before I should be captured by the Yankees and hung for the want of a good horse he would consider himself guilty of murder, and he could not bear the idea, and would never forgive himself if I should be hung on his account; that if I would accept the horse as a gift he would be pleased to present me with his favourite black. From the uniform meanness of mankind we generally expect something of the same sort in every transaction of life.

A sudden flash of grateful generosity takes anyone who has suffered much intercourse with his fellow-men by surprise. As neighbour, friend and physician I had known Mr. Via for seven years, and esteemed him as a kind, genial, honest, good man. But as Confederate morals when weighed in the balance with mercenary motives had declined *pari passu* with Confederate money, I was in no intellectual condition to expect a farmer of moderate means to bequeath valuable property in consideration for only a sentimental equivalent. I accepted the valuable present from my generous friend, with the promise that should I fall under the shadows of the black flag I would remember his unselfish liberality on the very threshold of another world, and if favoured by the god of war his kindness would be returned with compound interest.

The unequal valuation of property at this dark and uncertain era of civil strife could not be rationally explained. The soldier in the field, with breast exposed to the almost unceasing storm of death-dealing shot and shell, was rewarded by his government with twelve so-called dollars of Confederate money per month. A very small cup of bad whiskey (they had no glasses) would command a price equal to a half-month's pay of a soldier in the ranks. Five years' pay of an enlisted soldier would not buy a barrel of flour for his hungry family. November, 1864, I paid $480 (equal to a major's salary for three months) for a pair of boots—and very indifferent boots they were. Real estate did not rate with *useful* commodities. The price of two barrels of the most villainous apple brandy, or still meaner and more plebeian short corn whisky, would purchase an average Virginia farm, with dwellings, outbuildings, and agricultural implements thrown in.

A wide-spread, general insanity pervaded every department of business. Men of good reputation for industry and thrift—people who were never before even suspected of lunacy in any of its forms—would, under the excitements and hallucinations incident to war, sell their lands and houses for small prices in Confederate money, and forthwith invest the proceeds in Confederate bonds or slaves. The money received for the sale of many of the best and most fertile landed estates in Virginia can yet be found safely stored away in old *hair-covered trunks* in garrets and cellars of the South awaiting the blast of Gabriel's trump, or the more tardy approach of some equally reluctant financial redeemer.

The beautiful jet black steed presented to me would have sold for a sum sufficient to purchase several hundred acres of fertile land in the fairest portion of Virginia, and my appreciation of the generous act is in just proportion of its value at that time.

One incident of interest only I remember on my way to the county of Fauquier. The Piedmont counties of Virginia were at that time infested with many thieves, military and otherwise. Marauders and footpads frequently frightened, robbed, and annoyed the wayfarer. In passing alone on horseback through the northern borders of the county of Greene, two uncouth horsemen, with shabby uniforms, badly mounted, and armed with rusty carbines and unburnished sabres, halted me in the road. I observed that they were much more impressed with the appearance of my handsome black steed than with the looks of the rider. One, the uglier of the two, in a very rude manner, with a cracked voice that seemed to issue from a fractured bagpipe, asked in a decidedly impertinent method: "Whar did you git him?"

"Get what?" I replied.

"Git that fine crittur?"

I answered them in as Chesterfield-like manner as I could then command, if they were soldiers, deserters, or horse thieves? This question, and the earnestness with which it was put, changed their method of procedure. One of the men asked what regiment I served with. I informed him that his inquiry was impertinent, and I knew not by what right he made any demand on me; but I would condescend to satisfy his very unreasonable curiosity, provided he would tell me what officer had the misfortune to command such uncouth ruffians as they appeared to be.

Without seeming to be at all vain of his associates in arms, one of them, and the uglier of the horrid twain, said, "We is McCauslan's men; an' I'd like to git that hoss you's ridin'." Finding the interview growing more unpleasant and inclining towards a more serious turn than at first, I at once concluded that a bold front and some effrontery could be made to equal the value of a good horse. Taking a pistol from the belt, I announced that I belonged to Mosby's battalion, and proposed to conduct them to their command as prisoners if the distance was not too great; and if so, I would settle the legal right to our horses then and there. The uglier of the two barbarians assured me it was all a joke; and that he had heard a good deal about Colonel Mosby and his men, and he liked them mightily from what he had "heered," and he had no notion of interfering with any of them.

These fellows looked hungry, haggard, and desperately bad—something like two badly constructed ghosts in Hamlet, on a raid; but, unlike the ghost (so far as concerned my horse), they had some "speculation" in their eyes. I confess to a feeling of discomfort or unpleasantness while in the presence of these very hard specimens of the Southern soldier. As I moved off slowly, they were disposed to follow on their lean and jaded steeds. I turned upon them and made them understand in very plain language that their presence was not agreeable, and insisted on their speedy departure; which gentle insinuation they understood and reluctantly withdrew.

Though many years have passed since this trivial though disagreeable incident transpired, I yet distinctly remember the criminal expression that played upon the features of the uglier one. His dreadful face revealed coarse brutality, dull sensualism, and habitual crime. He seemed the living image of the man so graphically described by Mr. Thomas Moore: the old wretch discovered by the Peri, whose life was portrayed in the lines of his face, that told of *"The ruined maid, the shrine profaned, with blood of guests the threshold stained."* I can but think that if the devil or his war department had use for a standing army, he would be much pleased with just such recruits as this *specimen* private of McCausland's brigade. I galloped rapidly on, through a forest, endeavouring to obliterate from memory the mental vision of that uncompromising hideous face. I cannot truly say at this late period that "his bright smile haunts me still," but I have a sort of superstitious misgiving that the same demoniac physiognomy may confront me yet in another if not a better world.

It is pleasant to turn from the painful contemplation of so grim a subject, to view the brightest phases of human nature. There is something radiant as well as dark in our lives. I cannot well describe the contrast between the kind of character I have so imperfectly delineated here and the pure, intellectual, and social atmosphere that welcomed me on my arrival at the hospitable mansion of Major Richard Henry Carter, of Fauquier. I reached Major Carter's residence (Glen Welby) on the second night of my journey from Albemarle. I was fatigued by the travel of one hundred and forty miles. Mosby had notified his friends of my probable arrival. I shall ever gratefully remember the cordial welcome and warm-hearted greeting I received, and shall always regard my short association with the refined, gentle, and accomplished family of Major Carter as one of the brightest and most pleasant epochs of my life.

CHAPTER 6

# Major Blaizor's Expedition, Defeat and Capture

The hospitable and elegant mansion, that afforded shelter to Mosby and his staff was owned by Major Richard Henry Carter, and was situated in one of the most picturesque and beautiful regions of the county of Fauquier. There was something noble and elevating about the place and its occupants; a spirit of chivalry, hospitality, and immaculate patriotism seemed to pervade the very atmosphere of Glen Welby. Even in the very storm-centre of civil war, I found in this quiet and pure Virginia home the purest principles of religion mingled with the loftiest sentiments of patriotic self-sacrifice.

Major Carter was a Virginia gentleman of the old school. Before the invaders had stripped him of his wealth the broad, fertile acres and warm hearts of Glen Welby gave life to every charitable enterprise, and shaped the refinements of fashion for the aristocracy of Fauquier. I have never invested much faith in Utopias of government, dreamed of and sought by the ancient philosophers of the mythic ages of the world. Perpetual motion and perfection of government are equally difficult to attain, and only exist in bewildered imaginations and abnormal dreams. But, so far as Utopian perfection can apply to the domestic household, the happy circle of the bright and noble family of Major Carter offers an example so free from the contaminations of earthly selfishness that I must claim for that accomplished family all that humanity can attain towards the Utopian perfection of domestic life.

Major Carter was an officer on General Lee's staff. He had returned home on a short leave of absence to find a large portion of his fine estate laid waste by the barbarous cruelty of irresponsible soldiers. His farm had been pillaged of horses, mules, slaves and sheep; all his crops either stolen or destroyed by fire; fences and out-buildings burnt; and even his stately mansion had been set on fire, but saved by the superhuman efforts of its brave tenants. How cheerfully this noble family bore the accumulated misfortunes visited upon them, only because they gave shelter to the partisan leader, presents one more bright page in the history of martyrdom quite refreshing to the philosopher when contrasted with the usual soiled selfishness of mankind. No complaint or murmur ever escaped the lips of a single member of this oppressed family.

On several occasions, when Mosby's headquarters were attacked by the enemy, and all their provisions, jewellery and clothing stolen, and their furniture destroyed, the first question I have known the heroic ladies of that household to ask when the storm subsided was, "Did they capture any of our soldiers?" forgetting, as it were, themselves in the deep interest they felt for the cause of their country.

The cordial reception I met with at Glen Welby caused me to feel as much at home as if I had only returned to the presence of old acquaintances or well-tried friends. Major Carter introduced me to several officers of the battalion who were his guests, also to his estimable lady, accomplished daughters, and charming niece. Their graceful hospitality and refined courtesy caused me to feel more like a member of that delightful family group than a stranger within their gates. Charming conversation, a few games of chess with my noble host, and some of the sweetest music I ever heard soon passed the time away. Before retiring for the night my new comrades informed me of the best modes of escape should the enemy make a raid upon the house in the night-time. Without any kind of picket, guard, or other precaution than a weasel or a fox would put before his hole, we retired for the night.

This was the first night during the four years of war that I found myself within the enemy's lines, except when engaged in actual battle. With the full knowledge that the black flag was our only ensign, and that we had no guard on duty to give alarm at the approach of the enemy, and with the further information that a large force of the enemy was encamped only a few miles from our resting-place, and that our force at headquarters consisted only of two officers besides myself, altogether made up an association of ideas not calculated to act the part of a soporific upon the nerves of a newly-initiated partisan ranger.

The adjutant of the battalion was a brother of Colonel Mosby, a youth not quite twenty years of age, yet partaking, in a remarkable degree, of the peculiar characteristics of the great raider. Willie Mosby was my bed-fellow for the night. We conversed for several hours upon the stirring events in which he had taken part. He spoke lightly of the dangers by which we were surrounded, and assured me there was less peril fighting under the black flag than in the regular service. He argued that it made men fight much harder, and when they knew that no quarter would be granted them, they were much harder to catch, &c. I confess, even at this late date, that his arguments were neither soothing nor convincing.

The chances of being captured and hung any cold morning before breakfast, on an empty stomach, and by strangers with whom I had no sympathy whatever, was not calculated, in my opinion, to act as an incentive to a soldier's appetite, no matter how much he may enjoy the old belligerent system of long-range conflict, with a fair prospect of boarding on prisoner's fare at the expense of a hostile government. I was informed by Lieutenant Mosby that our headquarters were liable to be attacked at any hour; the enemy had recently made a raid on it; that they always attacked at night, and that our chances of escape consisted in being well armed, and either escape at one door as they broke through another, or cut our way through their columns if they surrounded the house, as they frequently did.

He gave me a very pleasant account of the last hanging of Yankees that took place at Rector's Cross-Roads, only three miles from our headquarters; and also the unprovoked hanging of seven of our own men at Front Royal, for which the cross-roads affair was retaliatory. With boyish glee he seemed to enjoy the cold-blooded butchery, by deliberate and barbarous strangulation, with as much delight as to crush out human life with the more dignified and gentlemanly method of shell, shot and bayonet. Juvenile warriors seem incapable of discriminating between a dignified and time-honoured system of murder and the new-fangled methods that reflect no credit upon the operator at all. If life must be taken to justify the whimsicalities of rulers, or to gratify the appetites of latent philanthropists, it should be taken by the methods that will do most good and leave to posterity healthy precedents that will save them much trouble in shedding what fashionable people are pleased to call this mortal coil.

But I never could see what special advantages could be derived from this peculiar innovation in belligerent ethics—of hanging a soldier after he has been captured. More particularly do I object to this barbarous precedence if I am to be the subject of this unwarlike experiment.

My first night at Glen Welby (Mosby's headquarters) was well spent listening to the narrative of the battalion's adjutant, William Mosby. He related with boyish vivacity many interesting encounters with the enemy, in which our brave boys were victorious. The adventure with Major Blaizor was one of the most entertaining as told by the adjutant. It seems that a desperado named Blaizor had offered his services to the old government, with the promise that he would volunteer to capture the cunning rebel partisan, Mosby, provided the government would permit him to form a company of one hundred picked men from the Federal army. The request was granted, and Blaizor selected his men. This command, it seems, was carefully composed of ruffians like the rough Blaizor himself. From the description of this specimen officer, I presume he must be one of the most uncouth bipeds that ever aspired to military honours. Hugo's description of the savage Cambronne reads like the picture of a carpet knight compared with the ambitious Blaizor.

Willie Mosby in his boyish style tells that this Yankee Major, with more daring than judgment or prudence, at the head of his desperate band, scoured the counties of Clarke, Loudoun, and Fauquier in quest of his prey. Mosby did not seem to be at all disturbed by the preparations and manoeuvres of Blaizor. About this time he was suddenly called to Richmond by order of General Lee. During Mosby's absence, Major Richards was placed in command of forty-five men, and ordered to find Blaizor, with his hundred picked veterans. The two commands met; Richards commanding forty-five rangers, and Blaizor in command of his one hundred men, chosen from a huge army of many thousands. The conflict was short, sharp, but decisive. Blaizor formed his command on a hill; Richards charged him with his small force. It was a clear field and a fair encounter. Blaizor lost nearly half his command killed and wounded; the remainder captured, including the boastful and desperate Blaizor himself.

The gallant Richards, having discharged the last shot from his pistols, unhorsed Blaizor by a heavy blow with the butt of the empty weapon, inflicting a severe wound upon the scalp of the aforesaid major of the desperate command. This unwise and venturesome officer and his surviving followers were placed under guard in the care of Sam. Alexander, and sent back to Gordonsville. Sam is said to have been in high spirits, partly from the hot blood engendered by the fierce encounter and partly from the contents of a tin can he always carried about him. He became instantly on intimate terms with the discomfited Yankee major, offered him assistance from his tin can, and attempted to cheer him up with strong apple brandy.

"Take a drink, Blaze," said Sam; "it will do you good and make you forget your troubles. I feel sorry for you, Blaze." Then, slapping the unlucky major on the shoulder with that insolent familiarity that only intoxication can impart, "Did you have the impudence to try and catch our Mose? Why, our Mose wouldn't condescend to fight such a fool as you. He sent little Dolly Richards arter you, with only half a company, and you see what you got. Blaze, you're a fool! Take a drink, Blaze; and if you ever get out of Libby prison again, let somebody else get up an army of a thousand men like you, Blaze, and then come and see us. Don't you feel ashamed, Blaze, to let our little Dolly Richards, with a handful of men, catch you and all your hundred wild men? Take a drink, Blaze, and don't try to catch our Mose again."

The dejected Blaizor followed Sam's advice by taking the brandy, but we never heard whether he returned in quest of Mosby any more. From the history Major Richards afterwards gave me of this engagement, it must have been one of the most remarkable victories of the war. No strategy could be used, no ambush or surprise, but a fair, open, field fight. The enemy numbered one hundred men, all selected because of their supposed fitness for the desperate work before them, and Richards's command numbered only forty-five of his regular rangers.

That such an engagement should result iu the smaller force destroying and capturing the larger one only tells of the determined earnestness of men fighting for a cause approved by an enlightened conscience and coarse hirelings who only fight for mercenary wages. The history of the world cannot point to a solitary page that tells of one hundred patriots being defeated by forty-five mercenaries. Blaizor's followers were prompted by the sentiments of fierce brutality and pecuniary gain, while the dash of the partisans was nerved by that high spirit that held the Spartans at Thermopylae or Stonewall's followers at Cross Keys.

CHAPTER 7

# Successful Pursuit of the Enemy

A few days before my arrival at Glen Welby one of the most daring officers of our battalion had been severely wounded. Lieutenant Charles Grogan, returning from a raid near Fairfax Courthouse, had stopped at the house of a *Union man* named Turner. While at the breakfast table a regiment of Federal cavalry (the Eighth Illinois) surrounded the house and commanded Lieutenant Grogan to surrender. The plucky old Roman, who attempted alone to defend a bridge against an advancing army may have paused to consider the chances of an unequal contest, but Charles Grogan fell in the desperate effort to cut his way through a regiment of armed men. His extraordinary courage won the sympathy and admiration of the brave fellows he so earnestly fought.

Surgeon Nelson, the medical officer of the regiment, examined and dressed the wound, advised and offered his services to amputate the limb. This kind offer the gallant Grogan refused to accept. I visited him the day after my arrival at Glen Welby. I found him suffering considerably from the severe wound he had received. His newly-made friend, the Yankee surgeon, had failed to remove the fragments of the broken bone, and the wound was in a very unpromising condition. I noticed my patient was in a very despondent mood. I carefully examined the fracture, removed the *spiculae* of the bone that caused much needless irritation, and left him more comfortable than I had found him. On my next visit I discovered that he was more depressed in spirits than before.

This is so unusual an occurrence with men of uncommon courage that I could not account for his mental condition. On my return home I noticed particularly one of the charming young ladies at headquarters manifested much interest in the condition of my brave patient. I immediately suspected that the heroic officer was attached to the fair lady, and made inquiries, with a view to a correct surgical management of the case. I soon learned enough to decide, with as little delay as possible, to remove my patient to Glen Welby, where he could be well nursed and scientifically treated. I have long ago observed that the mental treatment of diseases and injuries is as important as their physical management.

Apart from the romantic interest of this particular case, I can now assert as true that in a very active professional life of more than the fourth part of a century I have never known more perfect success to follow the psychological management of surgical injury. The soul has more to do with repairing physical disorders than even professional men with small souls can be made to comprehend. I shall ever believe that the fond attachment (or what young people call love) for a charming and accomplished lady had much more to do with the recovery of this brave officer than did the *armamentum medicum* at my command.

The extraordinary bravery of this patient, added to the softer sentiment involved, caused me to feel more than an ordinary interest in his recovery. Dr. Nelson, the medical officer of the Eighth Illinois regiment, whom I afterwards learned was an accomplished surgeon, had already given an unfavourable opinion. He had advised amputation as the only means of saving life. A compound comminuted fracture is always regarded by the surgeon as a dangerous wound. I caused him to be removed from Mr. Turner's to Glen Welby. Mr. Turner, at whose house he had received the wound, was a Union man. That fact alone I believe increased the despondency of my rebellious patient. The rebel nervous system, particularly in Mosby's command, was not very impressible to Union sentiments, and the patriotism of Lieutenant Grogan could not well brook the presence of a hostile nurse. The contrast between the tender care of a beautiful nurse, who already has charge of a patient's heart, with that of a hateful enemy to his cause, may well be considered as an important factor in the ultimate recovery of a doubtful physical injury.

I have never known a more sudden or a more remarkable improvement than Lieutenant Grogan experienced in the change from a loathed to a loving presence. Under the mystic influence of the pure and ethereal sentiment of unselfish love, the colour of life returned to his blanched features, and new vitality flowed merrily through the withered channels of his veins. Day by day this rapid convalescence was continued, until the success of perfect recovery crowned the efforts of psychological surgery. Let the learned votaries of material science object if they will, I assert it as the full conviction of mature reason, that this dauntless life would have been lost, without the agency of that potent though mysterious influence offered by loving hearts and ministered by gentle and tender hands. As his medical attendant I claim no other credit for this almost miraculous escape from the embrace of apparently certain death, than the common sense that directed the change from the care of a diabolic to that of an angelic nurse.

The reader may be naturally disappointed by the sequel of this rather romantic narrative. It would be easy enough to increase the interest of the reader in these sketches of fact were I to forget the demand of history and yield to the more pleasing creations of fancy. It matters not how bright the realms of imagination, and how beautiful the gems and the flowers of fiction, the unyielding demand of reality so shaped the lives and the destiny of the lovers, that the fairy hand whose tender care saved the life of the gallant soldier, with the loving heart of the fair giver, was reserved foe the happiness of another. The fearless, devoted and faithful lieutenant submitted to an ordeal infinitely more painful than wounds or physical anguish can bestow. He lived to see the beautiful Fairy Queen of all his earthly hopes of love become the bride of another, and that other a fat man of more than two hundred avoirdupois. A lover of such dimensions will blot the record of the most romantic sentiment on earth.

Mosby's battalion numbered eight hundred men. Lieutenant-Colonel Chapman, in command of six hundred, was stationed in that portion of Virginia known as Northern Neck. Major Richards, in command of two hundred, held and defended the counties of Fairfax, Loudoun, Fauquier, Culpeper, and Clarke.

Our soldiers were quartered in squads of four to ten men at each private residence, mostly throughout the county of Fauquier. When needed for action they were summoned by couriers to rendezvous at a given point. Within a few hours the entire command would always be ready for a "raid." Almost every dwelling occupied by Mosby's men was provided with trapdoors and other convenient subterranean hiding places. Whenever a house was attacked and surrounded by the enemy, a trap-door would immediately fly open, a few soldiers disappear through the floor, a piece of carpet or oil-cloth would then be thrown carefully over the hiding place, after which a fierce search for rebels would be made in vain. Major Richards lived with his father at Upperville. The old Richards mansion was of course supplied with the usual holes and hiding places, to be used in cases of sudden emergency.

With no more notice than a savings bank or an insurance company gives of its impending insolvency, a squad of several hundred Yankee cavalry from Winchester made a descent upon Upperville. Like many of the sneaking varieties of wild animals, the adventurous raiders would always select the most inclement weather for their unwelcome visitations. They found "Dolly" Richards at home, with several of his warlike companions. No sooner did the butt of a hostile carbine break through the panels of the door than Richards and his followers took to their holes through the floor. The surprise was so sudden and complete that the vigilant major and his comrades had no time to save their clothing and arms. Richards's beautiful new uniform, with hat and gay ostrich feather, fell an easy capture into the hands of the drunken Yankees.

Major Richards was a man of exquisite taste. His uniform was of the most unexceptionable finish; his hat and feather were considered the most stylish in the entire command. The drunken raiders held possession of the house for several hours, and our friends remained very quiet in their holes. "When the Yankees left, they carried away with them all the movable property found about the house, clothing, provisions, and such light or portable articles as could be conveniently tied to their saddles; leaving, indeed, nothing that could be of use to a fashionable officer in the way of clothing. I presume that the four years of war did not present, in a single instance, such a picture as this dashing, brave and handsome major offered to the public eye after he emerged from his hole in the floor.

An old suit of his father's clothing, with the blue coat of horse collar and sparrow-tail cut; an old bell-crowned, black beaver, boots several sizes too large for him, and of ancient make, and pantaloons like those worn by Chatelard when found in the chamber of Mary Stuart. These made up a *tout ensemble* altogether too strikingly grotesque to describe. The brave Richards—disgusted, incensed, enraged—gathered his followers with more rapidity than Rhoderick's horn could possibly have summoned his highland clans, and, in his picturesque costume, gave chase to the dishonest invaders of his quiet household.

The Yanks had evidently enjoyed their visit to Upperville. They had found and confiscated a large quantity of apple brandy, and from their physical condition had evidently used this contraband commodity to an injudicious if not a damaging extent. The entire command seemed profoundly intoxicated. They had captured a few prisoners in Upperville, and had also loaded their horses so heavily with stolen property of every kind, that even had they been sober they could not have escaped the pursuit of the incensed and avenging Richards.

A curious picture of war did this drunken cavalry present. Their horses, laden with bags, fowls, pigs, and small articles of furniture, tied to their saddles, yelling, singing obscene songs, and uttering disgusting oaths—hotly pursued by the handsome Richards, clad in his father's ancient habiliments. Two Chinese columns of hostile warriors could not have committed greater violence on the dignity of war than did this unique military display. Richards had gathered about fifty of his best men within a few hours. He sent a detachment of nearly half his force by a short route to obstruct the road beyond Paris. With the remainder he pursued the disordered drunken column until it was. driven into the murderous ambuscade prepared for it. The engagement was a one-sided affair. A large number were killed and captured. Several of our own men that had been captured at Upperville were recaptured in this engagement, and one or two of them wounded by our own bullets. Dr. Sowers, one of our best soldiers and most genial companions, was severely wounded in the fight. Major Richards recovered his stolen uniform, and expressed himself well satisfied with this adventure.

One of our scouts brought information that something could be captured in the vicinity of Alexandria. A force of forty men was immediately dispatched to that locality. When in view of that city, a long train of wagons could be seen winding its slow and tortuous course along in the direction of our position. There was generally a strong attraction—a sort of affinity—existing between the partisan battalion and a wagon train. Our boys waited, like a cat awaits the appearance of a mouse, until the coveted and tempting prize approached within short musket range, when, at a given signal, a rapid charge was ordered upon the devoted teamsters. A strong force of colored troops guarded the train, and the poor Africans fired at random, and were thrown into the utmost confusion by our sudden and unexpected t dash upon them.

The unfortunate creatures, in their extreme excitement and panic, fired their muskets in every conceivable direction except the right one. When "Our Boys" closed upon them, it was a sickening sight to see the miserable barbarians scatter and hide themselves under the wagons and in the adjacent brushwood. The fight, if it could be dignified by such a name, lasted only a few moments. Many of the unfortunate wretches were killed.

One of the number who escaped that fate was recognised as the property of Mr. Armistead Carter. He was captured. To the surprise and disgust of our brave raiders, the wagon-train did not afford a very rich prize. Instead of army supplies, the wagons were freighted with negro corpses, destined for a kind of African Potter's Field only a few miles from the city. Our boys soon recovered from their disgust and disappointment. They immediately detached the horses and mules from the wagons, and cremated the entire train, with its loathsome cargo.

Many valuable horses and one live negro were the results, all told, of this enterprise. The negro prisoner turned out to be almost as costly as Dr. Franklin's whistle. The contraband African was lodged for the night at our headquarters, and made to sleep in the same room with two of his captors. The guard was too much fatigued to keep a vigilant watch over the coloured prisoner. They were soon asleep, the negro escaped, took one of our best horses, and returned to Alexandria, a distance of more than forty miles, the same night. The night following this incident the hospitable roof at Glen Welby gave shelter to the following *dramatis personae*: Colonel Welby Carter, ex-colonel of the First Virginia Cavalry; Mosby's Chief of Staff, Colonel Joseph Blackwell; and a youth of twenty summers—all these occupying an upper chamber. Adjutant "Willie Mosby and myself shared a room with the wounded Lieutenant Grogan, on the first floor of the rear section of the house. The weather was very cold. A five-inch snow, with a hard-frozen crust, covered the ground. My friend Grogan complained of his wound, and desired me to get up and relieve him of pain.

I remember, with the distinctness of certainty, the incidents of that eventful night. It was not more than half an hour before the dawn of day when I had relieved the pain of my patient and returned to bed. I had scarcely settled down into a comfortable position for a morning nap, when a sound, but not a "sound of revelry by night," jarred most unmelodiously upon the rebel ear. The crushing footsteps of a thousand soldiers, breaking through the snow crust, as they stamped rapidly to warm themselves after a forty-mile ride through the frosty night air, mingled with the ominous thud of the carbine butt against the solid, well-barred doors of the stately old mansion, made altogether the most unpleasant combination of discordant and evil-boding sounds it has ever been my misfortune to hear. With a hasty, ill-considered, and not very gentle punch in the ribs of my companion, I aroused the adjutant. "Willie, Willie," I exclaimed, "the Yankees have surrounded the house!"

The word "Yankee" was alone sufficient to arouse my bed-fellow. In less time than I have ever known any animal to awake, Lieutenant Mosby had left me and disappeared in the dark. I shall not easily forget the feeling of utter helplessness that seized me at that moment. In our hottest and heaviest battles, when death seemed certain and inevitable there was no sensation half so unpleasant or dreadful as the horrible apprehension of a capture by night and a hanging in the morning. In that half-bewildered state that I suppose a stranger might feel when standing at the gate of Pluto's dark dominion, in gloomy contemplation of the greeting he shall receive, I appealed to Lieutenant Grogan for advice.

"They have got me, Grogan, I believe. What shall I do?"

"O, don't give it up, Doctor. If you can't do any better, get out on the house top."

I confess that I did not feel very wise just at that moment, but a hint to me was sufficient. I sprang from my covering, seized my clothing, boots and pistol, and hastened with all speed, first into the hall, then up the first flight of steps. It was very dark. Just as I landed upon the second floor, I ran against some small living and moving object. It turned out to be one of the little negro girls that waited on the ladies of the house. The young creature led me through the dark, up another flight of steps, and indicated, in a whisper, the way through the garret and out upon the roof.

CHAPTER 8

# Escape on the House Top

Groping my uncertain way through a garret, filled with broken furniture, old boxes and general rubbish, and guided by the indistinct light that proceeded from a small window, opening above an adjacent roof, I moved with cautious haste, inspired by the fear of capture and the attendant apprehensive certainty of an ignominious death. I succeeded in reaching the small window, and found it open. It was the labour of less than a moment to tumble my clothing and boots through the window and out upon the roof. I then crawled after my baggage, and closed the window behind me. I found that Adjutant Mosby, who had disappeared so suddenly from my bed and room, had preceded me to this elevated place of safety. The lieutenant was lying prostrate upon the roof. The snow had been thawed by the sun on all that portion of the roof not shaded by the gable-wall of the house, My comrade in misfortune was lying half way upon the snow; the remaining half of his handsome though meagrely clad person reclined upon the cold tin with which the roof was covered. With a view to the concealment of myself and friend, I assumed a horizontal position immediately upon him, and drew my overcoat over both.

While this very quiet and unostentatious process of "nest hiding" was being most faithfully executed, our boisterous pursuers were indeed making a great noise. Their harsh voices, mingled with oaths and diabolical threats, were heard in every room of the house. The rough, jarring and unmusical sound of the axe, as it crushed through resisting and well-barred doors, contained no melody for the sensitive ear of the nervous rebel. We were scarcely settled, and could not have been considered comfortable in our lofty perch, when a "Yank," out of several who had followed us to the garret, more adventurous and enterprising than his companions, came up to the very window through which we made our exit, and flashing his lantern in our faces, made use of the most undignified epithets I have ever heard. In stentorian tones he swore that many unsanctified and unblessed rebels were yet in the house and he would not give up the chase until all were killed or captured.

In my cold and helpless situation I could distinctly hear the uncouth and broken accent's of drunken foreigners, quarrelling over the stolen property they were dividing below. Presently, a loud voice, in the rough brogue of Erin, proceeding from the vicinity of the stables, proclaimed, "I say, b'ys, this is no scrub of an 'orse." I knew at once that my beautiful black stallion, the gift of my old friend Via, of Albemarle, was about to depart, like Ajut, never to return.

It is difficult to describe the sensations of a full-blooded rebel, as he crouched low upon the cold tin roof, with the lamps of the cruel and ferocious foe flashing in his face. Inspired by that extreme tension of the nervous system that only the terrible suspense of life or death can create, I was better prepared to resign my beautiful steed to the hands of the despised enemy than I would have been had my own corporate safety been better insured.

The scenes and sensations of that unpleasant night can be much better remembered than described. Willie Mosby was lying face down with his body partly on the snow-covered portion of the roof and partly on the naked tin. The morning air was cold and frosty. My comrade's costume would have been much more comfortable under the direct rays of a tropical sun than the frigid ordeal of the frozen house top. The lieutenant was as brave any youth could be. He had never flinched in the deadly charge. With boyish glee he would rush through the sulphurous blaze of battle and coquette with death at the cannon's mouth. But to respose with scant clothing on a very cold roof, with the skeleton Death in his most hideous and offensive garb looking him full in the face, was a refinement of mental persecution too far above the temper of nerve endurance for a youthful soldier to bear.

It is said that when a man in the flush of mental vigor and physical health is brought suddenly face to face with death, a panoramic view of all his past acts, both of good and of evil report, passes with the rapidity of an electric flash before his mind; that the scenes of a long life are condensed within a period of a few seconds of time. If the sublime and the ludicrous were ever compressed within a more concentrated focus of thought than the scenes that passed at Glen Welby on that night presented, the occasion has never come under my observation. The youthful and chivalrous adjutant of that gallant band of heroes, Mosby's battalion, was lying upon the snow and cold tin roof, with his toes keeping time to the rapid mutations of his foolings, like the gentle vibrations of the aspen leaf when moved by the soft current of the south wind.

I have ascribed the rattling sound of the adjutant's toes upon the tin roof partly to the extreme cold of our exposed position and partly to the varying emotions of hope and despair that alternately played upon his brave young heart. The surgeon, superimposed upon the prostrate form of the adjutant—both occupying as limited an area as possible upon the house top—presented a scene that would defy the accomplished genius of a Cruikshank or the more clumsy pencil of a Nast. In making my exit from the garret I had dropped my neck tie and collar.

The wretched "Yank" who followed so closely at my heels found these small articles, and I could distinctly hear his uncouth comments upon these unimportant though significant objects of his search. My cavalry boots, with huge brass spurs attached, had been hastily and carelessly thrown out upon the roof, immediately in front of the small window that had afforded us egress from the garret. I was anxious to remove the boots from their rather prominent position, for fear they would be seen by the enemy and lead to our discovery,

Adjutant Mosby was muttering something in a very low or subdued voice, while the light from the garret window was throwing its most unwelcome rays upon us. Everything was still as could be, so far as the fugitives were concerned, except the gentle though continuous rattling of the adjutant's toes upon the tin roof. At last I heard the voice of my comrade more distinctly, and could construe his almost inarticulate muttering into a most awkward effort at prayer. Willie was not a pious boy. He had evidently never before attempted to intrude upon the Throne of Grace with anything like a petition regarding his earthly wants or eternal aspirations. He was certainly as awkward in prayer as old Jim Bludsoe was said to be in a "row." But Willie did the best he could in his uncomfortable, if not desperate, situation. He was almost as ignorant in matters of theology as was the old sailor in a storm, who, when asked to pray, acknowledged bluntly that he knew nothing about it.

As the danger grew more imminent, he was again requested to do something pious, when the honest old tar offered his services to carry the hat around to take up a collection, that being the only duty appertaining to religion that he knew anything about. So it was to a certain extent with my anxious companion in tribulation. He certainly knew very little about preparing artistic petitions to the Giver of all mercies. He made a complete failure at the only attempt he proposed at the Lord's Prayer, struck one line of the sweet little nursery prayer, "*When I lay me down to sleep,*" &c., and seemed to appreciate the inapplicability of that sentiment to our unhappy condition. He then branched off upon detached portions of the morning service of the Episcopal church, and diverged upon the litany for a line or two.

While all these mumbling and decidedly unsuccessful efforts at extemporaneous piety were progressing, I was diligently endeavouring, with one hand, to remove my heavy boots, with their large spurs attached, from the rather ostentatious position they occupied immediately in front of the window. At each movement of the boots, their friction against the cold, dry tin-roof made an alarming noise. My poor companion, hearing the grating, would stop his earnest orisons and appeal to me, in whispered oaths, to "stop that d——d noise or we would be discovered and hung as sure as h—l." I would obey his command and desist for a few seconds of time. My peculiar position and state of mind at that time made me very obedient, and prone to accept any suggestion my more youthful though practiced partisan comrade might feel disposed to make; but when the big Yankee in the garret would throw the rays of his lantern through the small attic window full upon the boots, I would again act on my own judgment and discretion and make another effort to get them out of the luminous range of that annoying lantern.

With unusual and constrained earnestness would Lieutenant Mosby continue to offer up his broken fragments of borrowed and heterogeneous petitions. "Good Lord," he would say, with energetic though whispered unction, "We have done many things we ought not to have done, and there is mighty little help in us." On a slight movement of the boots, with the attendant grating sound upon the tin roof, he would change his tone and address me, in a sharp whisper, "Stop that d——d noise, they will hear you." Then he would mumble again into the merciful ear of Jehovah, "We have left undone many things that we ought to have done (let them d——d boots alone) and have mercy upon us, good Lord! (If these d——d scoundrels catch us, it will be your fault, d—n you.) Have mercy on all sick children and women in the perils of (them d——d boots will be the death of us. Stop that noise, by G—d, stop it!")

While this quaint commingling of sentiment and sin—of superstition usurping the place of religion—and that grotesque absurdity, faith born of fear, was acting the part of vicarious consolation for a terrified soul; while oaths and orisons were devoutly blended in all the mazes of fantastic confusion, on the housetop, scenes of no ordinary interest were transpiring in other portions of the hospitable old mansion. The room occupied by Colonel Wei by Carter, Joe Black well and young Waller was not altogether devoid of interest. Young Waller, a youth of twenty, was a near relative of the President of the Southern Confederacy. He had been with the partisan command but a few months, yet was experienced enough in H. W. Beecher's art of "nest-hiding" to elude the cunning search of the attacking party on that eventful night. With the assistance of a serving-woman of colon, who yet loved her old master too well to leave the generous and classic shades of Glen Welby to follow the *ignis fatuus* of Yankee promise, young Waller ascended to the top of an old-fashioned wardrobe, and there remained as secure as the infant Moses in his protecting bed of rushes, until the search was ended.

The wardrobe was inspected and removed some distance from the wall, with this young ranger on the top of it, yet he remained very quiet and said not a word until the rough, unceremonious and uninvited visitors left the house. He very quietly held his position until the storm subsided, then came down with an air of self-satisfied innocence difficult to imitate and still harder to describe.

The other occupants of the same room were not so fortunate as young Waller. Colonel Welby Carter and Chief-of-Staff Joe Blackwell slept together. Colonel Carter was not connected in any manner with Mosby's command. He had distinguished himself for extraordinary courage at the first battle of Manassas, while in command of a company of cavalry, and he won his promotion to the command of the First regiment of Virginia cavalry by gallant conduct in the field. Notwithstanding the fact that this officer won his spurs by that honest discharge of duty, and knightly courage, that demands the respect and admiration of his brave comrades, he was tried by a dishonest military court, and deprived of his rank, through the perfidy of a superior officer and the corruption of his subordinates.

Colonel Carter was the only regular at Mosby's headquarters the night of the raid. He was captured before he could get out of his room. His fat bed fellow, Joe Blackwell, known as Mosby's chief of staff, was not tall but very corpulent. He resembled the stage representations of Falstaff, only he was more obese and not so old as the gallant Briton whose numerous foes wore buckram. Joe Blackwell had an honest dread of Yankees. Though his aversion and dislike for the invaders was very great, his fear of these much abused people was much greater. They had burnt his dwelling and destroyed his other property, because he had given shelter to Mosby. He had formed an erroneous impression in regard to the enemy. He conceived that their purpose in visiting Fauquier county so often was not general, but personal He believed, no matter how large the hostile force that visited his county, they came with but a single object and that was to capture and hang the man whose property they had destroyed. His peculiar aversion, mingled with a morbid fear of the enemy, became the frequent topic of conversation and comment at the table, in the parlour, and at all the social gatherings of his friends. It was a well cultivated apprehension he entertained for the common enemy.

His peculiarly impressible condition, on this unpleasant subject, prepared him for more than usual excitement on the occasion of this unexpected attack on our headquarters. It is not an easy matter for the most lively imagination to conceive the sensations of Joe Blackwell when he discovered the startling fact that one thousand hostile horsemen, on blood intent, surrounded his defenceless sanctum. Nothing less than the certainty of immediate dissolution could have inspired the helpless, and almost hopeless, chief of staff, to the absolutely desperate effort before him. From my elevation position, I neard a great noise and commotion below. Rough oaths, loud laughter, and the sharp, quick reports of carbines told of some desperate or ridiculous incident.

Joe Blackwell had sprung from his bed, with only two articles of clothing about his person, and leaped from an upper window, not less than twenty feet from the ground, into the midst of his enemies. The Yankees shouted, yelled, laughed, fired on him, and gave chase. Blackwell weighed not less than two hundred pounds; he was very fat. I am satisfied no fat man ever made better time than the frightened chief. Propelled by the wild and gloomy emotion of utter despair, he dashed off like a frightened deer pursued by hounds.

With the force gathered by the avalanche in its furious descent from the cloud-capped mountain-top, the excited chief rushed headlong from his swift pursuers. He struck the garden fence in his mad career and broke through an entire panel. Rushing like Mazeppa's steed through the enclosure, he swept another panel of fence before him and gained an open field. Here the chase became as exciting and interesting as a first-class horse race. I could see, from the house-top, a large, white object, that seemed to roll rapidly forward like some huge snowball, followed speedily by many dark, fast moving figures, until the white thing seemed to strike a high stone fence, over which it rolled, without any perceptible diminution of speed, continuing its onward course until it disappeared over a distant hill. The dark objects in pursuit stopped at the stone fence and slowly returned to the house.

CHAPTER 9

# A Desperate Attempt at Rescue

About the time the chase of Joe Blackwell ended, the first faint rays of daylight could be marked along the eastern horizon. Lieutenant Mosby continued mumbling his heterogeneous prayers, while fresh dangers gathered around us. We knew that daylight would discover our hiding place, and just as I proposed to my unhappy companion the propriety of crawling back into the garret, the rattling fire of pistols in the yard beneath, told of another change in our kaleidoscope of chance. The bullets whistled distinctly and seemed to pass near us. I whispered to my companion: "Willie, they have discovered and are firing at us."

"Oh! My God, what shall we do, may the good Lord have mercy on our souls," muttered the lieutenant, in his most devout accents. Whether the fortunate sequel of this temporary unpleasantness can be ascribed to the efficacy of the prayers offered by my pious comrade, I know not, but he has frequently remarked since, that, if he were submitted to the same terrible ordeal again, he would certainly repeat the prayers with unshaken faith in the consummation of the same results. The firing in the yard below was occasioned by a desperate charge of three of our gallant boys upon the whole regiment of Yankee cavalry. When the column of cavalry passed White Plains *en route* to Mosby's headquarters, three of our brave boys, quartered at that place, suspected their purpose, and endeavored to reach Glen Welby before them and give the alarm.

But the negro prisoner who had escaped the night before acted as guide for the enemy and conducted them by the most direct route. When our three friends arrived, the Yankees had been with us more than half an hour. The brave boys were too late to give us notice of approaching danger, but were at last in time to save us from capture.

They rode into the midst of the enemy and fired a volley into their ranks. The whole regiment was mounted in an instant and pursued our friend in hob haste. This move I shall ever believe had much more to do with our safety than did the prayers and oaths of my pious young comrade, Lieutenant Mosby.

With profound sensations of relief that followed the departure of the enemy, we slowly descended from the house-top. Out of five rebels surprised that night, I was the only one fortunate enough to retain sufficient raiment to make a respectable appearance in the morning. I lent Lieutenant Mosby my overcoat to enable him to make a decent descent from the roof. Willie Mosby and Blackwell had lost everything "save honour." The former, in his night attire, badly concealed by my overcoat, with feet and head uncovered, made altogether no indifferent likeness to a ghost. The laughter and witty congratulations we received on our fortunate escape and grotesque habiliments by the amiable though facetious ladies of the hospitable household, retains yet a bright green spot in my memory. Every species of property had been injured, destroyed or stolen by the enemy. Nothing that could be utilised for domestic economy or comfort had been spared to this noble, generous and patriotic family. Yet their serious sacrifices did not diminish their joyous demonstrations at our fortunate though unexpected deliverance from the cruel and hated foe.

The sun rose in dazzling splendour over the wide expanse of snow. Its resplendent brightness seemed in contrast and mockery of the scenes and feelings of the preceding night. The landscape, as viewed from the gentle elevation of Glen Welby, is one of the most picturesque and beautiful in all Piedmont Virginia. The charming undulating azure of the distant mountain slopes distinctly outlined against the soft blue sky, with the modest aspect of less presumptuous hills in the fore-ground, mingling tastefully with the rolling surface of a fertile plain, chequered by stone fences and substantial farm houses, presented a lovely picture of this beautiful region. The ladies of the house had gathered in the front portico and were joined by Mosby, Waller, and myself. We were each relating the individual experiences, fancies and excitements of the night.

So far, only three partisans besides Lieutenant Grogan (who was not disturbed) had been heard from. Speculation ran high as to the probable fate of poor Joe Blackwell. He was missing, and I knew that a large white object had rolled with unprecedented velocity away from the Yankees in the early dawn; and we knew that this object in its course had swept two panels of the garden fence away with great power.

Yet we did not know that this object was Joe Blackwell; and from the number of carbines discharged at the receding spectre, we could not feel certain, even if it was Joseph, that he yet lived. The noble-hearted ladies expressed great sympathy and manifested some grief over the uncertain fate of the missing chief. When the topic of conversation had become almost painful in its gloomy interest, and a proposition had been submitted that we borrow a few horses and go in search of the lost one—an awkward apparition could be indistinctly perceived over a snow-clad hill in the dim distance. All eyes were instantly turned upon the figure as it slowly approached in the direction of the house. Some of our group suspected it was a Yankee scout in disguise, others suggested, from its white appearance, that it was a flag of truce.

The thing came forward steadily, but very slowly. It observed not the beaten track, path, or plantation road, but advanced over hills and across plains with the unerring accuracy of a perfect mathematical line. As the object came nearer, it looked more and more quaint in its outlines and odd in its construction. The curiosity of our entire group was excited, yet could not conceive the true nature of this singular phenomenon. We awaited patiently, but yet, in profoundest doubt, whether the thing was physical or metaphysical. Its strange *tout ensemble* could pass equally well for "spirit of health, or goblin d——d," and to a practiced eye more strongly, resembled the latter. Not with "Tarquin's ravishing strides," but with the broken gait of a lame horse, the thing continued to advance. From its tardy locomotion, and heterogeneous "get up," it looked neither hostile nor war-like.

It had approached within twenty-five, paces of our position, when the first indication we had that its "true inwardness" had been ascertained and its nature properly diagnosed, was a wild shriek, mingled with uncontrollable laughter, and the rapid retreat of our lady friends from the portico. The silver tones of merry laughter rang through the wide and echoing halls of Glen Welby before the members of our group of the male persuasion had discovered the cause of such a sudden stampede and extraordinary merriment. The genius of the gifted Dickens would pause in its effort to describe the figure that now presented itself. Joe Blackwell, with only two articles of "gentleman's wear" about his well-developed person, had eluded his baffled pursuers in the early morning's chase. With naked feet, over the frozen snow he had outstripped the swift following Yankees, and at the distance of two miles from the point he started, the alarmed chief had sought refuge in a dense forest behind the sheltering body of a fallen oak. Pinched by the merciless temperature of a cruel frost, he dragged his chilled body to the cabin of a friendly negro.

The poor darkey was not prepared to render any valuable aid to the fugitive chief. Relief such as he could afford was cheerfully given. The good darkey was the owner of a poor old horse. This species of personal property was cheerfully offered to the oppressed rebel, and as cordially accepted. With ingenuity demonstrating the old proverb, that necessity is the mother of invention, Joseph made a hasty change in the systematic arrangement of his scanty costume. He was compelled by the stress, or rather the distress, of circumstances, to protect one portion of his handsome person at the expense of another heretofore less exposed region of his physical economy. Having only two garments at his disposal, and neither of these, from their peculiar structure and customary application, affording the least protection or assistance to his frost-bitten feet, the chief deliberately divided one of his nether garments into two equal parts, and wrapped one half of said transposed linen carefully round his suffering pedal extremities.

In this guise, awkwardly mounted upon the old free negro's horse, without saddle or bridle, with a large rope halter around the animal's nose to guide him, he set out upon his return. The horse being poor, lame and badly galled by harness, looked not much happier than the rider. Without hat, with round, full face covered with short beard, holding the rope in one hand and blowing in the other to keep it warm, and each foot wrapped in half a linen garment, this, and only this, constituted the phenomenon that presented itself before the front portico at Glen Welby. Is the reader surprised that the ladies laughed and fled? If Sancho Panza had engaged in a prize fight, remained a week at Seven Points, spent one night in Babcock's ice-house, and then traded Dapple with his master for old Rosinante, he may possibly have made as striking an impression on a Sunday-school picnic as that made on the home circle of Glen Welby by the chief's return.

I was the first to go forward to assist him from his painful position and suffering steed. I remember well the significant nod of his head and the triumphant look he gave me as I extended my hand to help him down. It was with that unmistakable air of triumph and pain that he said, "Ah! Doctor, I beat them running, but I am mighty cold. Help me, for God's sake and give me a drink!"

CHAPTER 10

# Mosby's Return to the Command

A few days subsequent to the scenes and adventures described in the preceding chapter, the gallant partisan leader returned to his faithful command, after an absence of two months. Mosby was received by his brave followers with the wildest demonstrations of vociferous joy. His old well-tried veterans gathered around him with noisy manifestations of affectionate regard. The chivalrous and devoted retainers of Roderick Dhu could not have exhibited more admiration for their loved and trusted chief, than did this warlike partisan clan for their distinguished and dashing leader.

Napoleon the Great said that military success depends more on simultaneous thought and action, than on the tardy and deliberate methods of systematic calculations. These qualifications of the distinguished Corsican's criterion of true military genius, the partisan chief possessed to an eminent degree. With a thorough an intimate knowledge of his characteristic mental twists and peculiarities of disposition, I assert the belief that no man ever possessed a greater power of quick perception, or more promptness of thought and action, than did this meteoric genius of guerrilla warfare. Soon as he returned to the county of Fauquier, the officers of his command gathered around him, and plans were instantly perfected to organise the many volunteers that were constantly flocking to his battalion, into new companies, and rapidly filling the wasted ranks of the old. Mosby exercised the most arbitrary power over his immediate command, and also over the several counties under his military control. He was considered not only a military ruler, but also a civil power of unquestioned authority, over the several counties known at that time as "Mosby's Confederacy."

No caricatures of human justice, in the form of county or circuit courts, were then known or recognised by the people during Mosby's reign. He settled all disputes, and his decisions admitted of no appeal. Indeed, the opposing litigants were generally satisfied with his prompt and impartial decrees. If two old farmers quarrelled about a horse trade, or the sale of real estate, the court of first appeal and last resort, was the *drum-head* tribunal at Mosby's headquarters. From a hasty puerile quarrel, to the most important business transaction, the decisions of this arbitrary court were always considered the perfection of justice and the mature product of unquestioned wisdom. One great advantage contestants enjoyed before the martial judiciary of Mosby's administration was a "speedy trial" in its fullest sense.

One of the strongest elements of complaint in Hamlet's Soliloquy would not have annoyed the unlucky Prince of Denmark, had his case been tried in Mosby's court. There was no honest ground to complain of the "law's delay" before his prompt and inexorable bar. His scales of justice could not be made to change their even balance through the attraction of gain, or the force of prejudice, or malice; but when once the result was reached, not all the powers of earth could change the stubborn will or the inflexible determination of this arbitrary court. Quick perception, strong judgment, firmness of purpose and a determined self-possession, supplied the important functions of this tribunal of justice that are unfortunately so rare in others. Mosby detested red tape in every form. He recognised it as a deadly poison to military success, and often said to me that this contemptible relic of ancient stupidity, has retarded the progress of civilization more even than the vulgar superstition and hapless ignorance of the darkest ages of the world's history.

He frequently uttered his contempt for the circumlocution tendencies of all civil, military and legal matters in this country. He would hear the full evidence in any one case and decide the moment the testimony closed. He promoted his officers and soldiers on the single principle of merit. The most extravagant pretentions to aristocratic privileges, the boast of vulgar wealth, or the more common and contemptible claim of influence with the government, would alike fail in procuring a commission in his command. When a brave and intelligent soldier made a successful raid, and at a great risk, captured a number of the enemy, or obeyed the orders of his superior regardless of his own safety, and proved himself faithful, obedient, intelligent and totally fearless, he would find himself one degree higher in rank without the trouble of making a special application for promotion.

If all the officers of authority in the Confederate Government had possessed half the intelligence, patriotism, and innate justice that characterized the chief of the partisan battalion, surely our armies would have been severely purged of the traitors, cowards and impostors, that so often disgraced the official rolls of our unfortunate and ill-fated government. So strong was the attachment of his followers to their popular leader and his cause, that the only punishment he ever proposed for disobedience, was expulsion from his command. To be ordered back into the regular service was regarded by every man in the Forty-Third battalion of Virginia cavalry, as intolerable punishment and eternal disgrace.

The only sense of fear known to these brave raiders, was the honest dread of being remanded back into the regular army. I have known the intimation of this dreadful penalty to bring tears from the eyes of the most desperate and daring men in the partisan service. In all the history of human error, there is no impression yet made upon the public mind more wide of the truth, than, the general opinion regarding the honour and discipline of Mosby's command. The chivalrous leader of these gallant men, inspired them with his own high sense of honour, and their profound regard and admiration for him, commanded their strict obedience to his will.

Every man knew that the slightest suspicion of dishonesty, or cowardice, would consign him at once to the disgrace of expulsion; and although there must have been the usual modicum of human meanness always found in a given number of human beings, I am enabled to say, after three years of active field service in the regular army, that I have never witnessed, amongst eight hundred men and officers, more true courage and chivalry, or a higher sense of honour, blended with less vice, selfishness and meanness, than I found during my official intercourse with the partisan battalion. 'Tis true, acts of cruelty were sometimes committed—as will always happen when one man is placed at the mercy of another, and the base passions in common with all humanity, are lashed into fury by terrible and atrocious wrongs.

No lazy man, rocked in the cradle of luxury and nursed by the degrading spirit of indolence, can either comprehend or appreciate the fiery play of angry passion whipped into fury by the glare of burning dwellings, while the hungry and freezing little children of murdered parents are standing by the ruins of their homes, clinging to their pale though heroic mothers, pleading with blanched cheeks and tearful eyes for such protection as the feeble hand of a delicate mother can grant them, in the grim ordeal of murder, arson, starvation, and death.

I have read of civilized warfare, but that was not the kind the invaders waged against the defenceless inhabitants of Fauquier. General Hancock held the post of Winchester with a force of nearly forty thousand men.

A force nearly as powerful held the city of Alexandria and Fairfax Courthouse. Mosby, with his eight hundred veterans, held the several counties that intervened between these powerful forces of the enemy. Large commands from either post would make frequent incursions into our territory, and every advance would be illuminated by the ghastly glare of burning barns and dwellings. This is what certain pious writers denominate civilized warfare, conducted under humane regulations. If, under these trying circumstances, a squad of partisans should happen to advance upon a party of incendiaries, gloating over the ruin they have wrought—whose brutality crops out in their hideous, obscene jests and vulgar insults, hurled at the piteous pleadings of the poor mother and her frightened children—it would certainly not shock the genius that presides over the department of retaliatory justice, for the gentle partisan to seize the cruel incendiary by the neck and heels and add a small supply of combustible fuel to the fire, by hurling the vandal into the flames he kindled.

If the gallows prepared by Haman was a well-considered engine to raise its maker in the estimation of all just men, surely the hell created in Virginia by the hand of the barbarous incendiary was not too hot for the demon who applied the torch. If a "kindred spirit makes us wondrous kind," a demoniac act makes us wonderfully vindictive. This brutal conduct was probably more manifest in the county of Fauquier, than in any other region of Virginia. The savage cruelty of an Indian war was no more merciless in its barbarous atrocities' than that waged upon the defenceless women and helpless young children of this lovely section of Piedmont Virginia. The savage, in taking the scalp, shortens the agonies of his victim; but a huge army, that destroys the food and burns the habitations of defenceless women and young children, adds the protracted torture of gradual death by starvation, to the agonising pangs of mental torment in the feverish apprehension of cold and hunger.

The cold-blooded atrocities perpetrated upon the unprotected inhabitants of Fauquier and the adjoining counties, prove that the human animal is more ferocious than the wild beast in his jungle. The tiger is brutal by instinct, and takes life only when his own is in danger, or when he is pinched by the significant sense of hunger. But man (or at least such specimens of mankind as committed military arson and murder) makes use of reason, in brutality and calculates the sufferings of a tortured victim, prompted, not by hunger or even retaliation—for what brute would retaliate an injury upon a woman or a child? The gallant sons of heroic Virginia, were in the field, breasting the deadly storm of lead and steel in defence of their country. Her gentle daughters and her infant children, were left in the care of Him of whom it is said *"tempers the wintry winds to the shorn lamb."*

A general in a report to his commander-in-chief boasts of many thousand dwellings destroyed by fire. The ineffable Haynau was no doubt proud of the like hideous heroism of ordering Hungarian ladies, to be scourged with the dreadful knout.

If the history of atrocities in Northern Virginia is ever honestly or truthfully written, the descendants of the murderers and incendiaries will not be proud of the record of their unworthy progenitors.

A commissioned *officer* of a civilized government that can give or execute an order to burn thousands of human dwellings, that shelter only the most interesting and helpless of the human race—members of society that cannot bear arms for or against a government—that are in the fullest sense of the term non-combatants, must indeed be an animal without a soul. Or, if such a creature is the possessor of a soul, it is a very indifferent article.

The prayers of defenceless women and the tears of frightened children prevailed not with the cold-blooded brutality of the foul incendiaries. The heartrending picture of little children toddling out of a burning house and falling in their fright over its blazing timbers, failed to move the coarse black heart that would almost burst asunder at the raid on Harper's Ferry or break with pious indignation, at the hanging of old John Brown.

The cruelties and atrocities of the barbarous foe, inspired our partisan soldiers with more than human courage. When one hundred of these savages were engaged in burning a dwelling only ten partisan soldiers would often put the entire company to flight. A soldier who will insult a woman, frighten a child, steal whatever he can find to steal, or burn a dwelling, will not make an honest fight when danger looks him in the face. Cruelty and cowardice are inseparable companions. Show me a cruel tyrant, and I will discover a cowardly knave.

CHAPTER 11

# Union Men and Quakers

The county of Loudoun, one of the most fertile in Virginia, furnished some of the bravest soldiers in the Confederate Army and retained many of the bitterest foes to the Southern Cause. Amongst the Union men most active and acrimonious in their opposition to Confederate authority, may be noticed the brotherhood or sect, known as the society of Friends. The Quakers of Loudoun may have been friendly to each other, but they were decidedly unfriendly to the Southern soldier. These quaint, peaceful, and thrifty followers of Wm. Penn, possessed the most beautiful and profitable farms in the county of Loudoun. They were generally wealthy and lived well, yet refused to pay their taxes to the Southern Government.

The only method that presented a reasonable certainty of gathering the taxes of the Union Quakers, was that adopted by our battalion. Mosby ordered a detachment of one hundred and twenty-eight men to go down into their settlements, quarter the troops upon the rebellious Quakers, and send into the county of Fauquier one-tenth part of their grain, forage and bacon. The men deputised to execute this unpleasant order, were divided into squads of ten or twelve. Each squad was ordered to quarter upon some convenient Union man who had refused to pay his tithe of grain and meat, to the Confederate Government. I remember well riding through a beautiful and fertile region with my twelve rangers to the well-tilled and comfortable farm of Mr. R. T——. We found the old gentleman in his front portico. He was a fat and robust man. His red face and rotund appearance, bespake a thrifty agriculturalist. Everything about his domicile indicated ease, comfort, and plenty. Yet the first expression that escaped his lips proved beyond all controversy, that he was not happy.

Indeed, the Carthagenian had no stronger aversion to the Roman, than did this phlegmatic Quaker of Loudoun county, for the soldiers of Mosby's command. I rode directly up to the front door of the house and asked if he was the proprietor. In reply to a direct and civil question, the old gentleman asked if we belonged to that infernal band of freebooters, cutthroats and thieves commanded by the rebel highwayman, Mosby. The tone and gestures of the old man spoke more eloquently than his words. I had often heard of the quiet disposition and peaceful doctrines of the staid and gentle sect, of which he was a leader and was not prepared to witness such electric sparks of anger as seemed to flash from the old man's chin. I gently informed him in as mild manner as possible that we came into his county for the simple and laudable purpose, of collecting from himself and other Union men, the government tax of one-tenth of the products of their farms, that I demanded the keys of his stables and barns, for the purpose of examining hay, corn, &c.; also, I desired him to feed our horses and men for a few days.

A sprightly imagination may possibly conceive the intensity of anger that kindled the ire of old Douglass, when Lord Marmion called him a liar; but no one can picture the extreme rage that exploded the temper of this demure old man, when he fully comprehended insult added to aggravated injury. His chronic habit of economy was assaulted and his sense of prudence violently shocked, at the prospect of serious loss, and his pain was infinitely increased by the thought that the vile enemy inflicted the wrong. The old man yelled with rage at the bare idea of rebel horses feeding upon his valuable grain. He foamed at the mouth, stamped his feet, and exhibited more activity and vituperation than I had seen before in one of his advanced years. He accused us of all the crimes known to the law, and declared vehemently, that he preferred instant death to the surrender of his property, and he promised to die before he would give up the keys to his corn-house. I made the matter as plain as language could make it—that, in obedience to the orders of Colonel Mosby, we were compelled, no matter how painful the duty, to feed our horses and men at his expense for a few days, and send up to our headquarters one-tenth part of his crops as the tax he justly owed to his government.

This was more than Quaker flesh and Union spleen could bear. He screamed with rage and leaped into the air like some powerful wild animal shot in the head. He looked exceedingly comical, dressed as he was, in short breeches, heavy brogans, working jacket and broad-brimmed hat. His chubby figure and grotesque costume, did not coincide with his active and extreme manifestations of indignation and anger. He uttered whole volumes of abusive epithets with a rattling rapidity of sound, very much like that made by pouring a stream of dried beans upon a sonorous surface. He wildly shouted in despair his fixed determination to die in defence of his corn-crib. I endeavoured to explain to the infuriated Quaker, that even death could not protect his corn-crib, or save his bacon, and that it was our duty, in obedience to orders, to take his provisions whether he lived or died, and as good soldiers and patriotic citizens, we had no especial objections to his dying whenever his duty or pleasure prompted the sacrifice he then contemplated. I reminded him that he was at the mercy of the very men that he abused in such unmeasured and unreasonable terms, and suggested the propriety of prudence under the unhappy circumstances that environed himself and his coveted corn-crib.

In mercy to the old man I explained that even his death would not diminish the exact amount of tax we were ordered to collect from him, and it would be the part of wisdom, for him to live longer and raise another crop, as we would probably pay him one more visit for the same purpose the coming year. At this new insult he strutted awkwardly into the house and slammed the door with great energy behind him. A few loud raps with the butt end of a heavy pistol, aroused him from his profound indignation and brought him to the porch again. I now demanded the keys, with a warning that my men were becoming unmanageable, and I seriously apprehended that they would soon resent his insults in a manner to be deplored.

Trembling with anger and fear, he surrendered the keys, with the exclamation that God would inflict a distinct and terrible curse upon us for every ear of corn we dared to steal. The men proceeded rapidly with their work of measuring the old man's corn, while he poured out his vials of wrath and vituperation, upon all God-forsaken rebels in general and our little partisan flock in particular. The dull sound of his corn, as it rattled into the rebel measure, was wormwood to his Union soul. His rage seemed to wear itself out gradually as the deep sense of his loss, overspread his niggardly mind and parsimonious disposition. The sensitive old miser, crouched down upon the steps of his corn-crib and wept as bitterly over the trivial loss of a few bushels of grain as a true patriot would, over the loss of his country's rights.

When the rust of a metallic conscience oxidizes the microscopic soul of a contemptible miser, the sudden loss of a few pennies jars upon his sordid emotions with acutest agony. The sentient nerve structure of a base nature, will vibrate only to the touch of pecuniary loss. Such creatures feel no sympathy with the sufferings or misfortunes of others. They care not for their kind, kindred, or country. The old Quaker felt more acute pain at the loss of a few bushels of corn than the true patriot feels when he proudly offers up as a gift offering his gallant life upon the altar of his country's honour. The tears of a hungry crocodile make a respectable fluid compared with the lachrymal secretion of a chronic miser.

His paroxysm of passion had subsided into a wail of distress, when I again aroused his anger by demanding that my men should be provided with food. This demand he stubbornly resisted, and declared that if the infernal hell-hounds entered his house they should enter "over his lifeless corpse." I solemnly assured him that we would have no real objection to doing so, if it was at all desirable to him; that we were disposed to be accommodating, and would endeavor to please him either dead or alive; and were not very particular on that point, as indeed it was a matter of absolute indifference; but we were determined to be fed for a few days at his expense. I expressed the belief that he would find it more economical to prepare a dinner for the men, than to give up his keys to them—that we had no good cooks in our squad, and I feared they would be rather extravagant in an impromptu culinary enterprise. He comprehended this reasonable suggestion, and agreed to prepare a dinner for his enemies. Within less than two hours my order was obeyed, and a very excellent repast was ready for a dozen hungry partisans.

After dinner it became my *painful* duty to make another very unpleasant proposition to our antipathetic host. "Mr. T——, we are compelled to avail ourselves of your hospitality for the night. You will please prepare room and beds for twelve." When I uttered this sentiment, or "words to that effect," a torpedo under a camp-meeting would scarcely cause more confusion, consternation and noise. Even the ladies of this quiet abode manifested a lively interest against us. They gathered around a small table in the room in which we had dined, and by a given signal from the head of the household, that sounded like the discontented grunt of a wild boar in distress, this interesting family group, knelt down and prayed.

The old man led off in a devout growl; followed in indistinct murmurs by the younger and lesser members of this delectable group. The head of the house devoutly asked the merciful Ruler of the universe to condescend, in the infinitude of his power and mercy, to damn every rebel in the world; and, if he ran short of general curses, to please be kind enough to specially damn, without the power of revocation or appeal, the infernal devils in gray uniforms commanded by that hell-bound robber, cut-throat and murderer, Colonel John S. Mosby. The good Lord was petitioned, in most pious accents, not to spare any rebel; but if, in the discretion of Divine wisdom, anybody had to be spared the endless torments of a perennial hell, "do, good Lord, visit the extreme terrors of thy chastening wrath, upon those unconscionable scoundrels that stole our corn."

While this vindictive appeal was passing from the lips of a sordid miser, to the ear of the Great Judge, and some of our men were listening to the diabolical outpouring of superstitious folly, others were loitering about the stables, barns, and poultry houses. One of the wildest and most indiscreet of our boys had found in his rambles a hen's nest. It was evidently an old nest, or at least contained old eggs. The hardhearted young rebel had discovered that the old man's piety was not the only unsound thing on the premises.

The eggs he had found were unorthodox and as abnormal as the old man's prayers. We were listening to the devout family's expressions—so soothing and comforting to the rebel soul—and profoundly contemplating the disgusting sentiments of pious brutality, when suddenly our thoughts were turned from the group by a disagreeable noise, attended with a very unpleasant odour. The thoughtless wretch who had discovered the ancient hen-nest having no better sense of propriety than his *host* had of piety, and becoming incensed and disgusted with the old man's uncomplimentary insinuations against our command, this young savage had directed our oviparous battery against the pious group, with *smelling* if not *telling* effect.

After breaking a half-dozen of these unsavoury *shells* against the house and half-open door, this indelicate barbarian amused himself by quoting in a loud voice those beautiful though inappropriate lines of Tom Moore:

*You may break, you may ruin the vase if you will—*
*The scent of the roses will cling 'round it still.*

The indirect effort and the direct influences of the eggs brought the pious petitioners to their feet at once. They howled forth a torrent of unmeasured and ugly epithets with as much ease and fluency as Vesuvius or Ætna casts their ashes and lava. After rapidly delivering himself of all the sharp-pointed words that can be found in Webster and Worcester combined, the old saint folded his arms and stared at us with all the malignity that a fat man can possibly possess, and tried to look like an extinct volcano in his impotent wrath. But, with the exception of a few rum-blossoms, or coetaneous eruptions around his nose, I could see nothing volcanic about him. I now renewed my oft-repeated demand for a comfortable night's lodging, and the old man disappeared in great disgust without deigning a reply.

While engaged in holding a council of war with my followers regarding the best policy for the night, the lady of the house made her first appearance. She looked grand, gloomy and peculiar. It was made clear to the guerrilla boys, that the old woman was mad. She was also fat, but had more method in her madness than the old man had in his. She looked as if there was some milk of human kindness about her, though soured by adversity and rebels. With assumed deliberation and mock courtesy she asked, in measured and distinct tones:

"Is there a surgeon-doctor 'mongst you men?"

I politely stepped to the front and offered my services to the distressed dame.

"Are you a surgeon-doctor?" she asked.

I stated that I was the fortunate possessor of several diplomas and numerous certificates of distinction given me by the highest institutions of learning in America; besides, I claimed the proudest distinction yet of being the surgeon of Mosby's command, and would be still more proud were I fortunate enough to be able to render any valuable services to a lady of such distinguished appearance and surroundings as herself. She seemed unable to comprehend my statement, but understood enough to exclaim: "And you, a doctor, keeping company with such bad men! May the good Lord have mercy on your soul." She evidently enjoyed a very exalted opinion of the medical profession and placed a very poor estimate upon a rebel soldier, She informed me that she had a very sick child, and would be pleased if I would see the sufferer. I followed the fat dame into a comfortable and well furnished chamber, and to my surprise discovered that the sick child referred to was a beautiful young lady. I asked if the handsome figure before me was the patient. An affirmative response convinced me at once, that somebody was endeavouring to impose upon the surgeon. I knew quite well that such rosy cheeks, pearly teeth and rounded form could not mean disease.

"What are your symptoms, Miss, and what mysterious influence deludes you into the belief that you are an invalid ?"

"The hand of Death is upon me, Doctor," she replied. "I am dying; I shall soon leave this sorrow-stricken world, and I am willing and prepared to die, I have been sinking for many weeks, and shall soon go to the arms of our blessed Father in heaven. The destroyer, consumption, has baffled the skill of the best earthly physicians, and I have no hope to live. But before I die I make you this last request. I know that men of your calling are kind-hearted, and I shall expect you to grant my wish. I am nervous, my system is shattered and broken with long suffering. Will you be kind to a dying girl and prevail on those cruel men the soldiers, to leave our house? The noise they make will kill me, and my poor old father will become a madman under their cruel treatment."

I thought of the beautiful lines of Lord Byron:

*'Tis only in the sunny south*
*Such words are uttered and such charms displayed—*
*So fair a language from so-sweet a mouth,*
*To what an effort would it not persuade?*

I had for years paid great attention to the subject of malingering. I had made this particular branch of military surgery a special study. The experience of three years in the regular service, where men and officers continually pretend to be sick when they are not, prepared me to detect any effort in that line not perfectly considered. I perceived that my beautiful patient was more of an impostor than an invalid, and her motive was announced before her assumed symptoms were stated.

The universal rule, in a correct system of prescribing, would have answered as excellent a purpose in this case as in real disease. Remove the cause and the disease removes itself. Remove the soldiers, and the consumption of this pretty patient would not carry her to heaven as speedily as she pretended to believe. I wag too polite to insinuate the palpable fraud before me; I only expressed great sympathy for the sufferer, and promised to use my authority with my rude comrades for her sake, and counselled that her father should behave himself also, and desist from irritating the men.

My fair patient thanked me for my kind professions and offered up a very pretty little prayer for my rebellious soul. If I had to contract for a given amount of extemporaneous praying I would engage her services without hesitation, in preference to her more experienced parent. At least, it is to be hoped that the petition of this sweet young lady was heard and the barbarous appeal of the old man was lost on its way up to the celestial bar.

    My visit to the sick chamber seemed to act as a general pacificator. Even the old man smiled as I met him in the porch. The men were not insulted any more that night. Supper and lodging were ensured without more quarrelling on our part.

## Chapter 12

# Mosby's Successful Ambush

After supper I was again requested to visit the sick room. My fair patient asked me if I had ever shed human blood. (These Quakers are peculiarly averse to a lavish expenditure of sanguineous fluid). I told her I was sorry to confess I had, on many occasions. She rolled up her pretty, expressive eyes in great horror. I dissipated the painful impression as speedily as possible by defining my position, explaining that a profound sense of duty and humanity prompted me to shed blood. It was not through a savage or cruel propensity I did it, but my purpose was to save life and avert pain. My object was charity and good will to mankind, and my instruments were the lancet and the scalpel, not the murderous bullet, sabre, or bayonet.

"The good Lord will reward you for your kindness and charity to his creatures," was the fervent and apparently sincere ejaculation of my pious young patient.

I assured her that I looked alone to that source for reward, for surely men are rarely if ever known to pay a doctor's bill—that if the good Lord forgot me I most certainly would go unpaid, This playful turn of our conversation brought a very interesting smile to the handsome face of my fair patient, and she seemed to forget all about her fancied approximation to the gaunt arms of the grim old monster, Death. I was now on very good terms with the whole family.

Our men were made comfortable for the night. I parted with the several members of this Union family with reciprocal expressions of kindly feeling. Will the reader be surprised to learn that the old hypocrite sent a secret messenger many miles to a Yankee camp to betray us while we slept? Such was the fact. By sunrise the rangers were up and ready for a raid. Our horses were fed before the dawn of day, and the men were conversing in groups, awaiting their breakfast.

We observed the old man of the house very busy. He was actively engaged in carrying water from the spring, with a large wooden bucket in each hand, to fill a huge cauldron. This ponderous vessel rested upon a circular brick wall built for its support. The old man had deposited nearly one hundred gallons of water in this colossal kettle. I observed the activity with which he worked yet could not divine his purpose. I was leaning against a tree listening at the significant sound of our alarm bugle, when young Sclater, one of our most mischievous and witty fellows, approached me with a sly look and asked me if the boys might play a trick on the old man.

I asked him if it was a simple, or serious trick that he proposed to play. "It won't hurt him, and he deserves it," was the reply, followed with an air of injured innocence, by the remark, that the old cuss had been asked why he carried so much water to the cauldron, to which he had answered, with the same anger manifested on our first interview, that "it was to wash the bedclothes that had been soiled by those dirty rascals, Mosby's cut-throats and thieves;" that he would have to scour out the rooms they occupied, and boil the bedclothes to destroy the vermin; that he had been robbed and ruined by the infamous scoundrels.

"What trick do you propose Sclater?" I asked.

"When he gets his cauldron nearly full we want to upset it on him as he comes up the hill with a bucket in each hand, so he can't get out of the way."

After hearing this new and unprovoked insult, I readily gave my consent for the boys to amuse themselves at the expense of the old hypocrite.

Six strong men leaned against the huge iron vessel, prepared to lift it from its base, so soon as the old man came within proper range of this aqueous battery. It was a curious scene. The old man approached with a full bucket in each hand. He ascended a slight elevation to reach the point of his proposed deposit. When within eight feet of the cauldron, with a quick and powerful effort it was upset and its contents dashed against the approaching Quaker with such force that he was washed back almost to the spring from whence he came. Wet, mad, and covered with mud, he yelled with rage and ran around with as little method in his muscular functions as a small boy is expected to display when he has unexpectedly intruded upon the precincts of a hornet's nest, without the advantage of a formal introduction to those active, brave and independent insects. Before we had recovered from the merriment occasioned by this new entertainment, the alarm bugle could be heard distinctly in the direction of the Quaker church. A scout came in to inform us that the whole command was ordered to meet at the church without delay.

As our horses were being saddled, I was summoned to the front porch by the chubby old lady of the house. To my utter surprise, she thanked me for my kindness to the family, and, with one arm extended above her head, pronounced a blessing upon me, asking that the Lord might forgive me for associating with such evil companions and great sinners as Mosby's men; and that my kindness, charity, goodwill and valuable services to my fellow creatures, might bo rewarded in due season with plenteous grace and much more of the same sort. For all of these kindly sentiments I, of course, felt profoundly grateful.

Before the old lady completed her benediction, however, that obstreperous, uncouth, long-nosed young rebel, Willie Mosby, with his usual awkwardness, seriously marred the sentiments of her appropriate appeal, by the audible assertion that "the good old woman was mistaken in the subject of her prayer," and that "the doctor was decidedly the wildest and meanest man in the lot." This uncalled-for and provoking declaration of the adjutant, shocked my moral sensibilities so much that I have scarcely forgiven the young barbarian for his offensive suggestion to this day.

Bidding a hasty and affectionate farewell to the Quakers, we hurriedly mounted and rode rapidly to the place of rendezvous. On our arrival at the brick church we found the battalion ready for work, with the gallant Mosby in command. He instantly disclosed the circumstances that brought us so suddenly together. He said the old gentleman whose house had given us shelter the previous night had betrayed us by sending a messenger to General Hancock, commanding at Winchester. This messenger had informed the enemy that our force numbered five hundred men, and that we were robbing the Union men of Loudoun county; that the people were anxious for relief, asking that a large force be sent immediately to sweep Mosby and his men out of their county.

In answer to this appeal from my old host, the Quaker, General Hancock had ordered the Twelfth Pennsylvania cavalry and a Michigan regiment of infantry to do the old man's bidding. How Mosby discovered so soon and so accurately the facts in the case I have never ascertained, but all he told me on that occasion was verified by subsequent events. He pointed in the direction of the Blue Ridge mountains to a cloud of dust, and asked me if I knew the cause.

I told him I had often seen such phenomenon before, and that it indicated a moving column of troops. He said, "that is the force we've got to whip today." I told him that, from the amount of dust, I thought he must be mistaken; that the cloud was too large to be dispelled by only one hundred and twenty-eight men; that our force was entirely too small to meet two regiments; and from what he said the enemy outnumbered us more than ten to one; that I was not a graduate of any military school, but I had a right to my opinion, nevertheless, and though I did not have the impudence or presumption, to offer a successful leader like himself anything like advice, yet, if he would permit me to make a suggestion, I would most respectfully and anxiously recommend that we take our hundred and twenty-eight men back into the county of Fauquier, with all the promptness and speed consistent with a sound military reputation; that I had read of a great many battles where an inferior number vanquished a superior number.

I remembered distinctly the great Napoleon's statement that he never calculated the numerical strength of his enemies, but depended entirely on the discipline and organisation of his own army; yet I could not be made to believe, before the engagement, that we could defeat, rout, capture or kill one thousand six hundred men with only one hundred and twenty-eight; that I liked what people called "good nerve" as well as anybody—that I admired dash, and would not mind investing pretty considerably in a little second-hand glory if it didn't cost too much—but, when the odds were so heavy against us, I also had some regard for common sense, reason and prudence.

The great partisan chief laughed immoderately at my reasoning, and told me that his system had never failed him, and he felt just as certain of success as if his followers outnumbered the foe. He expressed such confidence and certainty regarding the results of this unequal prospective conflict that I felt somewhat encouraged by the sheer impudence of his assertions. He gave such apparently sound reasons why his small command, scientifically handled? could defeat a much larger force managed according to the old methods, that I began to regard him almost as much of a military genius as an irresponsible madman. He had already, in person, been within short musket range of the enemy's column, and told me that he knew, within one company, how many he had to fight. He had counted their wagons and ambulances, which property, he said, must be captured.

Also, he said, the Pennsylvania cavalry had some very good horses that would suit his men very well, and we must have them. I had been quite intimate with many of our most distinguished officers of the regular service and had the utmost confidence in their military ability, yet I must confess that there was something so absolutely preternatural in the assumption of power and the deliberate daring of Mosby I have never recognised in any other leader. I believe his presence before the enemy, would inspire the most abject craven, with almost heroic courage.

I had heard the thunder of all the greatest battles of the war, and had become accustomed to the noise, the carnage, and the peril of the hottest engagements on our continent; yet there is something about the quiet preparation of a small number of partisans to attack ten times their number of regulars, that gives more time for reflection, and consequently imparts to the soldier a more acute and definite sense of *cautious prudence* than the artillery storm of Gettysburg or the sulphurous hell of the Crater. Some men are born for particular callings with as absolute an instinct as a pointer dog is born with a nose for game. Mosby had the sharp, well-marked cunning for his desperate business that the sleuth hound has for the trail of a fugitive. He seemed to possess two distinct and separate natures. When in a state of repose and not in the presence of the foe, he was quiet, gentle and sociable, fond of jest and raillery, would laugh with boyish glee over a good joke, and enjoy with acute zest a witty anecdote or a lively narrative. I had never seen him when his true genius was ignited by the active excitement of the fray. He was not the same individual. He looked like a different man.

I remember well with what rapidity and caution he concealed his men in ambush that bright spring morning. One hundred and twenty men and horses were placed near the broad turnpike, so carefully hidden in their position behind the brushwood that an army might pass within fifty paces without perceiving them. With eight selected followers the cunning chief sallied forth and skirmished with the vanguard of the advancing foe. This ruse was intended to decoy the enemy into the ambush prepared for them. Many shots were exchanged, but the enemy did not pursue the decoying party. Mosby would sometimes ride within range of the musketry and expose himself to their fire, yet they would not pursue him.

He returned to his ambush and ordered us to proceed by a rapid and circuitous route a few miles further in the direction of the small town of Harmony. Here we were again concealed, awaiting the approach of the enemy. The same strategy was again attempted with like unprofitable result. Most of the day was spent in the effort to ambush and surprise the advancing column, but without success. Late in the evening we discovered that they were preparing to go into camp at Harmony. Mosby immediately placed us once more in ambush, one mile from the village, on the side of a broad turnpike. The head of our column rested within a few paces of a broad and well fenced road. He then selected ten men and dashed wildly through the enemy's camp, firing and yelling like madmen. The cavalry mounted in great confusion and gave chase to the desperate partisans. This was the result desired by the cunning chief. More than half the cavalry followed in hot pursuit and were led into the deadly ambush.

Mosby, in person, conducted the decoying squad. When the column advanced upon our concealed position, with the rapidity of thought he dashed out of the road and awaited the enemy at the head of his own column. Nearly one hundred men had passed the point of our intended attack, when the order to charge was given. I have never witnessed a more gallant charge or a more complete victory. Nearly one company of the enemy was entirely cut off from their column. They were captured without difficulty. The remainder of the regiment was repulsed and routed. Our gallant boys, with a yell and a shout, chased them back into their camp. The infantry had formed, and as their own cavalry came back in great confusion, opened a deadly fire upon their friends. From the number of wounded men I examined after the fight, and the nature of their wounds, I feel certain a large proportion of the wounded fell by the fire of their own infantry.

CHAPTER 13

# First News of the Fall of Richmond and Surrender of Lee

The brilliant affair at Harmony resulted in a decided victory for the guerrilla forces. Our small number of valiant raiders killed, wounded and captured a large number of Yankees. We also appropriated many very good horses, once the property of the United States Government, but unprofitably used by the Twelfth Pennsylvania cavalry. A reader unacquainted with Colonel Mosby's tactics, may indulge in an unnecessary display of incredulity when he reads that one hundred" and twenty-eight partisans did signally defeat and actually rout ten times their own number of well armed and trained regular troops. Yet, as remarkable as such a statement may appear, it is nevertheless a true history of the engagement at Harmony. What may seem still more startling to the peaceful reader, is the insignificance of our loss compared with the serious casualties on the part of the enemy.

In killed, wounded and captured, the enemy's loss did not fall far short of one hundred; Mosby's loss was one (the noble and gallant Binford, of Richmond), killed; Chew (a brother of Captain Chew, of the artillery) and Private Manning (once a captain on General Longstreet's staff), wounded. This was the first engagement I had witnessed on the true principles of Mosby's method of warfare. Had I not been present, it would have been difficult to convince me that one company of partisans could have routed two regiments of regular soldiers, inflicting a loss of several hundred and sustaining only the trivial loss of three men.

On many occasions I had listened to the roar of artillery and the incessant roll of musketry for many consecutive hours, with only a small number of casualties, to mark the murderous result of noisy warfare. On this occasion our boys were armed only with Colt's army revolvers. 'Tis true, each partisan carried twelve charges in his belt. The fight lasted only a few minutes, and the road, for nearly one mile, was literally covered with dead and wounded men and horses. Private Sinclair, in the hottest of the fight, discovered a Yankee lieutenant who wore a brilliant diamond ring. The partisan pursued him into the town of Hamilton and into the porch of a private residence, and shot him dead. The ring could not be readily removed from the finger. He amputated the finger and procured the jewel.

This remarkable encounter was really the last battle of the war. Our command was operating entirely within the enemy's lines. We had no certain or direct communication with the government of the Southern Confederacy. The stirring and significant scenes that marked the dying agonies of the Confederacy were unknown to the partisan battalion. We were gallantly contending against overwhelming odds, with a success unprecedented in the annals of modern warfare. We had not been informed of the events that were closing around our devoted capital. The last reliable intelligence we had received from Richmond, was a dispatch from General Lee informing Mosby that Sheridan was preparing a strong force of mounted infantry at Winchester for the purpose of sweeping the valley with fire and sword. With rare accuracy, the actual route he subsequently followed was foretold by that unerring and grand old general. We were at supper when Mosby received this dispatch. He smiled, and said to me: "Doctor, your old town of Charlottesville will soon be in the hands of the enemy," and gave me the dispatch to read.

This communication from General Lee—the last we ever received from him—informed us that the line of march proposed by Sheridan would embrace Harrisonburg, Staunton, Waynesborough, Charlottesville and Gordonsville, and finally unite with Grant's army, then at Petersburg. He requested Mosby to fall upon Sheridan's rear and retard his march up the valley. We struggled hard to cross the Shenandoah River, in a desperate effort to comply with this request, but fate was against us. The stream was immensely swollen by heavy rains, and we found it impossible to ford it at any point.

Totally ignorant of the events that were hourly sounding the death-knell of our government, we struggled on, with bright hopes of final success. During the month of March we had won victories against enormous odds. We had captured many prisoners and valuable army supplies, and had succeeded in inflicting severe loss upon the enemy wherever we met him.

The month of April now opened upon us with improved prospects. Lieutenant-Colonel Chapman had returned to us with his six hundred men that had wintered in the Northern Neck, and Mosby was making active preparations for a brilliant spring campaign. Our men were cheerful and our chief was in high spirits. Many of the bravest veterans of the regular army were rapidly filling the ranks of our companies, and Mosby was busy reorganising new ones. About this time there was a force composed of renegade Virginians, called Key's battalion, with headquarters at Harper's Ferry. These natural children of a spurious patriotism, commanded by an outlaw of nature named *Key*, annoyed the true people, called rebels, considerably, and from their knowledge of individuals and families betrayed many of the best citizens of the vicinity of Harper's Ferry into the hands of the enemy.

Mosby organised a company of veterans and placed the gallant Baylor in command. Baylor was one of the colonel's favourites. Mosby had a way of his own in forming companies and selecting officers. He always submitted his new organisations to severe ordeals. Baylor was a young man of uncommon courage. His new company was organised and placed under his command in the morning, and directed to visit Harper's Ferry that night to ascertain what could be accomplished in a collision with Key's Virginia renegades.

The morning following this event a messenger arrived at Mosby's headquarters with a dispatch from Captain Baylor, stating that he had obeyed the orders of his colonel; had visited Harper's Ferry; met Major Key and his command, and, though the Virginia Yankees outnumbered his company three to one, he had been fortunate enough to capture the party, and now held them as prisoners, awaiting further orders. This information gave great pleasure to the Colonel. He expressed the opinion that young Baylor was as able and as true as the best officer in his command, and he expected much from him in the future.

The news from Baylor put the whole command in a good humour. We rode rapidly, and in high spirits, to the quarters of the gallant captain. As soon as we arrived I gathered such Northern newspapers as were found on the prisoners. Mosby was in the best humour I had ever seen him. He was laughing and talking rapidly and cheerfully with Captain Baylor and his prisoners, while I gathered a package of Baltimore papers and retired to a seat upon a log to read the news.

Never shall I forget the shock and mortification that I received on opening the first newspaper. It was the Baltimore *American*. Double leaded columns told of the fall of Richmond and the surrender of General Lee. In the midst of our triumph over the capture of Key's battalion, I read the death warrant of the Confederacy. I was so suddenly and completely shocked that I could not realise the fact. Even under the startling announcement, that consoling element that clung to the bottom of Pandora's box, though considerably debilitated, clung to me. *Hope* was not dead, but dying. I still held on to the possible chance offered by the universal tendency of the enemy to lie.

I knew that most of their success throughout the terrible annals of war had been accomplished by their facile art of lying. They had lied under all circumstances; and had made public and private lying, professional and individual lying, general and local lying, legislative, judicial, and executive lying, civil, legal, and military lying, written and oral lying, perform all the functions of nerve, of numbers, of shell and shot, of artillery and musketry, and had so often succeeded, by their universal panacea of falsehood, in converting the most disastrous defeat into the most brilliant victory, that I yet hoped the startling announcement of the fall of our capital and the surrender of our army was a part and parcel of the same widespread and universal system of lying that had been displayed, with such wonderful success, for four long years of war. With that dreadful emotion, of hope contending against despair, that only a parent feels while watching the hurried breath and sunken eye of a loved child, I called Mosby to me and with one question, "Is that true," pointed to General Wetzel's dispatch from the city of Richmond.

The stern, brave, intrepid soldier gazed at the fatal lines that foretold the death of our country and our cause, and I gazed at him with the same intense feeling. When I saw tears gather in his eyes, I lost all hope. Other officers of the battalion gathered around us. Many of these hardened veterans that had faced death in every form that the monster could present himself, with unblanched cheek and steady hand, now dropped their heads in profound grief. The heavy sigh and moistened eye interpreted their deep feeling better than language could express it.

*Woe betide a country when*
*She sees the tears of bearded men."*

It was indeed difficult to realise that these men were the same that, only a few moments before, so joyfully cheered the victorious Baylor. To dream of the dazzling, resplendent glories of heaven, and awake amidst the burning marl and dismal fires of hell, may dimly portray the grim emotional contrast that played upon the hearts of these brave men.

The great leader of the valiant clan was dumb with grief. For the first time in an eventful life the quick fire of his fertile genius was suddenly extinguished by the startling violence of this terrible calamity. For years his whole heart had been wrapped in the fiery struggle for Southern liberty. No man ever offered up his life for any cause with more cheerful resignation than had our dauntless chief in hundreds of desperate conflicts. He had no other thought than the service of his country. His entire being was so engrossed with the dreadful work of the soldier, that the sudden and unexpected-downfall of the Southern Government, crushed him under its intolerable weight. His followers gathered around him, speechless, and shrouded in the dark mantle of unutterable grief. The great cause was *lost*. Virginia's motto reversed. "*Freedom shrieked when Koskiusco fell*;" brave men wept, when the glorious Southern cross went down. Mosby was the first in the group to break the painful silence. With the Baltimore *American* in one hand and pointing to the ominous report of General Wetzel with the other, he said:

> Our poor country has fallen a prey to the conqueror. The noblest cause ever defended by the sword is lost. The noble dead that sleep in their shallow though honoured graves are far more fortunate than their survivors. I thought I had sounded the profoundest depth of human feeling, but this is the bitterest hour of my life.

While uttering these sentiments that seemed to well from the deepest recesses of his overburdened heart, his faithful followers, mate with grief, gazed upon his fixed and rigid features. He looked the very image of despair. If the cubless tigress in her desolate jungle, could imitate her human cousin, by moistening her grim visage with tears of distress, she would doubtless resemble our mortified chief in haggard features and hopeless gloom.

Those faithful hearts that had followed the varying fortunes of the Confederate battle-flag were deeply wounded men when that glorious ensign fell to rise no more. The hallowed memories that cluster around the old banner will never be effaced from the heart of the true

Southern soldier. Yet, what strange emotions spring from the same cause, though prompted by opposite motives. While Mosby wept, and, like Rachel, would not be comforted because he had lost his country, my assistant surgeon, Dr. Dunn, complained bitterly from a different cause. The doctor had just returned from a successful raid in Maryland, where he had robbed some belligerent merchant out of a few hundred greenbacks, and was exceedingly jubilant over his spoils. Just as Mosby, with a tremulous voice and frame shaken by the deepest feeling, poured out his earnest lamentations from his aching and overburdened heart, Dr. Dunn arose in an awkward manner, and with expressive though uncouth gestures, said in a loud voice:

> This is just like all the rest of my d——d luck. If the world had been a cow I would have been its infernal tail, I expect. Now, I have been fighting for several years in bad luck not making a cent and just as I was getting in a good way of making money for the first time in my life, the d——d thing *busted up.*

This timely and ridiculous expression of my avaricious assistant, somewhat aroused our mortified comrades from their gloomy reflections. The glaring contrast between the mercenary mortification of Dunn and the patriotic anguish of Mosby, changed for the moment, the train of our melancholy thoughts. Now for the first time we were brought face to face with the most unpleasant realities that can possibly disturb the equanimity, or ruffle the temper of a true soldier. Our minds had been heretofore filled with only one purpose, and that was to oppose unto death a powerful enemy. Now we had to reflect upon the possibilities and probabilities of a good or a bad reception by the men we had fought so long and so earnestly. Will they receive us as prisoners of war or hang us as outlaws? *"To be or not to be, that is the question?"* Notwithstanding the clear and positive testimony borne by the Baltimore *American* that our capital had fallen and the noble old army of Northern Virginia had surrendered at Appomattox, Mosby once more disposed his men into several raiding parties to continue our unequal contest as if nothing of importance had transpired.

Chapter 14

# The Work Still Goes Bravely on

With that peculiar military audacity so characteristic of Mosby, he disposed his men in raiding squads, and sent them throughout Loudoun, Fauquier, Clarke, Frederick and Culpeper. His followers all felt that, Othello like, their occupation was gone. Yet in obedience to the orders of their chief, they seemed as earnest in their efforts to kill, capture and annoy the common enemy, as if nothing unusual had occurred. One bright Sabbath morning, Mosby and three of his followers, Sclater, Hern and another, were concealed in the brush-wood bordering the broad turnpike a short distance below Winchester; their horses were picketed a few paces from them in the woods. The chief was awaiting, as was his custom, to catch any stragglers or stray Yankees, that might possibly venture near his lair. By such means he frequently obtained useful information regarding the position of troops or the locality of wagon trains, also careless ambulances and army supplies.

He had a peculiar attachment to sutler's stores. He once captured the same sutler three times; on the third occasion the itinerant military merchantman exclaimed, in decidedly broken German, "Cur-nel, dees is de teird dime, end I vil not schtand mit it enny moor."

The three raiders were not long concealed in their cover when the inveterate Hern exclaimed, "Colonel, thar comes one live Yank and two town gals."

After waiting a few moments the laconic order was given, "Go out, Hern, and fetch them in." In less time than it takes to write this incident the uncouth, rugged and ragged Hern walked back into the brush, bringing with him a remarkably well dressed young man. This young man looked every inch a *beau* of the lower class, and, indeed, like anything else than a soldier. He was dressed in black and was as well jewelled as the best modern timepiece. He wore glittering rings and a flashy breast-pin, besides any quantity of gold watch-chains. It seems that he had indulged in an unusually long walk with two fashionable young females from the town of Winchester on that bright Sabbath morning. He had evidently put on his best harness and most costly jewellery.

Hern was one of the most daring of Mosby's fighting men, but, like Hugo's description of Cambronne, he was a very rough specimen of the *genus homo*. Most of our men were remarkable for cleanliness of person and exquisite taste in military dress. Hern was the opposite of this habit. He wore a ragged Confederate gray jacket, out at the elbows, and fringed by time in various places. His rough Confederate boots had seen their best days; they were out at the toes, and run down at the side, with short trousers, and an old dilapidated Yankee overcoat torn in many places. Hern looked every inch a clumsy clown in a sea of trouble. This was the figure that brought into the bushes the remarkably well dressed Yankee *beau*, and with an air of confused awkwardness, introduced him to Mosby, "Say, Kernel Mosby, here is the feller; what must I do with him, an' shel I fetch the gals in?"

At the sound of Mosby's name, the well dressed stranger trembled and stammered an expression of surprise. "Is this Colonel Mosby I have heard so much about, that kills and eats his prisoners?" The colonel grinned one of his most interesting and ghastly grins at this significant interrogation, and answered in the affirmative that he was the man. At this the unfortunate and alarmed prisoner cried out with a loud voice, "Oh! my God, Colonel, don't keel mee, I am a poor, miserable sinner and I ain't prepared to die. Colonel, forgive me, I ain't no soldier no how."

On bended knee with uplifted hands this frightened creature begged most piteously for his life. The trembling wretch seemed disposed to unbosom himself on all topics. The colonel, desiring to have a private interview with the stranger, touched him significantly on the shoulder and with that enlightened grin that only Mosby could execute, beckoned him to follow further into the dense woods. In passing near his horse Mosby carelessly reached out his hand, and shaking one of his huge cavalry pistols from its holster, said, "Now I want you to tell me the truth in answer to any and all questions I shall ask you." The frightened wretch, on seeing the stern visaged chief take the dreadful instrument of death from his holster, and feeling absolutely certain that he was doomed to immediate and certain death, fell on his knees again, and implored the savage looking colonel to spare his life.

"Oh! my God, I can't stand it; I shall run if you are going to *keel* me—you said you would not *keel* me, and now, now, now, you are going to do it. Oh! have mercy on me. I am a poor fallen sinner, and ain't prepared to die now."

The only reply the grim chief made to this pusillanimous appeal was, "You are very well dressed for a poor fallen sinner, and I have already told you that I shall not hurt you if you will only tell me the truth."

After considerable conversation in a low tone between the colonel and his frightened prisoner, both returned to the side of the road. Mosby turned to his men and said: "Hern, go through him." The unfortunate and frightened creature evidently regarded this order as his absolute and irrevocable death warrant. He did not understand the meaning of that much-used term in guerrilla tactics. The term "go through him" only means to relieve the sufferer of any loose greenbacks or superfluous jewellery that may cling about his person after the entertaining process of capture has been consummated. "Now, now, O Lord! you order that man to *keel* me, after all your promises. What difference does it make to me whether you keel me or that other man keels me? I shall run, I shall run, if you shoot. Lord! have mercy on my soul. Don't keel me! Oh, don't! for God's sake, don't! I will do anything you say if you spare my life."

Even the coarse, unfeeling and clumsy Hern felt sorry for the craven, cowardly wretch, and explained, in his primitive style, that he was ordered not to kill him but to appropriate his personal effects in a very peaceful and unostentatious manner; that if he would only keep quiet long enough and stop all that infernal begging and palavering he would soon show him by actual practice the difference between killing a customer and simply "going through him," *secundem artem*.

"Now let me show you," said Hern. "For instance, your coat is better than mine. I am gwyne to trade that garment wid you."

"Certainly, yes, by all means," said the alarmed customer. "I will swap coats with you; certainly I will."

"Well, then," said Hern, "your boots are better than mine, and that ain't right neither."

To this unjust assertion the accommodating stranger yielded a ready assent. He seemed altogether too willing to yield to every wish and approve every suggestion made by the barbarous if not villainous Hern. The rough guerrilla robber appropriated each and every piece of jewellery and article of clothing that suited his fancy, and insisted on the stranger wearing his old costume. The mind of the prisoner was very impressible to all the whims, desires and wishes of his inspector. Hern deliberately exchanged his several articles of clothing with his victim. No man ever manifested more pleasure in being robbed than did this unlucky *beau* of Winchester, when he discovered that his life was safe.

He would have been happy in the privilege of escorting his lady friends back through the streets of Winchester in no better raiment than was the progenitor of the human race attired when playing with snakes, robbing orchards, and flirting with Eve in the garden of Eden. In examining the contents of the stranger's pockets, we discovered the true cause of his great alarm in the presence of Colonel Mosby. One of the pockets contained a remarkable document. It was in pamphlet form, of the cheap dime novel order. It was printed on the cheapest and coarsest paper. The typography was dreadfully bad and the subject matter still worse. This curious specimen of cheap Yankee literature, was fearfully and wonderfully made. It pretended to be the life of Mosby and a history of his command. It was fancifully illustrated with the clumsiest wood cuts.

Some of the illustrations represented Mosby and his men at breakfast. Hideous pictures of rough Confederate soldiers around a camp fire, with dead Union soldiers before them in every stage of mutilation that the savage fancy of an excited fool could possibly suggest. Haggard, lean and famished men were represented with a slice of human flesh pierced by a bayonet or ramrod, and held over the burning embers to broil as a savoury dish for the palate of the wild and hungry partisan.

This quaint illustrated narrative of Mosby's command, if believed by the superstitious hoodlums of the North, must have impressed those benighted savages with intense horror and abnormal dread of the Confederate partisan. No savage ever conceived the horrors of war as they were described and pictured in this grotesque literary fiasco. Mosby was represented by the hideous wood cuts something in form between a centaur and a vampire, as he fed with ravenous gusto upon the choice steaks and tender cutlets of heroic Yankee prisoners.

After a perusal of this specimen of Northern fiction it is easy to comprehend why the well-dressed barbarian, was so dreadfully alarmed when he found himself suddenly in the presence of the great king of the cannibals. I have no doubt the unhappy fool believed that fate had fattened him as a choice repast for the horrid bloodsuckers of

Mosby's command. When he saw the Cassius-looking guerrilla chief take from his holster a murderous weapon and walk, with Tarquin's ravishing strides, through the brushwood, it is easy to imagine the inexpressible horror that darkened his terrified soul.

If 'tis true, as Caesar said it was, that brave men die only once, but cowards many times, this demoralised captive must surely have expired once a minute for the several hours of the fearful ordeal to which he was submitted in this dreadful interview. He had, no doubt, amused the charming young Union females during their promenade, with the blood-curdling stories of Mosby and his ferocious cannibals. He had probably shown them the pictures of hungry and savage rebels feeding upon the sweet tender loin flesh of youthful Union braves. He was young, green, fresh, and from his conduct and dress, must have been a successful ladies' man. What he had learned about Mosby and his men was evidently derived from the published record in his pocket, and that record was not only in print, which fact made it unquestionably true, but then its statements were corroborated by expressive illustrations, and the reader could see for himself that Mosby and his men were actually devouring the flesh of the Union prisoners.

Anyone could see them eating it in the pictures; then who could be so sceptical as refuse to believe, what could be seen even with the naked eye. Hern carefully and with great deliberation, divested the gaudy young dandy of every species of personal property that could be rationally utilised by a thoughtful warrior, and kindly assisted in dressing the victim in his own well worn and untidy articles of dress. When the work of exchanging garments was complete, the mother of the young Union dandy would not have known her son. He was of smaller stature than the robust and uncouth Hern; the stranger's black vestments fitted their new possessor very tight, while the raiment of the rough partisan, hung loosely on the more meagre person of the *beau*. Indeed the clothes of Hern fitted the fop too much, and the fop's clothing hugged the clumsy figure of Hern with the uncomfortable contraction that a straight jacket holds on to the limbs of a maniac.

The two females awaited patiently the return of their unlucky escort, with that blessed feminine adaptability so characteristic of the sex. They were amusing themselves with promiscuous giggling and walking around each other in total ignorance of the fate of their companion, nor did they seem to cure whether he returned to them again or not. Nothing could look more ludicrous than did the Union dandy after the process of "going through him" had been scrupulously accomplished. Hern's boots were much too large for him, and his toes peeped through them with a constrained air of retiring modesty, as if they were ashamed of their new and unaccustomed license. The old Confederate's trousers were too long for him, and they bagged about his unsubstantial limbs as if they wore hanging out to dry.

The dilapidated blue overcoat out at the sleeves and dangling in many melancholy folds over his narrow shoulders, wrought incalculable violence to the law that presides over the eternal fitness of things. The mournful slouched *felt* hat was not the only thing *felt* on that eventful occasion. The wearer felt happy, that he had only lost a few articles of worthless jewellery, exchanged a cheap suit of shoddy broad-cloth for the grotesque uniform of a modern cannibal, and had made a much narrower escape than Daniel had leisure to dream of in the lion's den. From the peculiar manner he wagged off in the direction of the females, I am convinced he felt happy in his novel and unbecoming costume. He did not depart with a strut, nor did the movements of his form betoken pride, but there was an airy swing about Hern's old blue overcoat, as it gracefully waved an *adieu* to the scenes of morbid fear and mortal peril, that told of blessed relief from great tribulations.

The appearance of the receding captive, was ludicrously monstrous. He seemed to think aloud:

"I was dead and am now alive. My flesh has escaped the digestive powers of voracious cannibals. Though decked in the ragged ugliness of a rebel uniform, I can once more breathe the pure atmosphere of heaven and live."

He did not walk the turnpike like a thing of life, but rather wriggled his slow course, in the direction of the two females. They awaited his approach with gestures and motions that implied astonishment and curiosity combined. As he came they gradually receded from him, as if alarmed at his changed appearance. He was so unlike their dandified escort of the early morning, that they seemed not to realise the change that had transformed a cheap and highly wrought *beau* of the morning to a hideous guy at noon. We could distinctly hear the screams and laughter that announced the recognition of our late prisoner. The two females seemed afraid of their *beau*. They moved slowly from him as he awkwardly approached them. The three figures receded in the direction of Winchester, and disappeared over a slight elevation of the road, the females still screaming with laughter and their disguised escort walking slowly after them.

CHAPTER 15

# The Chief Excluded from Parole

The legions of the North, like the folds of a monstrous reptile, had contracted upon the emaciated form of the Southern Confederacy until all evidence of vitality or hope of resuscitation had been extinguished. Eight hundred battle-scarred and war-worn veterans yet maintained a military organisation against the sovereign authority and well armed minions of Federal authority. Nothing could be more utterly hopeless than was our condition after the fall of our capital and the surrender of the Army of Northern Virginia. Yet true to the dire instincts of determined and inveterate purpose, our stubborn chief fought on. The blood-marked annals of diabolical war, tender no record of heroism, superior to that manifested by the officers and men of Mosby's command.

Let the future historian comment as he will upon the errors that marked the decline and fall of the Southern Confederacy. The maudlin sentimentalist may eulogize the victor and condemn the vanquished. The soulless sycophant may fawn and flatter the successful hero of the hour, the human parasite may cling to the corrupt tyranny of despicable fraud. The brainless snob may incur the contempt of true manhood by the pusillanimity that worships the living ass and calumniates the dead lion. But whatever may have been the faults or follies of the South during the great struggle for what she held most dear, no man of unsullied character will dare assert that her sons were inferior, in patriotism or courage, to any race or people that ever lived or died.

The month of April, in the year 1865, marked an epoch in the history of the North American Republic that will be long remembered by the victors and the vanquished that participated in that memorable struggle. Richmond had fallen, Lee had surrendered, and the ragged remnant of Confederate regulars, commanded by General Johnston, were surrounded as by a circle of fire, and were helpless, hopeless, under the ponderous guns of General Sherman. Shadowed by such gloomy auspices, Mosby continued to annoy the enemy by every conceivable method his fertile genius could suggest.

While the reverberations of artillery at Winchester resounded along the mountains and valleys of the lovely Piedmont country in honour of the Federal conquest, and as a solemn *requiem* of the dead Confederacy, our raiding parties were busy catching sutlers, frightening quartermasters, and capturing prisoners and supplies with a cool indifference to the decrees of fate that looms up as a crude and curious incident of transcendental audacity. Our leader was, in the fullest acceptation of the term, a man of character. Conventional laws, or the established rules of society, and the ordinary modes of thought were habitually ignored in his conduct and action alike. With uncommon quickness of conception and promptness of execution he followed alone the dictates of his own original and decided reason. What appeared irrational to other men he would assume as the perfection of wisdom.

On the 14th of April, a beautiful spring day, one of the most remarkable official papers ever written by one military officer to another, was received by Colonel Mosby from General Hancock. This extraordinary epistle was addressed to "Colonel J. S. Mosby, C. S. A.," and demanded the surrender of the partisan 'battalion on terms similar to those accepted by General Lee from General Grant, and an offer to parole all stragglers from the Army of Northern Virginia, but excluded from that benefit the "guerrilla chief Mosby." The significant fact that General Hancock should have been instructed by the War Department to conclude terms, with a military officer, and at the same time refuse to recognise or acknowledge him as such an officer, discloses and emphasizes the wild hallucination that inflamed and influenced the government at this interesting epoch of our history. The calamitous act of a lunatic in the assassination of the lamented Lincoln, only indicated the widespread insanity of that unhappy period. To treat with Colonel Mosby as an officer, qualified to transact important and responsible military functions, and consider him. an outlaw, qualified to sign his own death warrant, at the same time on contract, bears strong evidence of official insanity.

A government cannot be regarded *"non compos mentis;"* yet such an act would indicate unsoundness of mind in an individual. The morning this startling intimation of an ignominious death reached our chief, he was on the road, as usual. The powerful government had declared our chivalrous commander an outlaw.

Before departing from Colonel Carter's that beautiful April morning, the fair daughters of Glen Welby had decorated his hat with bright flowers and rare taste. His horse's head was also decorated with the same beautiful emblems of early spring. He looked as happy as a bridegroom before the honeymoon's eclipse. The gaudy appearance of our leader was in glaring contrast with the gloom of our environment and its dismal associations of disaster and defeat. I have never seen a more sudden change than his features expressed when he scanned the purport of General Hancock's letter. From high spirits to low, from brightest gaiety to black despair, from sunlight and spring flowers to the hangman and the scaffold, seemed the extremes of sensation that scaled the gamut of his emotions. With compressed lip and distended nostril, he looked the very embodiment of fierce determination.

It is difficult to conceive of a more painful situation than that of our brave commander. We had nerved ourselves to bear the most terrible calamities that a protracted and bloody war could bring us in its train of unnumbered woes. We were schooling our nerves to the stoic tension demanded by the sudden loss of that cherished liberty for which we had fought so steadfastly, so earnest, and so long. But now we were confronted with a new and cruel feature in the panorama of mental torture—the disgraceful death of our brave commander. In behalf of poor humanity, with all its errors, its crimes and its infamies, let it be said that Mosby's followers were not afraid to die, as men should die, before they would submit to surrender their chief to the scaffold.

Many plans and schemes were discussed by the officers and men. A proposition was made to keep the command in tact and cut our way through all obstacles into Mexico. We knew that the ill-fated Maximilian had offered strong inducements to officers of experience to join his army. Many expressed their convictions that Mosby would cut his way easily through the Federal forces and plant his well-earned military laurels upon the sunny plains of Mexico. Wild, extravagant and irrational as this suggestion may now appear under the luminous glare of recent history, it met with the almost unanimous approval of the officers and men.

Mosby knew well the unselfish devotion of his followers, and how ready and willing they were to sacrifice their lives in his defence. He decided to communicate with General Hancock. He appointed Lieutenant-Colonel Chapman, the surgeon of his command, his adjutant and Captain Frankland, to bear the following communication to the Federal general W. S. Hancock, at Winchester.

April 15, 1865.

Major-General W. S. Hancock, Commanding, &c.:

General—I am in receipt of a letter from your chief of staff, Brigadier-General Morgan, enclosing copies of correspondence between Generals, Grant and Lee, and informing me that you would appoint an officer of equal rank with myself to arrange details for the surrender of the forces under my command. As yet I have no notice, through any other source, of the facts concerning the surrender of the Army of Northern Virginia, nor in my opinion has the emergency yet arisen which would justify the surrender of my command. With no disposition, however, to cause the useless effusion of blood, or to inflict on a war-worn population any unnecessary distress, I am ready to agree to a suspension of hostilities for a short time, in order to enable me to communicate with my own authorities, or until I can obtain sufficient intelligence to determine my future action. Should you accede to this proposition I am ready to meet any person you may designate to arrange the terms of an armistice.

I am, very respectfully, your obedient servant,

John S. Mosby,<br>Colonel C.S.A.

Lieutenant-Colonel Chapman had recently returned with a large portion of the command from his winter campaign in the Northern Neck counties of Virginia, and was not present during our conference on the Hancock correspondence. Captain Frankland, Adjutant Willie Mosby and myself left Glen Welby in the evening bearing the letter of Colonel Mosby to General Hancock, and arrived at Colonel Chapman's before night. Colonel Chapman had been married only a few months. We found him in his parlour. He introduced us to Mrs. Chapman, and after a brief conversation I presented Mosby's letter and delivered the verbal instructions regarding our visit to Winchester.

I discovered instantly that I had committed a blunder in transacting this business in the lady's presence. But I was so pre-occupied with the grave purpose of our visit that I did not think of anybody's nerves but my own. I was soon made sensible of my error. Very naturally Mrs. Chapman was dreadfully shocked at the proposition to take her husband without warning right into a large camp of the enemy.

This was more than the nervous system of any reasonable lady could bear. She most earnestly and vehemently protested against our taking the colonel with us to Winchester lest he might be imprisoned or murdered by the enemy. I endeavoured to repair the result of my inexcusable blunder in not conferring with the colonel in the absence of his estimable wife. I made every possible effort to convince her that there could be no danger in our visit to General Hancock. She paid no attention to my repeated assurances, but persisted in her nervous reiteration that Colonel Chapman should not go.

The brave and chivalrous colonel, in as calm a mood as possible, tried to soothe her fears and make it clear that he had no alternative but obedience to the order of his superior officer. He also reminded her that the war was ended and no danger of any kind attached to the duty before us. His kind and affectionate expostulations had no other effect than to increase the nervous alarm of his wife. When she discovered that her earnest appeals were futile, and that she was powerless to save her husband from what her imagination had pictured as certain death, this estimable lady became unconscious from her great alarm. The gallant colonel quietly bore her off to her chamber and left us for a few moments to ourselves. Food was soon prepared for our journey and we were on our way to Winchester. The weather, that seems to attune itself in accord with the gay or gloomy feelings of humanity, was cold and cloudy, with a sufficient rainfall to depress the spirits of our party.

We crossed the Shenandoah River at Berry's Ferry. The water was, as usual, very high, and the ford very unsafe. By swimming our horses a short distance we succeeded in reaching the opposite shore, only wet enough to make us uncomfortable for the night. When we reached within four miles of Winchester, at 10 o'clock p.m., shelter for the night was obtained from a hospitable stranger. The proprietor of the farm was absent, but his kind lady, with that hospitality so characteristic of the good people of the valley, prepared us an excellent supper and made us feel grateful and comfortable. We were conversing sadly regarding the prospects of our chiefs deliverance, when the proprietor returned from a visit to Winchester. Subject to shock and surprise as we had been for four years of war, we could not be prepared for the sad and startling intelligence brought back by this hospitable stranger from Winchester. We had often endured the humiliation of defeat, and oftener revelled in the wild and glorious triumph of victory.

In efforts to secure what we earnestly thought and believed to be the dearest rights of our country, we had scaled the loftiest heights and explored the profoundest depths of human feelings; yet we were not ready for the shock that awaited us on that eventful night. The first word that escaped the lips of the stranger on crossing his threshold yet ring in the oar of memory like the melancholy vibrations of a funeral bell, and will not rub out from the tablets of the mind. "Bad news, gentlemen." Before he proceeded further I was suddenly impressed with the absurdity of any news being bad for us. We had lost all. Even hope had fled from us. We felt that death in any honourable shape, would be a blessed relief to a conquered rebel. What intelligence under the broad canopy of heaven could be tortured into bad news for us? We were groping in the dark. Our minds were so tossed and tormented by every variety of misfortune that we were almost incapable of normal reflections. The news was bad, and bad for us—a calamity to the civilised world.

Bad news. The President of the United States has been assassinated, and Colonel Mosby is charged with the horrible crime.

CHAPTER 16

# A Flag of Truce

With all our accumulated misfortunes we were not prepared to encounter this unexpected calamity. Our errand was one of extreme doubt, anxiety and uncertainty without this new unprecedented and accidental atrocity. We had fought earnestly for what we had conceived to be a noble and a righteous cause, and we were willing to. endure every form of human suffering for our country's honour. But we had never stooped to the contemplation of dastardly and atrocious crime for the accomplishment of our purpose. The intelligence of this hideous catastrophe of brutal and unprovoked assassination shocked and paralysed the veterans of honourable warfare.

We felt the blow as a bitter misfortune that must inevitably injure the fair name of the cause we had laboured so earnestly and so faithfully to maintain with the clean hands of patriotism, honour, and a courage that the truth of history is ever solemnly charged to vindicate. We felt that the unblemished character of those noble spirits that had passed from time to eternity on the bloody field of their country's fame, was compromised by the rash act of a lunatic, or the red hand of foul and unpardonable murder. We knew that our chief was innocent of the charge that connected his name with this dreadful crime, yet we felt that the suspicion was a base insult to our leader and his cause. We were confident that the excitement and fury the murder of the president must create would surely defeat that justice we were endeavouring to obtain from General Hancock in our almost hopeless mission to Winchester.

Without the power of foresight, or the gift of prophecy, we knew enough of furious hate to divine the probable result of this unprovoked and egregious crime. Though we could not conceive of the unmitigated brutality that did follow this great and hideous offence, we knew that the base passions of the thoughtless millions, whose malice had already been manifested in no uncertain manner by burning dwellings, indiscriminate plunder of defenceless women and the murder of young children, would not be soothed or abated by the maddening crime of butchering their idolised chief magistrate. 'Tis true, we did not think that a powerful nation would debase its good name by the judicial murder of an innocent woman, in retaliation for a crime she knew nothing about; but we did expect harsh treatment at the hands of an exasperated, merciless, and powerful foe.

The people of the South could not have encountered a more terrible misfortune than the untimely and violent death of President Lincoln. Of all the inhuman vampires that gathered about the Republican throne in Washington during the Reign of Terror that lasted from 1861 to 1865, the only philanthropic heart of that hardened crew was the heart of the murdered president. The hissing and seething cauldron of political corruption that distilled devil's broth for the American people during the administration of the unfortunate Lincoln became tenfold more virulent and unscrupulous in its malignancy when that kind-hearted political philosopher fell by the hand of the demented assassin. Of all the Northern millions that fanned the flames of hell during the war, Abraham Lincoln alone expressed sincere sympathy for his erring and unfortunate fellow-citizens of the South. And now that our fair country had fallen a helpless prey to the conqueror, to fill the bitter cup of all our sorrows we were informed that our only mediator and advocate had been foully murdered, and that, too, as we afterwards learned, by an irresponsible lunatic, in the name of the very people his unpardonable infamy, so fearfully outraged.

After a restless and wretched night we proceeded on our way to Winchester. We soon came in sight of a Federal picket, composed of a portion of the Twelfth Pennsylvania Cavalry. We halted and prepared a flag of truce by tying a white handkerchief to a stick. Now a new question presented itself. Who shall carry this emblem, of enforced humility? Colonel Chapman peremptorily refused. I offered the doubtful honour to Captain Frankland, who likewise refused. I then thought of Adjutant Willie Mosby. Notwithstanding his distinguished brother's life depended so much on this simple sacrifice of puerile pride, the adjutant also declined the honour of bearing the white flag.

I then discovered that our mission must end, or I must volunteer to bear this humiliating token of submission. To great souls it may appear as a trivial sacrifice of feeling to bear a flag of truce under the peculiar circumstances of our case; but I confess the emotions generated by the simple duty of transporting a small handkerchief, attached to a stick, into the dense columns of our old enemies was anything but flattering to a natural sense of self-esteem. I decided at once to perform this disagreeable duty. I seized the rude and hastily improvised emblem of temporary peace, and galloped, with as much show of indifference as I could command, up to the line of pickets.

About this time the roads were filled with Confederate soldiers as they poured in from every direction to surrender and receive their paroles. The first question asked, as I rode up to the picket line, was, "What command, Major?"

As I returned the answer, "Mosby's," a loud and prolonged shout went up along their entire line. One bronzed and weather-beaten old veteran stepped quickly to the front and reached out his hand. With honest face and sincere tears he said, with considerable unction: "Thank God! The war is over. I know the end has come when Mosby's men surrender." To see this old Pennsylvania soldier moisten his rough cheeks with tears and express with simple earnestness his unfeigned enjoyment at the flattering prospect of a speedy peace, caused me to forget my own grief and mortification. For the first time I was made to understand that these men were earnest, and had also made many sacrifices, for their cause.

We were met by the hostile troops in no bombastic spirit of insult to our misfortunes, but with a cordial and friendly grasp of the hand that seemed to say the past is forgiven, we are friends again. It is strange magic indeed, that can change the inveterate hatred and feuds of bitter strife one day for cordial feelings of warm friendship the next. We had expected a haughty, if not an offensive, reception at the hands of our old enemies. Our surprise was complete when those men we had fought with such savage ferocity a few days before now shed tears of joy as they greeted us once more as members of the great national family.

We waited only a short time, when an officer came and escorted us to General Reno's quarters. General Reno was in command of the troops we had fought so successfully at Harmony only a short time before. He seemed glad to see us, and offered us several kinds of liquors and the best Havana cigars. He addressed several questions to Colonel Chapman regarding the condition and numbers of our command. The colonel, being a much better fighting man than conversationalist, answered very slowly. The general seemed to be unable to keep up both sides of the conversation, and turning direct to me, asked if I was at that little affair at Harmony. I answered in the affirmative. "Will you be kind enough to tell me how many of your men were engaged in that fight?" he asked.

I assured him that I had no sort of objections to imparting whatever information I possessed. I considered the war at an end and our task as finished; we had nothing more to do but surrender; that it would give me pleasure to accommodate him with all the particulars of the engagement referred to. I assured him that our force on that occasion was very small. I remembered well the officers and men were counted several times on the morning he referred to, and that the number was the same. I was present, and on each occasion when they were placed in ambush they were counted, and the exact number amounted to one hundred and twenty-eight, all told. I could readily perceive that the general was very incredulous about my statement. He smiled and said: "Twenty-eight thousand, you mean."

I repeated that I had no interest or motive in deceiving him or misrepresenting facts, and if it was all the same to him I preferred that he should not consider me mean enough to utter falsehoods only for amusement. I told him that it was natural for me to presume, that he must have considered our force much larger than it really was, or else his two regiments would not have made such good time in hastening to the rear; and that it was more than probable, if he had known how weak we were in numbers, his troops would have fought better and would not have run away quite so fast. He seemed to take much interest in my account of Mosby's method of getting what he used to call the "bulge" on the enemy, and I thought it possible Mosby's system of the "bulge" from ambush, might have been mistaken by him for one or two extra brigades.

It was somewhat comforting in our forlorn situation, to compare notes with an officer we had so recently defeated, though even that consideration did not amount to a first-class consideration, in the face of our preparations to surrender to the very troops we had routed. The general made himself as agreeable as he knew how, by doubting all my statements and asserting some wonderfully plain ones on his own account. We had not waited long at Reno's tent, when two officers from General Hancock's headquarters arrived to escort us into that general's presence. The two officers wore the rank of colonel. One was Colonel Russell. I forget the name of the other. They were as courteous and affable as they could be, and much more so than General

Reno. They informed us that they were instructed to conduct two of us to General Hancock's quarters. Colonel Chapman and myself being of higher rank than Captain Frankland and Lieutenant Mosby, we were selected.

Leaving our friends, Willie Mosby and Captain Frankland at Reno's tent, we proceeded at once to General Hancock's house. A rumour had been generally circulated throughout the army that Colonel Mosby was on a visit to General Hancock, and the entire army turned out to see him. The road to Winchester was rendered almost impassable by the mass of soldiers gathering through curiosity to see the guerrilla chief. General Hancock occupied a large brick house on the north side of Main street in Winchester. With some difficulty we made our way through the dense crowd of soldiers in blue uniforms. We arrived in front of the general's quarters and dismounted.

Our polite guides proceeded up through an iron gateway overhung with a large United States flag. It seemed to me that this flag had been placed there as a kind of compulsory test of our loyalty to the new government now demanding our allegiance. Colonel Chapman, as well as myself, had been growing more tame and familiar with Yankees, yet this sudden call to pass under the old flag aroused the slumbering fires of our rebellious pride, and I moved slowly to a small side-gate that was also embellished with a more diminutive display of stars and stripes.

I deliberately removed the little flag and gently twirled it around its small staff, then laid it quietly down on the iron railing of the fence. This movement excited a smile on the handsome faces of our polite and courteous escort. One Yankee colonel looked at the other Yankee colonel and remarked that the rebellion was dying hard. We passed into the hall of a large brick house and was informed that the general was in his room and would soon grant us an audience. We were introduced to his adjutant, whom we found a very agreeable and pleasant fellow. In a few moments' conversation with this polite officer we were much impressed with his good manners and obliging disposition. He sent a messenger to the general's room to inform him that Lieutenant-Colonel Chapman and Surgeon ———, of Mosby's command were waiting to see him. We had no well-digested plan of action in the event the general refused our petition, and we were not so sure he would have much regard for our flag of truce.

Indeed, we were really at the mercy of our old enemy, and felt no certainty that we would be permitted to return. While conversing pleasantly with Colonel Russell and the adjutant, General Hancock walked into the hall. We were introduced by Colonel Russell. Fourteen eventful years have been gathered to Time's bosom since that interview, yet I have a distinct and vivid mental vision of General Hancock as he approached us and cordially grasped our hands. There was a self-possession, ease and benignant dignity about him that I will never forget. A benevolent expression, illumined by a powerful intellect, spoke volumes of meaning from his bright and handsome face.

It may be that an association of ideas, caused by receiving kind expressions of sympathy and regard, when I expected a harsh, cruel or haughty reception, impressed me so favourably with this true gentleman and distinguished soldier. Be that as it may, I have never met a man for whom I have a higher regard, or more profound respect than I have even at this date, for General Hancock. I had never before felt at all ashamed of my old gray uniform, but when this true soldier held my hand and looked kindly and squarely into my face and said, in a firm and earnest voice:

"I sympathize with you in what you believe to be a great misfortune. You have fought bravely, and have nothing to be ashamed of. You have, like gallant soldiers, left your cause to the God of battles, and the arbitrament of the sword has decided against you. Let us once more kneel down at the same altar and be like brothers of the same household."

I felt I suppose as the Prodigal Son ought to have felt when he dropped the corn husks and abandoned his riotous living, to return once more to the home of his father. On finding such a man as General Hancock, a great leader, an accomplished officer and a perfect gentleman, against us, I for the first time encountered a doubt as to the righteousness of our cause. This noble old hero was so kind, considerate and gentle in his manner to us, when we had so little to expect of him, that he conquered me more effectually by his manly sympathy and noble sentiments than could have been done by brute force and military despotism.

CHAPTER 17

# A Negro Slave's Conception of a Yankee

Throughout the dark and stormy annals of our I bitter and earnest struggle, all the worst feelings and attributes of that wonderfully incomprehensible paradox, Confederate "humanity," had been kindled into a living blaze of active hatred for all Yankeedom. In Dixieland the word *Yankee* was a generic term that implied the enlarged significance of all and everything that is low and mean, loathsome, contemptible, disgusting and despicable. The Southern soldier, like all other men when sorely tempted, has been known to steal, but never with the readiness or alacrity of a member of Congress. I have known even commissioned officers of the Confederate States army to take what Shakespeare called *trash* that didn't belong to them; I have known some low-born followers of the Lost Cause, to do other disreputable things, and amongst others, to submit to charges of dishonesty, and even cowardice, without resentment; but I have never known during the war, a single instance of a Southern soldier submitting to the intolerable indignity of being called a Yankee. No other epithet in the language conveyed such intensified insult to the Southern ear.

It is the general opinion of mankind that a sense of guilt constrains a criminal to submit without resistance or resentment to the charge of crime. But the most hardened old offender of the Southern army, would not brook the insult of being called a Yankee. So keenly was the Southern mind cultivated by prejudice, hatred and passion, against the public enemy, that the most ignorant citizens of our rural districts believed the Yankee a kind of quadruped with crooked horns, cloven hoofs and hairy tail. I remember well my own servant, a fat, young, burly African, to express great surprise at the appearance of a brigade of Yankee prisoners captured at the seven days' battle of the Chickahominy. Henry was a good negro, a badly spoiled slave, and a great coward. He had carefully concealed himself during the hottest of the fight—like some of our more distinguished brigadiers—and when the thunder of artillery and the rattling of musketry had subsided, crept quietly out of his cover, to join the herd of human jackals in their ghastly raid upon the pockets of the dead.

I remember well when, with white eyes and glistening teeth, contrasting widely with the midnight hue of his jet-black skin, he crawled through the underbrush, cautiously and slowly, to inquire, with an air of intense anxiety mingled with fear, "Massa, is dey gwine fit agin soon? If dey is, I gwino way fum dis he-er place."

"No, boy," I replied, "the battle is over; here comes a large number of Yankee prisoners; come and see them."

The bewildered African gazed with anxious curiosity at the approaching column of prisoners, until they came very near, then turning suddenly to me, asked, "Is dem Yankees?" I answered him affirmatively. With a ludicrous expression of astonishment and glee that only a young untutored African can assume, he said: "Why, lor! dey is folks, just' like our folks, only dey close is blue. If dey dress like de res' uv us you couden' tel' um fum our sodjers."

I discovered, during the progress of the war, that my benighted servant was not the only man in Dixie that questioned the humanity of Yankees. Not only the negroes of the Southern States, but a great many unsophisticated *white folks*, had grave doubts as to what classification of the animal kingdom the Yankee properly belonged. They entertained a vague conception that a Yankee was something not well defined in natural history, but generally considered to be a monstrous compromise of nature, between a fish, a bird, a reptile or a beast of prey. Neither did many of our uncultured people care to inquire whether Yankees inhabited the earth, the air, or the deep sea.

The general impression was that the Yankee could be amphibious if he chose to be, and that he could crawl, run, fly or swim; that he fed mostly on young negroes, and was especially noted for being very numerous and in great many places at the same time. Scarcely anybody doubted that he was a voracious and ubiquitous animal, with decided prowling and nomadic proclivities. Everybody believed that his ruling passion was to take what did not belong to him, and that he was exceedingly hard to please.

From the fact of his being to a certain extent a sort of unknown quantity, as well as quality, the imagination of the more ignorant, and consequently the most superstitious, portion of our people enjoyed great latitude. It was no uncommon thing to hear the boast of some visionary young warrior proclaim, that he had broken a Yankee's wing or knocked off a Yankee's horn in a desperate hand to hand fight. There was a great variety of opinions regarding the habits of the Yankees. Many thought they fought to greater advantage by climbing trees, and if overpowered they would, take to their holes like squirrels. Others declared that their habit was to burrow in the ground, after the manner of the prairie dog, or the Florida gopher, and always to turn up when they were least expected or desired.

The impenetrable mystery that gathered around the true nature of this remarkable and badly understood animal, exercised a great moral effect upon the public mind. Women who promenaded the lower walks of Southern society, would frighten their young children into obedience by telling them wonderful stories of Yankee cruelty and barbarity. Many a boy has grown up with the fixed and changeless impression that there is no perceptible difference between a meek and pious Yankee, a shark, or a Bengal tiger. Whatever variety of opinion may have existed regarding the physical condition, shape, size, or appetite of a Yankee, there was one point on which all men, women and children agreed with an unanimity as remarkable as it was determined, and that was, that the Yankee was deceitful above all things and desperately wicked.

Repugnance, contempt and acrimonious hatred for the despised Yankee were not solely confined to the inferior classes of Southern society. I have heard a Confederate Brigadier-General, who was also a graduate of West Point, declare, in the presence of his staff, and that a large one, that every Yankee prisoner ought to be shot or hung; that they were entitled to no more rights or immunities than so many stray dogs. 'Tis true, a brave young officer replied instantly and sharply to the brigadier that "mean as the public enemy might be, no Yankee could be meaner than the officer who could utter such cruel and disgusting sentiments."

It is difficult to comprehend the ugly feelings of aversion, antipathy and hatred that animated the individual members of the opposing armies. The Southern people had educated themselves into the abnormal belief that the Yankees were the most relentless, cruel and dishonest animals on earth, while the coarse, untutored millions of the North were carefully taught by their professional liars, that the rebels were not only barbarians far beyond the reach of civilization, but that they added the hideous feature of cannibalism to their otherwise savage accomplishments. Thus the hellish fires of fratricidal strife, were fanned into a blaze of fury, by the tortured imaginations and excited passions, of a brainless and ferocious multitude of unthinking, superstitious and misguided zealots. This was the general state of preternatural antipathy that existed between the contending sections of this great country at the time of our visit to General Hancock.

Notwithstanding the fact that Colonel Chapman and myself did not participate in this foolish and ferocious hatred, for the common enemy, we had breathed the hot atmosphere of Dixie too long to feel an entire Christian resignation, to the irrevocable decrees of "outrageous fortune." We had never indulged in a senseless, savage, spiteful, thirst for revenge, yet we could not, with any healthy regard for truth, declare that we had either a very tender regard, or sincere affection for the people that had so persistently killed our friends, stolen our property and burned our dwellings. I have always admired that beautiful Christian injunction to *"love our enemies,"* but have never yet discovered the exact method by which that divine doctrine, can be rationally applied to Yankees, without committing an indecent assault on conscience or doing violence to another divine law, of a decidedly mandatory kind, that *commands* obedience to the law of truth.

As a Christian man, I cannot say that I ever did, or that I now do, love Yankees; but I do confess that the excess of virtue that made me a criminal in the eyes of all Yankeedom—the principle of patriotism, that was so admired in Washington and abhorred in Lee—grew beautifully less in the presence and under the influence of that courteous gentleman and distinguished officer, General Hancock. His manly bearing, kind words, unfeigned regard and unexpected sympathy, changed at once whatever feeling of aversion or antipathy I then harboured for himself or his cause, into sentiments of sincere esteem, not unmixed with a grateful sense of just admiration for this noble old soldier.

The general placed before us choice wines and cigars, and spoke feelingly and fluently of the prominent features of the great struggle about to be closed forever. He seemed to be as familiar with the lives and characters of the leading Confederate officers, as with his own, and evinced an intimate knowledge of all the leading incidents of the war. The conversation progressed pleasantly until I suggested the propriety of dispatching the business that brought us to Winchester.

## Chapter 18
# A Cruel Order Countermanded

General Hancock carefully perused Mosby's communication, and for a brief period of time seemed wrapped in profound thought. He said that he had been awaiting a reply from our commander for several days, and he was glad to receive it even at so late an hour. The response to his letter was just in time to save our people from great loss and suffering. He had given an order only a few hours previous to our arrival, and said it was with great reluctance that he ordered ten thousand men into the counties of Loudoun and Fauquier, as the last terrible resort, for the purpose of destroying every house that continued to give shelter to Mosby and his men.

The general manifested much feeling for the people whose fidelity to their convictions of patriotism demanded this cruel alternative of submission or destruction. He insisted now that our cause was utterly hopeless; any effort to continue the war on the part of Mosby and his followers, was savage stubbornness and irresponsible madness; that since he had demanded the surrender of our forces, we had annoyed his outposts in a most outrageous manner; that we continued to kill his pickets and capture his quartermasters, commissaries and medical stores every night. His patience was now completely exhausted, and he was compelled to use the harshest measures to force us to honourable terms of surrender. He assured us that the cruel order would be immediately countermanded, and that our visit had saved our generous and faithful friends the ordeal of having their houses and property destroyed. On how little does the happiness or destruction of a noble and self-sacrificing people depend! The mere whim or fancy of a fool, the passion, eccentricity or caprice of a madman, a false sense of duty or an erroneous sense of honour, may often produce the most serious consequences for weal or woe.

We did not think that the decision of Mosby, in sending us to General Hancock, would result in saving the houses of hundreds of our best and most self-sacrificing friends in the counties of Loudoun and Fauquier, from the vandal and cruel torch. Yet such was the fact as told by General Hancock himself. Our visit, made only a few hours after his cruel order was given, saved a large number of our devoted friends the dreadful scourge of military ferocity and destruction by fire. The general reasoned well, and argued the point that "*extremos morbus, extrema remedia,*" and asked me, with a significant smile, if that was not one of my professional dogmas. It was very evident, from the military prescription, of this true soldier, that he considered Mosby's tactics an extreme disease that required heroic remedies.

Though General Hancock possessed the stubborn and iron nerve of the true and trained soldier, he also possessed the acute sensibilities and refined emotions of a good man and an accomplished gentleman. He manifested as much feeling and sympathy for the people he had prepared to punish with such extreme severity, as any one naturally hardened by the needless cruelties and brutalities of military life could possibly feel. The purely military man is nothing more nor less than a trained brute. I have always entertained the same regard for a well-trained mule. If a mule obeys the order of his driver or master he is looked upon as a valuable animal, and the same rule holds good with a military mule, be he general, colonel, major, captain, lieutenant or a high private in the rear rank of an army. What is such an animal but an unthinking mass of organic matter that has some other animal, and oftener a brute than otherwise, to think for him? To obey the rein or voice of a driver is the highest duty known to a well-trained mule.

To obey every order given by a superior officer, is the highest duty known to the military animal. Then does not that faithful domestic animal (the mule) deserve just as much credit and glory for his submission and obedience, as does his human military co-labourer, in the campaign, or field of battle? The simple performance of a brainless duty characterizes both these noble and patient creatures. I know the world claims much more glory for the patient biped, than the stubborn quadruped; for the stolid, stupid soldier, than for his more useful cousin—the mule. But is it right, just or equitable? Can intelligence furnish the degrees, or grade of true glory that mark the disparity that divides the faithful quadruped, from the prouder and more faithless biped? So far as the disposition to do right or wrong indiscriminately is concerned, the military man is far superior to the mule.

But for constancy, patience and endurance, under long suffering the mule ranks first. When a free citizen suddenly becomes transformed into a well-disciplined soldier, he is metamorphosed into a human mule. He is not expected to have an opinion, has nothing to say on any subject; the man is as much of an automaton as the mule. Why the simple machine with two feet should be entitled to more fame or glory, than the more useful, faithful and constant machine with four feet, no writer, or philosopher has yet explained. The world has produced very few soldiers with high claims to the sort of admiration that is directed by an enlightened conscience.

The good citizen that becomes a soldier through the pure motives of patriotism when his country is in danger, when he offers his life, his fortune and his honour for the cause he holds most dear, deserves a better fate than his fellow mercenary, who fights only for his wages, and cares nothing for his cause. The mere professional soldier who fights against his convictions or his country, seems only an automaton, without brain, conscience or soul, and is lower than the honest and patient mule, who works only for his food. Indeed, the mule is not complimented by the comparison. It is alone the cause, for which he fights that gives true fame to the soldier; that makes him a martyr when he falls and a hero when he survives. The creature in uniform that fights for or against liberty, as his master commands, sinks lower than the level of the brute.

God has placed the human animal a little higher in the scale of creation, and when he falls, he passes lower than his fellow-brute, because he gained in the impulse of his descent, a power in his fall, while his follow-beast holds with serene instinct the place his Creator assigned him.

When the true soldier is illumined by the higher virtues of chivalry, patriotism, humanity and charity, that marks the character of a Washington, a Lee, and a Jackson, or a Hancock and a McClellan, we look upon their unspotted names as bright green spots 'in the boundless desert of war, that extends all the way from the siege of Troy to the capitulation at Appomattox. There is a constant propensity in man to worship something. The ancient mythologists had their passionate gods—Bacchus, Jupiter, Mars, and many other unmitigated old ruffians, of that classic age. The modern heathen enjoys with exquisite emotion, the worship of his uncouth, mug-headed and bow-legged monstrous idols. The devil-worshipers of India perform their hideous rites around a sort of diabolical altar erected in honour of the devil himself, and in soft and mellifluent accents address the old "He Fiend" as the "Injured One." The good and true men of all countries worship the ever living God, and admire only the noble specimens of their own race who elevate themselves above the base and degrading passions, appetites and sensualism, which man shares in common with the brute creation.

The character of the worshiper is estimated by the purity of the being worshiped. The worshiper of Bacchus, is presumed to be a drunken sot. The worshiper of Mars is reasonably presumed a bull-headed ruffian, with as much soul or sentiment as we would expect to be manifested by a brace of Kilkenny cats. The degree of admiration displayed by some men for others also expresses a kindred feeling between the admirer and the admired. Men that admire the name, fame and character of John Brown, of Potowatomie, are surely not superior in intellect, wisdom, virtue or character, to the admirers of George Washington. A calm review of ancient or modern history will clearly establish the fact that the bubble, reputation or fame is not worth seeking at the cannon's mouth. As only good men are admired by good men, and bad men worshiped by bad men, it inevitably follows that bad men are in the majority throughout the world; hence a distinguished bad man is much more popular than a distinguished good man.

Benjamin Franklin Butler and old John Brown, will be remembered and admired by a much larger number of people (of a peculiar kind) than will such Virginia rebels as Washington, Jefferson, Jackson, and Lee. General Hancock was both gentleman and soldier. Any man can admire him without compromising his own intelligence or degrading his moral perceptions. Colonel Chapman and myself were entirely at his mercy and subject to any caprice or whimsicality a weaker officer's fancy would suggest or exercise with irresponsible impunity; yet he treated us as gentlemen and as officers, and as if we were entitled to equal consideration with himself.

He said, with much affability and kindness, that he would be very glad to receive Colonel Mosby and his entire command as prisoners of war, and assured us that we should be treated with all the civility and respect that gallant officers and brave men were entitled to, and that we would all be paroled and permitted to return to our respective homes. We received the following communication for Colonel Mosby:

Headquarters Middle Military Division,
Winchester, Va., April 16, 1865.

To Colonel John S. Mosby, C. S. A.:

Colonel Major-General Hancock directs me to acknowledge the receipt of your communication by the hand of Lieutenant-Colonel Chapman, of the 15th instant, in reply to mine of the 11th. The general does not think it necessary to designate an officer to meet you to arrange an armistice, as you suggest.

Understanding, however, your motives in hesitating to surrender your command without definite intelligence from your former superiors, the general is very willing to allow a reasonable time for you to acquire the information you desire. It is not practicable for you to communicate with General Lee, as he is no longer in authority. Lieutenant-Colonel Chapman, the bearer of your communication, has been furnished with such evidence as will undoubtedly satisfy you that further resistance on the part of your command can result in no good to the cause in which you have been engaged.

In view of these facts, the general will not operate against your command until Tuesday next at 12 m.. provided there are no hostilities from your command. This agreement to be understood to include the Department of Washington and the Potomac River line. It is possible some difficulty may arise from the operation of guerrilla parties not of your command, but the general hopes you can control the whole matter. On Tuesday at noon the general will send an officer of equal rank with yourself to Millwood to meet you and ascertain your determination, and if you conclude to surrender your command, to arrange the details. Lieutenant-Colonel Chapman will be able to give all the information you desire as to the probable terms.

If you consent to the above arrangements, please notify Brigadier-General Chapman, at Berryville, as soon as practicable.

Very respectfully, your obedient servant,

C. H. Morgan,
Brevet Brig-Gen, and Chief of Staff.

CHAPTER 19

# Colonel Chapman Mistaken for Mosby

After a prolonged and decidedly pleasant interview with this polite, courteous and accomplished officer, I arose to thank him for his magnanimous kindness and rare generosity before taking our final departure. He politely asked us to dine with him, and at the same time informed us that General Torbett had sent a special invitation to take dinner at his quarters. With a pleasant gesture and a significant expression of his handsome features, this fine looking old Federal chief said:

Gentleman, as you have been on much more intimate terms with General Torbett than myself, and as you have given him recently such good evidences of your regard, and always received-his visits with such warm if not affectionate cordiality, it may be more pleasant during your short stay with us to accept his invitation. Though General Torbett claims the right to entertain you, I will be very much pleased if you will do me the *honour* of accepting a soldier's hospitality and break bread with me today.

This was said in such a kind manner, and with such pleasing grace, that the most callous and obtuse rebel, would have been softened by the smooth and touching sentiments so appropriately expressed.

For two poor, forlorn, helpless, conquered rebel soldiers, who presented themselves at the throne of Federal power, as humble petitioners for mercy and justice to our outlawed chief, to be treated as distinguished visitors by the august representative of absolute power, was a shock to our previous calculations that threatened to take the atmosphere out of anybody's lungs. This great and unexpected condescension of potent military authority, almost overpowered us. To think of two hungry and friendless supplicants in gray uniforms being asked to confer an *honour* on a great, big, powerful major-general of the victorious Federal army by taking dinner with him, was more than the best trained nervous system could bear. If we could have been educated slowly and gradually to accommodate ourselves to this change of feeling we would have exhibited less awkwardness under the shock we received, if the startling compliment had been administered in broken doses. But taken all at once, it made us feel something like the poor relations in the Pickwick papers—"*all smiles and shirt collars.*"

My comrade, Colonel Chapman, was not a talking man, and General Hancock's extraordinary and almost oppressive kindness left me bewildered and confused. I endeavoured to say something pretty, but stammered something probably the reverse. Kind treatment was what Confederate soldiers knew nothing about. We had never received any of it from our own officers or government, and had no reason to expect it from our old enemies. At the death of poor old Peg Sliderscrew, the housekeeper of Arthur Gride, the miser, many suggestions were made by the people as to the cause of the old woman's sudden taking off, when a youth, who knew something of the true inwardness of old Gride's household habits, said that "it was probable that the old woman had seen something good to eat, and the surprise killed her."

Good treatment to a Confederate soldier would do as much violence to the law of chronic habit as the appearance of dainty food was suspected to have inflicted upon the lean, hungry housekeeper of the inveterate miser, Arthur Gride. I tried to be as thankful and polite as I could. I talked a good deal. My quiet friend Chapman afterwards told me that I talked too much. I remember the feeling of gratitude that prompted me on that occasion much better that I can remember the words by which I endeavoured to express it.

It occurs to me that I looked the old general squarely in the face while he held my hand, and told him that if ever fate decreed that I should live to get the better of him as much as he seemed to have the advantage of me, I should do my best to return all his distinguished favours with compound interest—that is, if the laws and the Constitution of the new government, known as the United States at that time, should be so kind as to permit favours, or any other currency to bear compound interest or any other kind of interest—that if I was unfortunate enough to live several hundred years more than Methuselah ever did, I should not then outlive the profound gratitude I felt for his exceptional kindness and unmerited generosity; that should fortune ever turn his footsteps in the future towards the good old county of Albemarle, where I had a home when I last heard from it, I would assuredly kill the fatted calf; and if the calf was not fat enough, or if General Sheridan had not already killed it, he should have the first choice of all the pigs, chickens, ducks, or any other thing that was good to eat or drink, that was yet left in that hospitable old county, provided that infamous marauder, General Sheridan, with his hungry swarm of human caterpillars, known as Sheridan's mounted infantry, had left enough in his wake to feed so distinguished a Federal general as himself upon; that provided General Sheridan had left anything in my old county, I would see to it that General Hancock should have it.

Feeling a full and clear certainty that my intentions were first-class, I was not very cautious in the words I used on this occasion. I have, ever since that eventful epoch, believed that my earnest effort to please only succeeded in sadly boring my distinguished host. The general had implied a handsome compliment to our command in his reference to the several warm receptions we had given his friend, General Torbett, as we had recently repulsed him in a lively and splendid engagement at Warrenton. He had also complimented our courage, skill and bearing as gallant soldiers, and eulogized Mosby's extraordinary genius and unprecedented daring.

All these things were exceedingly flattering to our vanity. All men have vanity, even a vanquished soldier, and human vanity always enjoys a good appetite and can digest an enormous amount of the crudest and toughest flattery. Though conquered we were like other men— vain even of our defects and proud even of our follies. But, with all our human follies, when General Hancock told us he would be *proud* of the *honour* two friendless, helpless and lonely rebel officers would confer by dining with him, it was rather more than the very voracious appetite of human vanity could well receive or comfortably digest.

Colonel Chapman wore one more star on his collar than I wore on mine, and I left it to him to decide whether we should *honour* General Hancock or General Torbett with our distinguished presence at dinner. The colonel being somewhat slow, I put the question, "All who are in favour of dining with General Torbett will say aye; those to the contrary say no." The colonel not being contrary said nothing. I voted in the affirmative, and as the colonel did not vote on either side I decided that the meeting had voted unanimously for dining with General Torbett. The noble old general smiled at this method of taking the sense of our delegation on the interesting question of dinner. With an air of condescending though majestic dignity he walked with us to the door. The street in front of the house was densely packed with Federal soldiers in blue. General Hancock said, with a smile: "It is rumoured that Colonel Mosby is here; observe the curiosity of the army to see your leader. Gentlemen, it is impossible for you to go out by the front gate."

Then turning to Colonel Russel he asked him to conduct us out by the back way and escort us to General Torbett's quarters. Colonel Russel kindly guided us through the rear way into an alley that led into a cross street. No sooner did the Federal soldiers observe our movements than they made a great rush into the cross-street in a desperate effort to see the famous fierce fighter, Colonel Mosby. We worked our way as best we could through the dense mass of uniformed humanity that surged and rolled around us as blue and restless as the sea. In answer to the many questions as to "Which is Mosby?" I would point to Colonel Chapman and the colonel would point them to me. Many were the comments made, and some not of a decidedly complimentary character, as to our appearance.

Some of the men expressed great surprise that "sich an 'unery' man should have made sich a fuss in the worl'."

Others said they thought "he must hav' bin an ugly cuss frum the way he behaved heself, but he wuz re'ly wus lookin' than we had spozen he wuz." "Lor! what a hard-lookin' feller! No wonder he fout so, frum his looks. He looks like a foutin' man, he do." "I ain't never see no wus lookin' man, I ain't; he looks like he wuz bought outen a drove of wild men, he do. He don't look like he tame yet, he don't." "He dang'rous feller to turn lose now, you bet." "He don't look like a bad man, he ugly though." "I woulden like to trus' him now, if he has gin it up, I woulden." "No wonder we coulden ketch him befo'; he look like a fox, he do." "Thank God hie done gin it up, I say." "I didn't think he looked like that, I didn't."

Such were the running commentaries passed upon us as we moved through the dense mass of Yankee soldiers from General Hancock's to General Torbett's headquarters. As the various reflections fell equally upon, myself and my comrade, Colonel Chapman, we divided the doubtful compliments between us the best we could, and felt any other sentiment than vanity as we received this running fire of criticism from the rank and file of blue uniforms before us. Colonel Chapman insisted that I was the man mistaken for Mosby, and I with equal contumacy insisted that, as the colonel was equally as ordinary looking an individual as myself, and at least an inch or two more conspicuous, the doubtful compliments must "have been intended for him."

Without any further difficulty than the wild creations of Yankee fancy that greeted us on our way, we arrived at General Torbett's quarters. We found the general reclining on a couch. He informed us that he had been seriously indisposed for several days, but was glad to receive us as his guests. He spoke pleasantly of the interesting encounters he had had with us on previous occasions, and mentioned the affair at Warrenton as one of peculiar interest, particularly to his medical director. He introduced me to that officer, and informed me that his doctor had lost two very valuable horses on that occasion and would like to know something about them. The medical director seemed so deeply interested in the fate of his favourite quadrupeds that he gave me a graphic description of the animals in question, and anxiously asked if I thought there was any prospect of his ultimately recovering them. From his minute description I recognised the fact that our gallant Captain Glasscock was the officer who had captured the doctor's horses.

I told him it was very probable he would finally recover his property. He said they were great pets, or favourites, and he was willing to pay full price for them. I had formed an opinion that as we were conquered we had no right to anything. We had unfortunately lost our liberty and could not conceive how we could maintain any legal right to property. I therefore assured him that Captain Glasscock would doubtless take great pleasure in restoring the horses to their legal owner, without money and without price. I very much regret that I have forgotten the name of this medical director. I remember his appearance well. He was a small man with small eyes and small side whiskers, of small stature and still smaller ideas. His whole soul seemed to be totally absorbed with the hope of recovering his lost property. Every other officer at General Torbett's headquarters was thinking of the great events of the closing struggle that had shaken a continent and bathed a nation in the best blood that ever flowed from patriots' veins. But this remarkable military M. D. seemed wholly absorbed with his horses.

It occurred to me that unfortunate indeed must be the brave soldiers whose welfare in sickness and wounds would depend upon such an officer. A commissioned officer who could think only of his private property in the throes and agony of a great nation, in the storm and convulsion of the hideous civil war that shed its horrid glare around us, must surely be unfit for the high and responsible duties of his almost sacred office. What a great curse it is—incalculable in its cruel damage to humanity—for the medical department of an army to be incompetent and indifferent to the discharge of important functions, stupid, unjust, or depraved! Whenever or wherever I discovered incompetency, folly, and cruel injustice, I always thought of the thoroughly organised hell of the medical department of the Confederate States Army, with its implements of torture in the irresponsible hands of ignorant and cruel impostors. The medical department of our army, with its Gorgon head, was well described in *The Devil's Drive* by the great lord of British poetry:

*What shall I ride in, quoth Lucifer then,*
*If I follow my taste, indeed?*
*I will ride in a wagon of wounded men,*
*And smile to see them bleed.*

The horribly shocking picture in Lalla Rookh, drawn by Tom Moore, when Mokana lifts his veil upon the ghastly scene of his poisoned victims, and discloses for the first time to mortal vision features too hideous to describe, and plainly tells them:

*Now see if hell with all its powers to damn,*
*Can add one curse to the foul thing I am—*

is nothing more nor less than the picture of thousands of mangled human bodies—the sick and wounded myriads of Confederate soldiers—looking intolerable anguish and despair into the face of the stolid representative of Confederate surgery. The veiled prophet of Korassan was more merciful to his deluded followers than was the Confederate medical department to its unhappy victims. "The Moon Maker" poisoned and killed without torture; but it was left for the prophet of the nineteenth century to transport thousands of living, mangled soldiers hundreds of miles for no other purpose than cruelty, torture and death.

CHAPTER 20

# Description of the General and his Surgeon

We found General Torbett a very pleasant fellow. He was excessive in his politeness, though his excellent address did not entirely conceal a vein of inordinate vanity that cropped out from his every word and gesture. My preconceived ideas regarding the good looks and behaviour of Yankee officers prepared me to expect a very different impression and reception from these antipathetic gentlemen. General Torbett was of medium stature, more gaunt than robust, of erect figure, a large jaw and expressive features. The prominent facial muscles, compressed lips, high curved nose and steady eye, betokened strong will, determined purpose and intellectual power. This was the officer that commanded the Federal cavalry against us at Warrenton a short time previous to this interview.

He made some very pleasant observations regarding that engagement, and seemed to think as General Reno did of the affair at Harmony—that our forces were much larger than we acknowledged them to be. I soon discovered that these Yankee officers believed Mosby's command to be about as numerous as the Persian Army under Xerxes. Falstaft's foes in buckram did not increase in numbers with half the rapidity of Mosby's men when multiplied by the abnormal imagination of Yankee generals. No doubt, when partisan pistols prattled so lively in the streets of Warrenton, and Torbett's braves "skedaddled" in a manner that caused any other system of rapid transit to fade into insignificance, those nimble warriors conceived that rebel partisans were as countless as twinkling stars in the firmament.

The general informed us that we were just in time for dinner. lie expressed much regret that he had no opportunity of preparing a suitable banquet for his distinguished visitors, but desired that we accept his good intentions under the circumstances for a more elaborate and ceremonious reception, but yet hoped that the best efforts of his commissariat would at least satisfy the natural requirements of a reasonable appetite, and insisted with marked politeness, that we make ourselves at home and partake with cheerful freedom of a soldier's hospitality. One glance at a table well covered with every luxury that a tropical or temperate climate could produce convinced me at once that all the polite though superfluous verbosity of the general was only a peculiarity of his modest method of boasting in regard to his lavish and profuse alimentary display.

He apologised to us for the meagre repast, but said it was the best he could do on so short a notice, and added that soldiers were from the very nature of their calling subject to occasional privations. I did not desire to appear surprised or overcome at the extravagant profusion of boned turkey, chicken salad, savoury lamb, veal, fish, flesh and fowl, surrounded with tropical fruits and vegetables, and costly wines. I did not feel like "a, poor boy at a frolic," nor did I wish to appear like that melancholy and despondent young animal; but feeling to the contrary I waited for Colonel Chapman to reply to the feigned and laboured apologies of our august host.

The colonel, with his usual marked economy of language, remained silent. Finding it absolutely necessary and proper to say something, I deliberately gathered all the dignity the situation and its *outre* surroundings admitted of and tried to look as much like a Federal cavalry general as possible. Feeling quite assured that everybody present expected me to say something in response to General Torbett's studied misrepresentation of an excellent dinner, I straightway told him that we had for several years been occasionally subjected to hardships and temporary privations of different kinds; that I had once read of a noted Continental officer of the old Revolutionary war inviting a British general to dine with him, when much to the surprise of his distinguished guest, he presented him with a roasted potato on a platter of pine bark.

I informed him that we had, during our many campaigns just closed, on several occasions been forced by unavoidable circumstances to put up with almost as indifferent and meagre a dinner us his many misfortunes had now caused him to offer us, but I hoped he would not permit a nervous or supersensitive conscience to further disturb him on the score of his extreme poverty or inability to provide more suitable or savoury viands for his guests, but desired him to feel assured that we were to a certain though limited extent children of sorrow and slightly acquainted with grief ourselves; and furthermore, our mothers and Lord Chesterfield had taught us manners sufficiently civilized not to complain aloud about any mere temporary hardship; we had fully made up our minds to bear up under all such afflictions as best we could; and also, that it gave us unfeigned trouble to observe his pain because of his inability to provide better for us.

I made it as plain as possible to him that we had travelled far and could truthfully claim a very good appetite, and although his table was not an fait, and did not present as good articles of diet as we had been accustomed to in the commissariat of the Confederate States army, we were prepared to submit to the awkward infliction of a poor dinner with firm resolve and Christian resignation. I consoled him with the truthful observation that we were prepared to enjoy this interview with him even without dinner more than we did the last time we met; that I much preferred meeting himself and friends in a spirit of fraternal regard, as at present, even on an empty stomach, than as we had last met after a full and hearty meal of Nassau pork and bean-meal bread.

I hoped he would not distress himself further on our account because of his scanty repast. He could, of course, imagine that the variety of his meats, vegetables, fruits and wines differed somewhat from our accustomed fare within the Confederate lines during the maintenance of his blockade; that we could not well avail ourselves of the luxuries of foreign markets, and also, the culinary art by which we prepared our delightful Nassau pork and compounded our monkey-pudding differed somewhat from his more stylish yet less palatable modes.

The general seemed as much astonished as amused at the cool effrontery and deliberate manner in which I agreed with him in depreciating his extravagant and lavish display of dainty viands. When I explained to him the *modus operandi* of constructing Confederate monkey-pudding, composed of hard-tack, sorgum and gravy from the everlasting Nassau hog, compounded in a camp-kettle, he laughed aloud, and said if we enjoyed the monkey-pudding as much as he relished my description of it, it must have been very excellent food indeed. After making every reasonable effort I could to cause the general to feel comfortable and at homo in his own quarters, I observed he still manifested some awkwardness in the presence of such rough rebels. We had partaken of several glasses of strong Ohio whiskey at General Reno's tent and repeated the same potent prescription at

General Hancock's.

Of course we had not refused to be equally as sociable with General Torbett. The exciting scenes and inspirations of our mission, added to the potency of Ohio corn-juice of the best quality, prompted me to use many words where probably only a few would have sufficed. I told General Torbett not to look so sad on account of his indifferent dinner; he had cause to rejoice at the termination of the war. He was a victorious general and we poor conquered rebels; that he ought to feel glad even if everything on his table was sour except the pickles and vinegar; that much better men than himself had often eaten worse dinners.

According to my view of the situation, a great general ought not to set his whole heart on the mere animal or sensual pleasures of appetite, more particularly at such a time when his military aspirations and martial pride had been so signally gratified and his ambition as a soldier crowned with glorious victory; that he might excuse the expressed freedom of my opinions and sentiment if he thought proper, and if not, I was as indifferent as Mr. Toots himself: it was "a matter of no consequence;" and that if I had said anything I was very sorry for I was exceedingly glad of it.

My laconic friend and comrade, Chapman, afterwards informed me in his usual quiet way that my conduct, conversation and general behaviour on this occasion was a most sublime exhibition of human impudence. I noticed the general was not as talkative after my assault on his unprotected vanity. He continued to look as pleasant as any man in a blue military uniform could look, but complained of physical indisposition, and requested his adjutant-general and medical director to entertain us at the table. I have forgotten the name of the adjutant, though I remember he was a very polite and agreeable gentleman. I was seated by the side of the medical director, and would have enjoyed the conversation of the staff-officers very much, but for the constant and annoying questions of the medical director.

This officer would constantly interrupt our conversation—no matter what the subject or how interesting—with interrogations about his captured horses. When more intelligent officers were discussing the entertaining subject of our approaching surrender, he would invariably lug in Captain Glasscock and his horses—his pet horses, his poor horses, how he would like to recover his horses. Were he a savage he would be more likely to assume the name of Boston Charley or Shack Nasty Jim than "Young Man Afraid of his Horses." At least, he was not afraid to talk about his horses to the exclusion of every other topic. I would occasionally interrogate him upon the subject of military surgery, hospital gangrene, erysipelas, pyemia, gun-shot wounds, and refer to the rapid progress made in our profession during the war—the scientific wisdom hived by our brethren—as the only profitable result of the great struggle.

Yet, in reply to such questions as related to the approved modern methods of treating formidable diseases and injuries, he would say that he was willing to pay Captain Glasscock any reasonable price for the recovery of his horses. Surely Captain Jinks, of the Horse Marines, did not have a more affectionate regard for his favourite quadruped that was so tenderly replenished with "corn and beans" than did General Torbett's surgeon manifest for the animals captured by Captain Glasscock.

Chapter 21

# Return from Winchester

Having faithfully and successfully accomplished the purpose of our mission to Winchester, we at once bade *adieu* to our newly-made Yankee friends with many wishes for their future welfare and continued happiness, and, in company with our polite escort, the two handsome Yankee colonels, galloped back to General Reno's quarters. We found our friends, Captain Frankland and Willie Mosby, patiently awaiting our return. Their general appearance indicated that they had enjoyed General Reno's society and shared freely of his good *spirits* during our absence. Willie Mosby smiled pleasantly, as only a very happy young man can smile who smiles often; he seemed to be profoundly under the influence of General Reno's improved laughing-gas.

The general had been kind to our friends, and had evidently moistened his lavish hospitality with a very liberal allowance of Ohio whiskey. Willie, at all times demonstrative, became more so under the variety of disturbing causes by which he was surrounded. His expressive and youthful features expanded into an immense wealth of expression under the influence of mixed excitement. More stern and aged tissues are not as flexible under the strain of mental emotions or alcoholic pressure. He welcomed Colonel Chapman and myself back with a wild and explosive exclamation of delight, that sounded more like a solitary rebel yell than any other noise I have yet known to escape from human lips. It was not altogether a civilized sound; he seemed to forget that we were yet the guests of our old enemies.

Much to the surprise and mortification of my silent companion, Colonel Chapman, he loudly proclaimed in the presencs of General Reno and his staff officers: "This is the first time in my life I have ever seen the derned live Yankees in a natural state. By G—d! we can kill a thousand of them and then get away." Then taming down his ardour, he asked me, in that croaking, gosling voice so peculiar to youthful inebriation, what I thought of his suggestion.

I told him that, judging from the unquestionable evidence before me, I was forced to believe that whiskey was indeed a potent factor in the destruction of human reason, and I had already seen cause to believe the same agent was also a formidable engine of death; that I thought it exceedingly probable the Yankees, whether in the natural or artificial state, could be slaughtered by thousands; if they used that agent as freely as he had, they would kill themselves, and would hence save us all the unnecessary trouble in the vain effort to accomplish the sanguinary purposes he so patriotically recommended. This singular mode of reasoning seemed to console and quiet him very much. He took only one more glass of Ohio consolation, stuck one of General Reno's largest cigars between his teeth, and announced himself ready for any emergency. From his improved appearance I thought he was quite ready.

Slowly and sadly we returned to the county of Fauquier. Mosby had awaited our arrival at Glen Welby with feelings of uncertainty as to the result of our mission to Winchester. When we gave him the communication from General Hancock granting him all the privileges and immunities we had asked under his own instructions, he very promptly decided that it was not his intention to surrender his command at all, but thought it was his duty to disband his forces and permit officers and private soldiers to return to their respective homes.

One of Mosby's peculiarities when engaged in profound meditation was the habit of picking his teeth with a wooden toothpick, gazing at nothing with great intensity, then deliberately chewing the toothpick until it was entirely destroyed. Until this process was ended it was useless to address him, as he was never known to make a reply, even to the most important question, while any of the toothpick remained. I have known him, when absorbed in deep and anxious thought, to destroy two or more toothpicks in this way. He would sometimes use a small twig in place of a toothpick, and it seemed to depend somewhat on the size of the material he was engaged in chewing how long his spell of total abstraction would continue.

On this occasion, as well as I can remember, while engaged in the unpleasant contemplation of surrendering his faithful followers, he consumed three or four toothpicks, and said not a word until the last vestige of wood had disappeared. It was his custom when recovering from one of these protracted reveries to speak of some subject entirely foreign to whatever theme furnished the topic of his last conversation. So it was in this instance. After thinking severely in earnest for a long time he turned to me with a vacant expression and a most unmeaning grin and asked me, with the air of a sick man just awaking from a profound and protracted sleep, "Doctor, what do you think of the widow?"

"Confound the widow," I replied, "What in the name of the paternal ancestors of all the mules in creation has the widow to do with the serious question before us?" The widow referred to was a lady of considerable beauty and many accomplishments. She was one of the colonel's favourites. When I first entered his "confederacy" he had introduced me to this lady, and had recommended me as one of his warmest personal friends; and to have a good joke and a little fun of his own, he represented me as a *beau* and quite a catch. The lady was attractive, charming, and had decidedly winning ways. But she was that kind of a *belle* that probably old Nebuchadnezzar would have fancied in his day and generation more than any prudent surgeon would prize in the nineteenth century. Mrs. F—— was a *grass* widow with a live husband a long way off, way down among the gold-diggers of California.

Not many days previous to our visit to Winchester the colonel and myself had dined at the hospitable and delightful residence of Mrs. W——. This amiable and patriotic lady lived with her beautiful, graceful and refined daughters and nieces only three miles from Salem. The widow in question was her guest. This hospitable abode was an Elysium for Mosby's men. It was a place of light and life, of music, laughter, beauty and bliss. Whenever Mosby was sad or disheartened by misfortunes to his command or his country; whenever he was depressed in spirits or any disaster cast its shadow of gloom across his pathway of duty, he would invariably visit the delightful precincts of Waveland and have there the dark foreboding of sad thoughts laughed out of him by the bright and cheerful magic of that charmed circle of lovely and lively young ladies.

At the dinner-table the fascinating and fashionable grass-widow, believing, as she had been informed, that I was yet in the market of matrimony, and feeling, no doubt, quite at home in the adroit use of those irresistible charms that the genuine widow habitually directs with such marvellous power, addressed herself particularly to me, and succeeded in getting off some very excellent specimens of original wit. As I was somewhat awkward in making known my real status, thinking that it would be unpleasant to the colonel for me to state plainly that I was not in the hymeneal market, as I would thereby spoil his little joke and destroy the innocent fun he had manufactured for his own amusement, I hesitated, and the widow advanced her sharp-shooters all along the line. With the skill of a true and practiced archer she threw her arrows, feathered with cunning wit and directed with unerring aim. Mosby was delighted with the success of his ruse. It was working finely.

Everyone at the table knew I was invulnerable except the charming widow, and all seemed to enjoy with great zest the stolid manner in which I received the splendidly directed and incessant fire from this sprightly and brilliant fortress. Mosby had his stern features kindled into an expressive smile that gradually expanded into a fixed and significant grin; the young ladies laughed by platoons; even the graceful and dignified lady of the house exhibited more symptoms of mirth than I had before witnessed on her calm and handsome face. The widow said she had been favourably impressed with me from the moment her friend, Colonel Mosby, had introduced me; that she had seen a good deal of the world in her travels, but she believed she had at last discovered her *beau ideal;* that my being a warm personal friend of Colonel Mosby increased her regard for me so much that she had concluded to set her cap for me.

I thought this sort of fun had gone just about far enough, and whether it was pleasing or offensive to my chief I determined at once to put an extinguisher upon it. I at once advised my charming and vivacious female friend that in the event she concluded to set her cap for me to set the largest one she had; that I had good reason to believe I would be able to fill it. She quickly asked why she should set a larger cap for me than for any one else. I told her she was fishing in deeper water than usual, and if successful she would catch more than she bargained for, as I could promise as much as a wife and seven children for the first haul, on my part, and if the executive officer of her own household should come in from the Pacific *slope* it would amount almost to a certainty that somebody else would have to slope also.

I have never known whether it was the sudden discovery of my own *multiplication* or her domestic *division* that so startled and shocked the fair widow. She blushed an honest blush, and gave me a fierce glance, that conveyed all the meaning of a whole battery of Gatling guns, supported by a Chinese man-of-war. She threw down her knife and fork, and with an air of majestic though savage grandeur, flirted out of the room with a storm of laughter from the young ladies and Mosby's fixed and rigid grin to cheer her exit. This was the last interview I ever had with the fascinating widow, and I have never learned whether her cap is still setting or not; if so, it is very still so far as my knowledge or interest in it is concerned. With a distinct recollection of the elder Mr. Weller's advice, I am at all times prepared to "beware of the widows."

But for the fact that she gave Colonel Mosby an opportunity of exercising his peculiar habit of changing a conversation to a subject that no one could possibly be thinking of but himself, it is more than probable I should never have thought of this fascinating personage again. I earnestly urged him to ignore for the present all frivolous subjects and proceed at once to the serious work before us. He said, with a provoking laugh, that the widow was not a frivolous subject, and he believed I was afraid of her. The truth of Mirabeau's assertion that Frenchmen are composed of equal part of monkey and tiger, applies, I believe, to other people than the natives of Gaul. To think that a distinguished military leader, who had inscribed his name so deservedly high on the column of martial fame, and who now was engaged in the serious and sad contemplation of parting perhaps forever with those brave followers who had contributed so much to the glory or his record and had shared so many dangers with him, caused me to feel too solemn to participate in such ill-timed and badly digested jokes about any giddy-headed or light-hearted widow.

There was much talk but very little certainty among the officers and men as to what the erratic genius of Mosby would determine. We knew that only a few hours remained for us to consider any plans for future action. Judging by the opinions expressed among the officers, it was clear that the majority were in favour of surrender, while a few considered it more consistent with the dignity and honour of the command to disband and permit every man to act for himself. Only a few days of disastrous news had produced a wonderful change in the spirits of the brave followers of the lost cause. Each man felt that he had faithfully performed his part even under the most trying and adverse circumstances, and could bear the humiliation of disaster and defeat with the fortitude and strength that a clear consciousness of duty faithfully performed will ever bequeath to the brave and true soldier.

## Chapter 22

# The Curtain Falls upon the Last Act

The sands in the hour-glass of the doomed Confederacy were fast fading from the anxious gaze of her devoted and chivalrous defenders. The last faint ray of hope was descending rapidly below the horizon. Fate, with the blackness of an Arctic night, filled the Southern soul with unutterable gloom. Solitary, dismal, blackened chimneys and deserted homesteads marked the decline and fall of our ill-fated system of self-government. To those brave spirits that had followed the varying fortunes of our cherished cause through, sunshine and storm, through victory and defeat, through evil and through good report, the ordeal was indeed one of' unprecedented and transcendental cruelty. When the endurance of the soldier is submitted to the severe test of physical pain, hardship, privation, want and peril; when in the heat and hell of battle he is nerved by dauntless courage and patriotic impulse, the better elements of his nature predominate over the baser emotions, and the latent philosophy of his being overcomes alike the cowardice of fear and the sense of pain.

> There is something of pride in the perilous hour,
> Whate'er be the shape in which death may lower;
> Fame is there to see who bleeds,
> And honour's eyes on daring deeds.
> But, when that is done, it is humbling to tread,
> Over the weltering field of the tombless dead;
> While worms of the earth, birds of the air,
> And beasts of the forest all gathering there—
> All regarding man as their prey—
> All rejoicing in his decay.

When the undue strain and tension of a terrible and protracted struggle against fearful odds for four long years gives away suddenly to the abnormal reaction of hopeless defeat, relaxation assumes the form of mental torture that the most cruel savage might envy in his barbarous though impotent rage. The ripe resources of human iniquity have been exhausted in the vain endeavour to discover or accomplish a more hideous form of acute suffering than the murderous blow from the mailed hand of insolent, haughty and defiant despotism, that curses the prostrate form of defenceless liberty. So earnest was the fight, and so absorbing the clash of arms, that few men paused to contemplate the possibility of defeat. Now that war and mental chaos, with all its elements combined, submerged the hope of liberty in the black sea of irrevocable anarchy and desolation, we were peremptorily commanded by inevitable destiny to submit to the ugly decrees of a fate far more intolerable than death without the cheering promise of final resurrection.

Mosby directed all his commissioned officers and a few of his most trustworthy scouts to rendezvous at Paris, a small village in the county of Fauquier about three miles from Berry's Ford, on the Shenandoah river, punctually at 10 a. m. the following day. At the time appointed about twenty as brave men as ever met the shock of battle, well mounted and equipped, patiently awaited at Paris the coming of their chief. We started punctually at the appointed time, and fording the river without difficulty arrived at Millwood thirty minutes before the hour fixed by General Hancock that our truce should expire. We found General Chapman and staff, with several other Federal officers, awaiting our arrival.

General Chapman expressed much regret that the time allowed us by the terms of our truce was so limited; that he had some doubt that we could accomplish our purpose and arrange the final terms of surrender before the hour of twelve. He was acting under orders from General Hancock and had no option in the matter. General Hancock had fixed the time for the truce to expire with Mosby, and his only duty was obedience to the command of his superior; that he did not possess the power to alter terms of truce fixed by the commanding general, but would take the liberty of arranging another truce for the period of twenty-four hours, if agreeable with Colonel Mosby; and suggested that we return at an earlier hour on the following day. This arrangement was finally accepted by Mosby, and we once more departed for the county of Fauquier.

The distance from Millwood to the several abodes of Mosby's men would average twenty to thirty miles. Many of them, fatigued by the previous day's journey, slept late on the morning of the final meeting. We met at Paris a half hour later than on the previous day, and consequently arrived at Millwood almost at the exact hour that the second truce expired. We found fifteen Federal officers again awaiting us. They were seated in a large room, called a parlour in the only hotel in the little village of Millwood. Mosby walked in rapidly, followed by twenty of his officers. Taking a seat by one of the Federal officers, whose name I have forgotten, he entered into an earnest conversation with him. The first words were spoken in such low tones that, though sitting near them, I did not hear what they said.

While we were engaged in this interesting interview within doors, some excitement was going on outside. The irrepressible Hern had accompanied us without any special invitation. He was a rough diamond in his own way, and did not recognise the difference between a diplomatic military mission and a regular raid. Hern had formed some acquaintance with the Yankee soldiers immediately on his arrival, and his ruling passion for the turf prompted him at once to propose a horse race with his new made acquaintance. The challenged Yank accepted, and a spirited race was the immediate result. Hern had a vague suspicion that the Yankees had planned this meeting for the purpose of capturing Mosby and his officers. He had never mentioned his suspicions to any one; but in the race with his Yankee competitor an event occurred that ripened his suspicion into a certainty true as "proof of holy writ."

Hern and his rival turfman, after testing the speed of their horses nearly a mile, ran into the solid ranks of a Federal brigade. No sooner did this faithful and zealous soldier discover the hostile array of blue uniforms than his suspicion of foul play became a fixed conviction, he abandoned the race and returned with an earnestness and speed that would have reflected some credit upon the Knight of De La Mancha in his memorable charge upon the insolent wind-mill.

Hern was a rough but ready partisan. Like many other people, he was not handsome, neither did he dress well. No careful observer would ever discover any very striking resemblance between Solomon in all his glory and my fellow-soldier Hern. Yet he was faithful, reliable, and earnest; determined, daring, and brave. When he rode into a strong body of Yankee cavalry just beyond the limits of Millwood he felt sure he had made a far more wonderful and important discovery than Christopher Columbus or Isaac Newton ever did. He came back breathless, excited, and alarmed for the safety of his admired and beloved leader. Just as Mosby and the Yankee general had entered upon the most interesting and important phase of their mission, with the strained attention of thirty or forty officers bearing upon them, eagerly catching every word that escaped their lips; just as the potent and grave representative of Yankee authority announced to Mosby the fiat of his omnipotent judgment; just as he announced the imperative decree (looking the subtle and active guerrilla chief full in the face), "The truce has ended; we can have no further intercourse under its terms"—at this moment Hern rushed into the room.

With frantic gestures and hasty speech he reported the important result of his personal observations. "Colonel, Colonel," he exclaimed, "the infernal devils have sot a trap for you; I jist now run out about a mile and I found a thousand uv urn a hidin' in the bushes! They're in ambush! Less fight um, Colonel; darn urn! It's a trick; it's a trick to capture us, by G—d, it is."

Taken altogether, the several incidents of this remarkable interview in the parlour at Millwood were well calculated to test the moral courage, determined pluck, or military skill of any leader. With the significant voice of the great mouth-piece of Federal power imparting the irritable intelligence that we were no longer protected by the flag of truce, simultaneously with this bad news came the startling apparition of the rough and clumsy Hern announcing the clustering outside perils of our alarming situation. With a look that I shall never forget Mosby sprang to his feet, instantly grasping one of the murderous weapons in his belt, and glaring upon the Yankee officers with an expression that reminded me more of a tiger crouching to spring upon his prey than anything I have ever seen appertaining to the human race, he said, in a loud and sharp voice, "Sir, if we are no longer under the protection of our truce we are of course at the mercy of your men. We shall protect ourselves."

With that inimitable sign and gesture that so often had sent his gallant followers like a thunderbolt into the serried ranks of the foe, he led the way with long and rapid strides to the door, closely followed by twenty silent bat as determined officers as ever bore a military commission. It was a scene difficult to describe but never to be forgotten. Every partisan was well prepared for instant death and more than ready for a desperate fight. Had a single pistol been discharged by accident, or had Mosby given the word, not one Yankee officer in the room would have lived a minute. With Hern's warning voice ringing in our ears we mounted our horses in silence and Mosby led the way. His only word of command was, "Mount and follow me." We galloped rapidly from Millwood to the Shenandoah River, closely followed by a cloud of Yankee cavalry.

This was the final interview of Mosby's command with the Yankees. Thus closed the last scene of this remarkable drama on the guerrilla stage. The day following, the battalion was summoned for the last time by command of Colonel Mosby. It met at Salem, in Fauquier county, to hear the farewell address of its brave and beloved commander:

> *Soldiers*: I have summoned you together for the last time. The vision we cherished of a free and independent country has vanished, and that country is now the spoil of a conqueror. I disband your organisation in preference to surrendering to our enemies. I am no longer your commander. After an association of more than two eventful years I part from you with a just pride in the fame of your achievements, and grateful recollections of your generous kindness to myself. And now, at this moment of bidding you a final *adieu*, accept the assurance of my unchanging confidence and regard. Farewell!

This address was delivered in a voice tremulous with emotions of grief to eight hundred brave partisans, who listened with bowed heads and moist eyes to the sad words that dissolved and severed forever the strong bonds that bound them to their gallant chief.

Thus the curtain fell, the footlights were extinguished, and the actors in this exciting drama moved slowly from the stage!

Chapter 23

# Sketches of Prison Life by a Guerrilla

1

On the 14th inst. Col. Mosby struck the Baltimore and Ohio Railroad, at Duffield station, and destroyed a U. S. mail train, consisting of a locomotive and ten cars, securing twenty prisoners and fifteen horses. Among the prisoners were two paymasters with $168,000 in Government bonds.
Signed,                               R. E. Lee, General.

While Mosby was engaged in the raid referred to by the above report of Gen. Lee, Col. Gansevoort, commanding two regiments of cavalry and the first regiment of Pennsylvania infantry, guided by a traitor to our cause and a deserter from Mosby's command? named John Lunsford, made a raid on Emory's, on the Cobbler mountain, and captured four pieces of artillery. This was the only battery of artillery attached to Mosby's command. The guns were in charge of Capt. A. G. Babcock, one of the most able, trusted, and faithful officers of our command. A few days before this event, Capt. Babcock, with his artillery and only one-hundred and fifty men, defeated and put to flight a large force of the enemy at Salem, in Fauquier County, killing a considerable number and capturing two hundred prisoners.

Captain Babcock informed me that the Yankee force defeated in this engagement consisted chiefly of Pennsylvania!! ninety-day soldiers, and that they were splendidly equipped, "many of them having both hands full of gold watches and other jewellery and fine things in proportion." One hundred and fifty partisans, with two pieces of artillery, captured two hundred prisoners and much valuable property.

The artillery ammunition being exhausted in this fight, Col. Mosby ordered Capt. Babcock to remove his battery to Emory's, in the Cobbler mountain, to conceal his guns and replenish his caissons. The roads were in such bad condition that the battery had to be moved across fields and through that region of the world known as the Free State. Not being familiar with the route and topography of this region, one John Lunsford was detailed to act as guide.

Two days after the pieces were concealed in the ivy bushes of Cobbler mountain, the gallant Capt. Babcock, Nathaniel Pontier, A. G. Wharton, D. S. Smith, E. M. Jones, and John Ayler were basely betrayed by John Lunsford, and captured by Col. Gansevoort. An extract from a Washington paper not many days after this capture, under the head of "Guerrillas Sent In," says:

"Six guerrillas, all of Mosby's light-horse artillery captured near Rectorstown about a week ago, were sent in last night and committed to the old capitol. Babcock claims to be a private, but he is a captain, and the commander of the battery of Mosby's artillery, which was captured by our troops some time ago."

When Capt. Babcock was captured in the Cobbler mountain, the first question asked him after his name was ascertained by the Yankee officer making the capture: "You are the very man I am looking for where are your guns and ammunition?" proved beyond all doubt that the deserter Lunsford was the traitor. The captain refused to tell him where the guns were concealed. But the desired information was extorted from one of the drivers, who readily pointed the way, under the promise of being liberated and paroled. This creature was released, as the price of his perfidy. He was a weak and recreant recruit from the county of Fairfax. Capt. Babcock and his gallant comrades were sent from Emory's to Piedmont station, thence by train to Alexandria, and there lodged in the Slave Pen, a prison established for Yankee criminals and bounty jumpers. This place is described by the gallant captain as being as unlike paradise as its uncomfortable occupants could possibly imagine. It was a huge pen, with a brick floor, and rough planks as beds for prisoners to repose on.

After spending one night in this purgatorial retreat, they were carried before that distinguished individual, Military Governor H. H. Wells, for investigation. A close and interesting interrogation of Capt. Babcock ensued. The *brave* Wells expressed great anxiety and much curiosity to discover the exact number of guns and guerrillas yet extant in Mosby's "Confederacy." His many questions were all answered after a manner not perfectly satisfactory to this *great* man. The captain, with eminent gravity and as much deliberation and exactness of language as he could well command, instructed Gen. Wells carefully as to the most reliable methods of acquiring exact military information regarding any really important business, and cautioned this excellent though inexperienced officer against placing too much reliance upon any intelligence received through the instrumentality of hostile informers. The captain expressed to the general the belief that he would be enabled to get the desired knowledge in no better or more trustworthy manner than by going down to Mosby's command in person and thus make the necessary inquiries; that if it was not too unpleasant or disagreeable he could count Mosby's guerrillas and guns himself.

A few days before Capt. Babcock and his brave comrades were captured, a squad of guerrillas had attacked a train on the Manassas Gap Railroad at White Plains, destroyed two locomotives and a large number of cars, killed the superintendent of the Orange and Alexandria Railroad, captured a number of Yankees, and recaptured a few of Mosby's men that were prisoners on the train. Gov. Gen. Wells ordered Capt. Babcock and his fellow prisoners to be recommitted to the Slave Pen and kept as hostages; and as an additional security for the good behaviour of Mosby and his command. Gen. Wells notified Col. Mosby that he should place some of his prisoners on all the trains leaving or returning to Alexandria; that if he did not behave better in future than he had done in the past, the next time he tried any of his foolishness in throwing trains off the track he would kill some of his own men—to all of which Mosby replied that he should continue the even tenor of his way, and that if his own wife and child were on the train and it was necessary to attack it, that simple fact should not deter him from fulfilling his duty.

Wells thereupon issued a brutal and cowardly order that several prominent southern sympathizing citizens and Mosby's prisoners should be placed upon all the trains. Dr. Robinson, and Messrs. Snowden and Dangerfield, with Capt. Babcock and his comrades were crowded into a box-car next to the locomotive and sent up and down the Railroad from Rectorstown to Alexandria for five weeks. The unjust and brutal malice of Wells was visited upon these innocent and unoffending citizens because their wives were kind to the hungry prisoners and sent them food and clothing. The traitor Lunsford was frequently seen at Gen. Auger's headquarters at Rectorstown by our prisoners. Pontier, one of the prisoners, would never forget to say ugly things to the traitor wherever seen. Two trains were run daily from Alexandria to Rectorstown, with citizens and prisoners as a safe-guard. The only safety and rest the prisoners and unfortunate citizen hostages enjoyed was on the Sabbath day. No trains were run on Sunday. The creatures that could play heathen or savage in their unprecedented cruelty and barbarity to innocent men and helpless women were far too pious to allow the steam horse to labour on the Lord's Day.

About this period of their prison life our friends were frequently visited by the curious old maids and schoolmarms of the North. These primped up female oddities, would come to the Slave Pen every Sunday. The New England schoolmarm is a peculiar animal. She is as trim as a starved race horse, with a waist like a consumptive wasp, and she is always anxious to see a rebel prisoner, particularly a caged guerrilla. These attenuated specimens of New England female humanity were escorted by officious and foppish Yankee officers to the portion of the slave pen occupied by Capt. Babcock and his partisan comrades, called in the affected nomenclature of the school marm dialect the "Guerrilla Corner." One of the most curious and inquisitive of these female nondescripts advanced to the front, raised her glasses, and stared the captain full in the face for sometime and exclaimed, with an air of great surprise, "Good gracious! they look just like our people."

The spinster had evidently made as important a discovery as the great philosopher of England when he found the paving-stone with "Bill Stump his mark" engraved upon it. Capt. Babcock, one of the largest and most conspicuous of the prisoners, enjoying upwards of six feet of altitude and one hundred and eighty *avoirdupois*—feeling to a remarkable degree a just sense of disgust at being exhibited and glared at like some recently captured wild beast—arose to walk away from the uncomfortable gaze of the ugly basilisk. As he put his huge anatomy in motion he seemed to alarm his unwelcome visitors still more. As, if by a given signal, the old schoolmarms all at once raised their shrivelled arms before their elongated withered, and homely faces, and with a shrill voice that passed rapidly into a gentle and excited scream, cried out "Good gracious! what a big guerrilla." Ever since that memorable scream of the schoolmarms Capt. Babcock was known by his Yankee keepers as the "Big Guerrilla."

From the Alexandria slave pen the prisoners were removed to the old Capitol prison in Washington. At this prison all the guerrillas were kept together and separated from other prisoners. Rations here were much better than at the "slave pen." Every prisoner had his due allowance of boiled beans, though no man was allowed, under the pain of severe punishment or certain death, to carry any beans out of the mess room. Among the prisoners was a man named Prosser, who hailed from the same State that furnished a president to the Confederacy. This prisoner, to use the unembellished Saxon of his own comrades, was a "great hog" and exhibited a most extraordinary proclivity for "boiled beans," and, in short, for any alimentary article that could by any possibility be digested. Beans were good, and Prosser, like Oliver Twist, wanted more. But the men were not permitted to carry any beans out of the mess-room.

So Prosser armed himself with a quart bottle, and the bottle had a mouth nearly as large as his own. He emptied his first cup of beans into his bottle and like little Oliver, passed his cup for more. The greedy fellow had played his trick successfully for some time without being discovered. Old Rickett, the steward of the prison, was very suspicious regarding the disposition of Confederate soldiers in his charge to take beans that did not belong to them. He was exceedingly watchful and one day he arrested Prosser on his way out of the mess-room with his bottle of hot beans under his jacket. "What have you got there " asked the lynx-eyed Rickett. Prosser, who was as much addicted to lying as stealing or devouring beans, promptly and positively declared that he had nothing whatever on the outside of him. Rickett was not so easily satisfied of the soundness of his veracity.

Some time was lost in the interview. The bottle that concealed the beans was a large little used for preserving pickle. The beans had been hurriedly emptied into it while yet steaming hot, and had no time to cool. While the medacious glutton was using his best efforts of reason, logic, and sophistry to convince old Rickett that he had no extra beans about him, the bottle exploded by the moist heat and expansion of the beans, and a full stream of hot boiled beans came pouring down on the floor in the very presence of the watchful Rickett. Much to the surprise of the lying Prosser, the Cerberus of the mess-room laughed heartily at the ludicrous accident, and considered it so good a joke that he permitted the Mississippi glutton to depart in peace.

Not long after this event, Prosser made a descent upon the provisions of an officer. Old Clark, one of the rulers of the prison and consequently a very prominent and much respected officer, enjoyed great authority and many privileges. Among others, he kept his own private mess-room. This distinguished patriot lived much better than the prisoners—as of right he should have done, being a much better man, no doubt in many respects. The prisoners, on leaving their *bean* room, had to pass directly by the door of old Clark's mess-room. Prosser, in passing the old man's door, like any other dog, could smell something very savoury u the old man's table. He slyly entered the room, and without difficulty captured a nice, fat, well cooked ham and a pot of fresh butter. Prosser wore an old and somewhat dilapidated Confederate jacket, yet this garment was strangely elastic and could be made to cover any reasonable amount of provisions at a moment's notice.

On this occasion Prosser retired in good order, with a large ham and a pot of butter well covered by his short though serviceable uniform. The hungry thief made good his retreat and concealed his stolen provisions safely under his bunk. When old Clark returned to his room—hungry no doubt, as all good patriotic officers are expected to be when arduously engaged in defending their country against the fierce attacks of incarcerated rebels—the heroic old warrior missed his provisions and made a great "fuss." The entire prison was carefully searched, and the prisoners punished by a special order depriving them of supper. Yet the old man could not recover his bacon and butter. The prisoners were too true to turn State's evidence, even against such a despicable fraud as the gluttonous and dishonest Prosser.

## 2

It was amusing to notice with what rare success Prosser would raid upon the sutler's store. He regarded the art of stealing as a virtuous and reputable accomplishment, and exhibited the same regard for tobacco, apples, cakes, and other contraband commodities, that a cat has for valerian. Indeed, every article of food seemed marvellously adapted to Prosser's digestive machinery, while the fact of stealing his food seemed to add a powerful incentive to his otherwise excellent appetite. Beans, apples, raw potatoes, and ginger-bread would vanish before his wonderful voracity like snow flakes before the scorching rays of a tropical sun.

If every man could be made to comprehend, and was prepared to appreciate, the facility with which people through habit can adapt themselves to the most painful circumstances and associations, even the threatened torments of hell would be divested of half their terrors. Mosby's men in the old Capitol prison, as I have before stated, were not in a condition either physically or mentally to enable them to enjoy perfect happiness; yet they were kept so constantly occupied in the arduous effort to preserve their cleanliness and remove the various causes of filth and disease, that they were too busy to regret their misfortunes or lament their sad condition. To such readers as have been deprived of the pleasures of incarceration, it may not be totally uninteresting to review the habits and rules of guerrilla life in the old Capitol prison. Mosby's prisoners had accumulated from time to time for many months, until the old Capitol had received nearly one full company of these daring and resolute *Rebels*. Forty men occupied one large room, and were arranged in bunks one above another. They divided themselves out into committees of various kinds; there were scrubbing committees, sweeping committees, committees of vigilance, and washing committees.

Dennis Darden, of Washington city, was elected by the prisoners as prison sergeant and *ex-officio* judge of this oppressed commonwealth. His decrees were like the laws of the Medes and Persians, irrevocable and without appeal. Any delinquencies on the part of a prisoner, or the slightest violation of prison rules, would be summarily punished by a process quite disagreeable to the offender but very amusing to spectators. The *bastinado* of the East or the Russian *knout* was not more feared than the dreadful cobb. The peculiar process of inflicting the penalty for the most trivial infringement of prison rules was called cobbing, and as the unsophisticated reader may be ignorant of the *modus operandi* of this highly civilized method of enforcing obedience, it may be interesting to describe it.

The victim or prisoner when convicted was led out of his bunk by three or more strong men, and carefully stretched across a table or bench, then one of the most muscular members of the *committee of retribution*, armed with a lath, a narrow plank or the stave of a barrel, would proceed deliberately but forcibly to execute the decree of Judge Darden's court by inflicting the prescribed number of blows set forth in the sentence, upon the prostrate form of the often der.

Should any prisoner make resistance to the just execution of the sentence he was entitled by the common law which was the custom of the prison to an additional number of from three to six blows without extra costs to the prosecution. For the same reason, possibly, that some men are more fortunate than others, some of the prisoners were more prone to the cobbing process than their less enterprising comrades. Old Prosser was one of the most popular candidates for *cobbing* honours. Whenever it was rumoured that cobbing was about to commence every eye was turned to Prosser's bunk, with the full expectation of seeing him laid upon the table.

I have mentioned before, some of the peculiar characteristics of Prosser besides his remarkable propensity for boiled beans and indiscriminate lying. With a robust disposition to steal, he was like the fat boy described in Pickwick—always asleep when not engaged in stealing. Prosser was captured while asleep. He had been ordered by Mosby to guard several Yankee prisoners, and of course became drowsy. While asleep, the prisoners disarmed him and he became their prisoner. Mosby at the time was so disgusted and incensed at Prosser's want of vigilance, he declared he would be glad if they would hang him. So strict was the discipline arid so evenly balanced the scales of justice in the prison that any man who carelessly spit on the floor, or in any other way intentionally or otherwise soiled or defiled the room, would be guilty of conduct unworthy of a partisan and gentlemen, whereupon three cobbs would be his portion, with the unerring certainty of fate.

Each man had to wash his own clothes, or if he was fortunate enough to have money, he could hire some one poorer than himself to do it for him. If any one became unclean from indolence or choice, and failed to immediately purge himself of the implied contempt of Judge Darden's court, he could rely on the certainty of at least three cobbs. When the scrubbing committee held its meeting, (and the floor was thoroughly scrubbed twice every week,) all the prisoners had to ascend to their bunks, and there remain until the floor was dry again. In those days, and in the old Capitol prison, there were men called *oath-taker's*, and there was a room separate and distinct from the other apartments of the prison, called the *oath-taker's room*; and it came to pass that several Confederate prisoners, who had become weary of prison life, determined, without the fear of the Lord before their eyes, and possibly by the instigation of the devil, straight way made application to take the oath.

And it came to pass that when these *weak* and *weary* Confederates made their application to the good and great Yankee authorities, for the rare privilege of once more swearing to be good boys and wipe their weeping eyes with the old flag again, they were at once separated from the old offenders, those impenitent sinners, that stood more in need of a good square meal than all the oaths in Judge Jeffrey's court. When once the young convert advanced to the anxious bench and expressed a willingness to "jine," he was sent to the oath-taker's room and not permitted again to associate with the hardened and impenitent sinners that were yet lost in their sins, and like Ephraim, were wedded to the idols of the land of Dixie. The saints were permitted to mingle with the sinners only in the mess-room. As it has always been when the ungodly are permitted to have intercourse with such sanctified, meek and submissive spirits as the lamb-like oath-takers, many disagreeable incidents marred the pleasures that should naturally spring from a free and friendly association of soldiers, lighting under the same flag, for the same cause, and caught in the same trap.

Whenever the lambs came forth from the oath-taker's room to get their boiled beans, the hardened scoffers at the shrine of Yankee Doodle, would invariably say ugly things to them. Then the sensitive and repentant children, whose tender consciences could allow them to swear allegiance to two hostile governments with the same breath, would often lose their patience, ruffle their gentle tempers, and say many things back at the rough old veterans, that manifested no especial meekness on their part, yet were unmannerly enough to show the badness of their morals. On one occasion an oath-taker, while eating his boiled beans, was so keenly insulted by young Monroe Heiskell, (a kinsmen of President Monroe) that though a man of small statue, the oath-taker unhesitatingly proposed to fight the little fellow.

At this Capt. Babcock, one of the coolest men that ever handled ice, quietly asked the belligerent oath-taker if he would fight a man of his own size who would not take an oath. The oath-taker said he would. At once Capt. Babcock offered his services, when the fellow declined the honour because the captain was too large. He was probably correct in his view of the case, as the captain had already been dubbed by a delegation of New England schoolmarms the "Big Guerrilla."

As the man who had sworn to support the United States Government seemed to be in earnest, Capt. Babcock nominated his young friend Sclater, of Baltimore, who was of marvelous proper size and a clever representative of the Confederate Government in general and Mosby's command in particular, who would be pleased no doubt to decide by a fair fight the merits of hard swearing or no swearing at all. The fellow asked young Sclater if he would fight, and Sclater replied by a blow in the face that sent the penitent rolling over the prison floor.

This adventure caused some excitement among the Yankee authorities; to see one of their young converts punished and belaboured by an unredeemed Rebel, and guerrilla at that, was more than Yankee patriotism was prepared to tolerate. Capt. Babcock, Monroe, Heiskell, and Henry Sclater were at once arrested and put into a dungeon.

Babcock, Sclater, and Hieskell were probably the most perverse, obstinate, and incorrigible Rebels in all the old Capitol Prison. What would have been intolerable punishment to weaker minds or more unstable souls was a luxury to those hardened reprobates. Even Lafayette, the great friend of human liberty, did not enjoy his dungeon life during the long five years of incarceration at Almutz more than our desperate partisans enjoyed the old Capitol dungeon during their brief imprisonment. These brave and resolute fellows were no sooner separated from their comrades and environed by the dark, damp walls of the gloomy dungeon, than they immediately cast about for some method of escape. The body of a partisan may be confined by chains and prison walls, but his brave soul cannot be cribbed, cabined, or confined, by all the chains of slavery yet forged by the genius of tyranny. Weaker souls yield a ready obedience to the dictates of diabolical despotism; but such spirits as Babcock, Sclater, and young Hieskell, cannot be tamed by brute force or arbitrary power. No sooner were the ponderous doors closed upon them than they began, in activity and earnest, to cut their way out by burrowing under the floor of their cell.

Never did men work with more energy. Surrounded by foul air and damp, dark walls, they tunnelled under the earth a great distance until their progress was obstructed by the solid masonry and frame work of the outer wall of the dungeon. During the twelve hours of their close confinement within the dungeon walls, they had worked with great activity. They were greatly disappointed when relieved from their intended punishment and returned to the more comfortable precincts of the common prison. Injustice to old Clark, the Pluto of this modern Hades, he was kind to the prisoners, in his own peculiar modes of kindness. He favoured them in their prison rules and discipline, and furnished every facility at his command to keep themselves, their clothing, and their rooms in cleanly and decent order.

Among the various agencies and instrumentalities of regimen and police, one man was appointed—or to use the army vernacular, "detailed"—for the special though onerous function of "bug hunting," as it was called in the prison. Each man assigned to this unfashionable though necessary duty had to ascend to his bunk and pursue his calling as best he could. But if he failed or was declared a delinquent in this purifying process, nothing could be more certain than that the "cobbing" apparatus would surely await his return.

Cobbing always took place after roll call. One of the most original and interesting organisations of the prison was known as the "Owl Club." This club consisted of forty members. Each member was selected because of his supposed merits. There were several rooms in the prison, besides the "oath-takers'" room, and the "Owl Club" was formed of the best material of the several rooms. The habits of this club, as its name implies, were not unlike those of the nocturnal bird that bequeathed a name to this lively organisation. The several members of the Owl Club would sleep occasionally in their bunks by day and sit up before the fire all night.

Their every hour was occupied in laying plans and devising ways and means of escape from the strong walls and vigilant guards of the prison. The ever watchful members of the "owl" fraternity had overheard certain conversations between the officers of the prison and messengers of the government. They had been able to ascertain the probable removal of the prisoners from the old Capitol to Fort Warren, in Boston Harbor; their vigilance had discovered the intention of the authorities, and this wide-awake club had laid its plans accordingly.

Many of the owls were well informed as to the topography of the country through which they would pass on their way to Boston. Their well digested scheme was to escape from the train when near the Relay House, between Washington and Baltimore. The plan was for the Owl Club to get into the rear car of the train, and when the train approached the Relay House, at a given signal to seize and disarm the guard, cut loose the rear car from the train by removing the coupling pin, make prisoners of the guard, cross the Potomac on the ice, and return to Mosby's command.

## 3

There were spies and traitors in those days. And it came to pass that some of the "oath-takers" had been eaves-dropping and discovered the plans of the "Owl Club." And it came to pass that when the time was ripe for the prisoners to be removed to Fort Warren the guard came into the prison, armed with a huge supply of improved handcuffs in addition to their 'other accoutrements. The irons were strong and so was the guard. The guard was more numerous than the prisoners, and carried a pair of handcuffs for each rebel. This new feature of well-considered safety extinguished alike the hopes and plans of the organisation. "*The best laid plans of men and mice aft gang aglee,*" thus was "*the winter of our discontent*" made anything but glorious summer by this untoward event. It was a sorry sight to see seventy-five daring and dauntless men heavily ironed and guarded by nearly one hundred guards, marched through the streets of Washington *en route* to the city of Boston—to them, the most detested spot on the earth, under the earth, or above the earth.

The Guerrilla prisoners enjoyed a highly cultivated contempt and well considered detestation for everything in or about the hated "Hub." There was at that time as much congeniality of feeling between the Boston and Mosby's men, as was supposed to exist between St. Paul and the devil, and for that reason alone, they believed the malignity of the Federal authorities sent them there. Notwithstanding their hopeless chance for escape when placed upon the train, several of the most desperate prisoners managed to slip their handcuffs and prepare for certain death or a speedy deliverance.

The few that had removed their irons gathered in one corner of the car and held themselves in readiness to receive the signal for a general conflict with the guard. As only a few of them had shaken off their fetters, the signal was never given. Passing through the city of New York, from the foot of Courtland Street to 4th Avenue the guard was frequently taunted for their seeming cowardice by all manner of people from stage drivers to pedestrians. They were frequently insulted for using so strong a force to guard a small number of prisoners heavily manacled with chains and irons.

At Fourth Avenue the prisoners, with their strong guard and large throng of street-followers, encountered old Horace Greeley. Many of them recognised him by the well known historic white hat. The kind-hearted apostle of negro liberty stood on the kerbstone and gazed at the throng of manacled prisoners. When the old man recognised Capt. Babcock in the unhappy group, the captain raised his clanking chains and iron bracelets, and shaking them significantly in the old man's face, said; "Good morning, Horace, how is this for a prisoner of war?" The old man moved not a step and said not a word, but gazed earnestly through his good old emancipation spectacles, that saw the handcuff's slough off from the dusky limbs of the docile African slave.

The prisoners were embarked at the New Haven Railroad Depot and conveyed direct to the Hub of the universe. Arriving in Boston at night, they were confined in a warehouse until the next morning. They had been well prepared to expect a hospitable reception in this great centre of Puritan civilization and they were not at all disappointed in their anticipations. In passing through the streets they were insulted on every side, and assailed with extreme barbarity and brutality by the cowardly denizens of this ancient town. In their transit through the market-place at Faneuil Hall, the butchers and their ragged, bloodstained apprentices headed a large mob of the basest and most brutal looking inhabitants even of Boston, and cried out, not as their progenitors did of old, "crucify him" but in savage tones and shrill, croaking voices they shouted, "drown the d——d Guerrilla Rebels! kill um' hang urn! cut their d——d livers and lights out, d—n um." And many other unmelodious expressions that displayed with great clearness the average obliquity of Boston morals.

Fort Warren is a much worse place, and very much more uncomfortable for Rebel prisoners, than the Old Capitol prison even claimed to be. If the malice and ingenuity of all the speculative devils, that contract for the combustible materials of the infernal regions, had conspired in their fiendish malignity, they could not have succeeded better in administering the penalties of the damned than did the authorities of Fort Warren, in torturing both mind and body of the unhappy guerrilla prisoners.

A creature curiously shaped and cruelly stamped, with a rare expression of unmixed brutality, one Lieutenant Woodward, had sole and unrestricted control of the prison, which he succeeded in converting into a modern hell. This military Pluto was the officer in charge. Woodward was an ex-shoemaker of Boston, and may have owed his plutonic promotion to his extreme cruelty to the prisoners. He was a low born, cruel cowardly and despotic wretch. This unclean and heartless creature, increased, by every means in his power, the pain and privations of prison life, under the pretence that Northern soldiers were maltreated in Southern prisons; this fiendish military cobbler, with uncontrolled power, starved many brave and gallant men to death.

The prisoners were closely confined in damp and dark casemates, so foul that every material exposed to its poisonous atmosphere would mould, rot, or rust, in a few hours. When on rare occasions the prisoners were permitted to breathe a less deadly air, they were allowed to gather in a circumscribed area, of thirty by one hundred feet of ground, and stagger about for exercise as best they could. A dead-line was drawn close about this limited space, and no prisoner dared to pass, by accident or otherwise, beyond the confines of this fatal circle. Any man that passed beyond this line, even if he was delirious from starvation or disease was shot down like a dog.

Bread was exceedingly scarce in Fort Warren prison. Often by the strict ruling, of the merciless lieutenant in what he called "retaliative measures" there was a total suspension of bread, and the prisoners were not permitted to buy salt from the sutlers. The food of the suffering prisoners consisted of a small loaf of musty bread, for each days allowance, a small piece of salt beef was given each man for his dinner, with a small tin-cup of dirty water, in which the poor stringy beef had been boiled. No coffee or tea was given under any circumstances.

On Wednesday's and Sunday's, they were given a tin-cup of boiled beans in addition to their sumptuous and extravagant bill of fare. These rigid rules of certain death by starvation, filth, foul air and fouler water, were scrupulously enforced, for. many long and weary months, until the capitulation of the Confederate Capitol, and the surrender of the army of Northern Virginia. The starving prisoners ate all the rats they could catch. When compared with prison fare, a fat rat was considered a great luxury, and, when skilfully prepared a dainty dish indeed.

After the fall of Richmond, and the surrender of Lee, such fortunate prisoners, as had money or friends that could extend them credit, were permitted to purchase food from the sutler, at the most extraordinary price that a soulless extortioner could possibly demand. Under the harsh and cruel treatment, by enforced starvation and irremediable filth several of our bravest and best men perished in this dreadful place. Young Glasscock, a near relative of Captain Alfred Glasscock, one of Mosby's most knightly and dashing officers, was deliberately starved to death, by the wilful malice of the prison authorities.

Unlike old Clark at the Capitol prison, in Washington, the ex-shoemaker in charge at Fort Warren, laboured to augment the hardships of prison life, and his success was marked by loathsome methods of deliberate murder. After the capture of Richmond several distinguished prisoners were sent to Fort Warren; Regan of Texas, and late of the Confederate Cabinet, with Vice-President Stevens, and many other high officers of the ill-fated Southern Confederacy; were received within the foul embrace, and putrid atmosphere of Fort Warren. About this time the cruelty, severity and barbarity visited upon the prisoners seemed to relax. As an interesting feature of the late civil war, the future historian should not ignore such startling events as transpired within the sickening precincts of Northern prisons.

The reading portion of the world has been surfeited with repeated misrepresentations, and slanders, of the prolific political press. That huge engine of falsehood and perversion, groaned under its dreadful burden of slander. The charge of Southern cruelty to Northern prisoners; was invented for a malicious purpose. The thought was hatched, from the egg of envy, hatred and malice. By raising the cry, against the unfortunate South, it tended to obscure the fact of dreadful cruelty visited by the authorities of Northern prisons, upon the. unhappy Southern victims under their care. When the emotional public insanity engendered by the war subsides, it will be right and proper, to turn the clear and unbiased lens of history upon the uncouth features, of Northern cruelty to Southern prisoners. In justice to both parties, be it said, that neither were as merciful to prisoners of war, as the Christian pretensions or professions of both parties would persuade the outside barbarians to believe.

Now that the hot blood, and the ulcerated consciences of North and South, have had time to cool and heal, and the soothing influence of reason can be felt, what rational candid man, will dare risk his reputation, by the doubt, that Northern prisoners were treated with more humanity in Southern prisons, than Southern prisoners were in Northern dungeons? The false plea of retaliation on the part of the rulers of Northern dungeons, is the veriest consummation of genuine hypocrisy. During the earlier periods of the war, no complaint was heard of cruelty to Northern prisoners. But when the fair Southern lands were encircled with fire and famine, when the countless legions of foreigners, swept over the Southern States, like the locust, the vermin, and the plagues of Egypt, when the brave Confederate soldier, stood naked and starved on picket, when his costume consisted of a cartridge box and musket; when he could not even procure raw corn and bean soup, to quench the raging fires of maddening hunger, when his own commissary had stolen his scanty rations, and his aristocratic quarter master had purloined his raiment to invest in whiskey or eight *per cent*. Confederate 'bonds, then and under these flattering conditions, the devastated South was called on to feast the Northern prisoners on dainty viands that were totally inaccessible even to the President and Cabinet of the Confederate government.

The Southern soldier was starving in the rifle pits. His perishing government had, levied with its skeleton fingers, upon the last bushel of grain, or pound of meat, that the public enemy had failed to destroy or appropriate to his own use. Writhing within the gaunt embrace of famine, the torch of the military incendiary, casting its lucid glare of desolation over our hopeless and starving people, we were called on to furnish rare luxuries to prisoners of war, when we could obtain only crusts of bread, or husks of corn, to feed the, brave defenders of the South. The civilized and decent inhabitants of the earth, will not forget the fact, that the Southern government urged the Federal authorities, to exchange prisoners, because the government could not provide them proper food and medical supplies. This was a very humiliating confession, and a great military blunder on the part of the Confederate authorities, as it exposed our helplessness and encouraged the perseverance of the enemy, yet with cruel contumacy, and murderous barbarity, Northern despots refused to save the lives of their own soldiers, from the dreadful death that awaited them, through unavoidable want and privation. Merciless and emotionless rulers of the North, had waged a relentless war, against, the lives, the property and the liberties, of our people.

Military murder struck down the tottering aged sire, and the smiling toddling babe with the same demoniac blow. Hundreds of thousands, of hirelings from the crime stained and pauper crowded, shores of the old world, came torch in hand to burn the dwellings, barns and provisions of the people, and when they had performed their devils task of death and desolation so well, how can even the unthinking Northern hypocrites, with brain of lead and brow of brass, expect the absurdity they demanded that their prisoners should revel in luxury while the captors starved to death.

The meanness is incalculable that prompts human creatures, clothed with arbitrary power to commit foul murder upon helpless prisoners of war, by torture and starvation. Falsehood added to murder only aggravates the crime. The plea of retaliation, is infamously false. This is the point where history should turn its light upon demons in the shape of men. It is well known, that the South, was unable to supply healthy food and raiment, for its own soldiers in the field, yet with unparalleled generosity divided its last crust, its bean meal bread and Nassau bacon with its unfortunate prisoners.

While the rich North with its ports open to all the markets of the world, starved its prisoners to death by thousands, with the infamous, pretence of retaliation. The world may roll on through all the ages of time, and move on through the endless cycles of eternity, yet it will not bear on its broad surface a baser record of cowardice, cruelty and crime, than were the foul murders by starvation, inflicted upon Southern prisoners of war in the military dungeons of the North, "Killing by poison" or "killing by lying in wait" fills the laws definition of murder in the first degree. This sort of killing implies premeditation and malice. How much more cruel and cowardly is the killing by starvation and enforced filth? Legions of brave men—of gallant soldiers, that offered up their lives on the battlefield in defence of what they believed to be the right, have perished by the slow torture of starvation, and the poisoned atmosphere of military prisons, their last hours were tortured by the pangs of hunger from within, and crawling vermin from without, and all this in the name of patriotism and Christian charity. The Northern press with its six thousand tongues, has laboured in season and out of season, to

*Distort the truth, accumulate the lie,*
*And pile up the pyramid of calumny.*

But prejudice can disarm history, only for a season, "murder will out,"

*Truth crushed to earth will rise again,*
*The eternal years of God are hers.*
*While, falsehood wounded writhes in pain,*
*And dies amid her worshippers.*

# ALSO FROM LEONAUR
## AVAILABLE IN SOFTCOVER OR HARDCOVER WITH DUST JACKET

**AN APACHE CAMPAIGN IN THE SIERRA MADRE** by *John G. Bourke*—An Account of the Expedition in Pursuit of the Chiricahua Apaches in Arizona, 1883.

**BILLY DIXON & ADOBE WALLS** by *Billy Dixon and Edward Campbell Little*—Scout, Plainsman & Buffalo Hunter, *Life and Adventures of "Billy" Dixon* by Billy Dixon and *The Battle of Adobe Walls* by Edward Campbell Little (*Pearson's Magazine*).

**WITH THE CALIFORNIA COLUMN** by *George H. Petis*—Against Confederates and Hostile Indians During the American Civil War on the South Western Frontier, *The California Column, Frontier Service During the Rebellion* and *Kit Carson's Fight With the Comanche and Kiowa Indians*.

**THRILLING DAYS IN ARMY LIFE** by *George Alexander Forsyth*—Experiences of the Beecher's Island Battle 1868, the Apache Campaign of 1882, and the American Civil War.

**THE NEZ PERCÉ CAMPAIGN, 1877** by *G. O. Shields & Edmond Stephen Meany*—Two Accounts of Chief Joseph and the Defeat of the Nez Percé, *The Battle of Big Hole* by G. O. Shields and *Chief Joseph, the Nez Percé* by Edmond Stephen Meany.

**CAPTAIN JEFF OF THE TEXAS RANGERS** by *W. J. Maltby*—Fighting Comanche & Kiowa Indians on the South Western Frontier 1863-1874.

**SHERIDAN'S TROOPERS ON THE BORDERS** by *De Benneville Randolph Keim*—The Winter Campaign of the U. S. Army Against the Indian Tribes of the Southern Plains, 1868-9.

**GERONIMO** by *Geronimo*—The Life of the Famous Apache Warrior in His Own Words.

**WILD LIFE IN THE FAR WEST** by *James Hobbs*—The Adventures of a Hunter, Trapper, Guide, Prospector and Soldier.

**THE OLD SANTA FE TRAIL** by *Henry Inman*—The Story of a Great Highway.

**LIFE IN THE FAR WEST** by *George F. Ruxton*—The Experiences of a British Officer in America and Mexico During the 1840's.

**ADVENTURES IN MEXICO AND THE ROCKY MOUNTAINS** by *George F. Ruxton*—Experiences of Mexico and the South West During the 1840's.

AVAILABLE ONLINE AT **www.leonaur.com**
AND FROM ALL GOOD BOOK STORES

## ALSO FROM LEONAUR
### AVAILABLE IN SOFTCOVER OR HARDCOVER WITH DUST JACKET

**LIFE IN THE ARMY OF NORTHERN VIRGINIA** by Carlton McCarthy—The Observations of a Confederate Artilleryman of Cutshaw's Battalion During the American Civil War 1861-1865.

**HISTORY OF THE CAVALRY OF THE ARMY OF THE POTOMAC** by Charles D. Rhodes—Including Pope's Army of Virginia and the Cavalry Operations in West Virginia During the American Civil War.

**CAMP-FIRE AND COTTON-FIELD** by Thomas W. Knox—A New York Herald Correspondent's View of the American Civil War.

**SERGEANT STILLWELL** by Leander Stillwell —The Experiences of a Union Army Soldier of the 61st Illinois Infantry During the American Civil War.

**STONEWALL'S CANNONEER** by Edward A. Moore—Experiences with the Rockbridge Artillery, Confederate Army of Northern Virginia, During the American Civil War.

**THE SIXTH CORPS** by George Stevens—The Army of the Potomac, Union Army, During the American Civil War.

**THE RAILROAD RAIDERS** by William Pittenger—An Ohio Volunteers Recollections of the Andrews Raid to Disrupt the Confederate Railroad in Georgia During the American Civil War.

**CITIZEN SOLDIER** by John Beatty—An Account of the American Civil War by a Union Infantry Officer of Ohio Volunteers Who Became a Brigadier General.

**COX: PERSONAL RECOLLECTIONS OF THE CIVIL WAR--VOLUME 1** by Jacob Dolson Cox—West Virginia, Kanawha Valley, Gauley Bridge, Cotton Mountain, South Mountain, Antietam, the Morgan Raid & the East Tennessee Campaign.

**COX: PERSONAL RECOLLECTIONS OF THE CIVIL WAR--VOLUME 2** by Jacob Dolson Cox—Siege of Knoxville, East Tennessee, Atlanta Campaign, the Nashville Campaign & the North Carolina Campaign.

**KERSHAW'S BRIGADE VOLUME 1** by D. Augustus Dickert—Manassas, Seven Pines, Sharpsburg (Antietam), Fredricksburg, Chancellorsville, Gettysburg, Chickamauga, Chattanooga, Fort Sanders & Bean Station.

**KERSHAW'S BRIGADE VOLUME 2** by D. Augustus Dickert—At the wilderness, Cold Harbour, Petersburg, The Shenandoah Valley and Cedar Creek..

AVAILABLE ONLINE AT **www.leonaur.com**
AND FROM ALL GOOD BOOK STORES

www.ingramcontent.com/pod-product-compliance
Lightning Source LLC
Chambersburg PA
CBHW031616160426
43196CB00006B/155